THE MYSTERY OF THE CHURCH

CONTEMPORARY COLLEGE THEOLOGY SERIES

 GENERAL EDITORS: J. FRANK DEVINE, S.J.
BOSTON COLLEGE

RICHARD W. ROUSSEAU, S.J.
FAIRFIELD UNIVERSITY

THE MYSTERY OF THE CHURCH is one of the volumes in the Ecclesial Theology section of this series.

THE MYSTERY OF
THE CHURCH

by JOHN POWELL, S.J.

THE BRUCE PUBLISHING COMPANY / MILWAUKEE

IMPRIMI POTEST:
Robert F. Harvanek, S.J.
Praepositus Provincialis

NIHIL OBSTAT:
JOHN A. SCHULIEN, S.T.D.
Censor librorum

IMPRIMATUR:
✠ WILLIAM E. COUSINS
Archbishop of Milwaukee
July 25, 1967

The Nihil obstat and Imprimatur are a declaration that a book or pamphlet is considered to be free from doctrinal or moral error. It is not implied that those who have granted the Nihil obstat and Imprimatur agree with the contents, opinions, or statements expressed.

Library of Congress Catalog Card Number: 67–28214

© 1967 THE BRUCE PUBLISHING COMPANY
MADE IN THE UNITED STATES OF AMERICA

Editors' Introduction
THE CONTEMPORARY COLLEGE
THEOLOGY SERIES

This series begins with the presupposition that theology is necessary.
It is necessary if Christian intelligence is to search for meaning in its
dialogue with God, man, and the world. Since Christian intelligence is
not the exclusive possession of the theological specialist or the cleric,
the search must be carried on in all those areas of life, secular as well as
religious, including the college situation, where meaning is to be found.

This search is a peaceful one, for in some mysterious way it has
already achieved its goal: the vision of faith and the fullness of love.
Still it remains a relentless and universal search. Its inner certainty must
radiate out not only to the edges of the mind but also into the farthest
recesses of the world. We could call it "lay" theology, but this word
seems too pale a description for such an exciting enterprise of the
Christian life.

In view of this, the editors of this series are convinced that new questions had to be asked, new structures created, and new books written.
These books would be neither catechetical nor apologetic. They would
be purely and simply theological. The primary audience would be
believers, but all thinking men would find them useful. In scope they
would be broad enough to ensure perspective. They would be scholarly
enough to be intellectually relevant. They would avoid pedantry. In
short, they would try to present a rich and deep understanding of Christian revelation in such a way that today's college students would be able
to respond with a Christian faith and life that are both culturally mature
and scientifically precise. Finally, the authors of these books would be,
for the most part, teachers in colleges and universities where much of
the contemporary theological dialogue is now going on.

The series falls into four parts: biblical, historical, ecclesial, and ethical.
The divisions were not predetermined by the editors. They follow the
shape of the most vigorous theological work now being done.

The books in the biblical section are intended to go beyond the
traditional treatment of Bible history and the now familiar perspectives

of salvation history. They concentrate on various books of the Bible. Their method has been especially designed for college work. Tentatively it might be called "exegetical theology." Every verse is not considered after the fashion of a commentary, nor are narratives developed as a biography, nor is there any attempt to create large theological syntheses. Rather the individual books are studied in chronological sequence; key passages are treated in detail and the rest are summarized. At the same time some attention is paid to the growing theological synthesis.

Since scholastic theology is already represented by individual works and sets of textbooks, the books in our historical section study dogmatic questions from a developmental point of view. In this way the editors hope to make the college students more aware of the great wealth of theological thinking that recent historico-theological studies have uncovered. This method which is more inductive than deductive should happily coincide with the thought processes of the college student. The three basic poles for synthesis are: God, Christ, and Man. In each area the historical development will be studied and a significant number of basic source texts presented. The problems raised in these studies will range all the way from Augustinian pessimism to Teilhardian optimism.

The textbooks for the third part of the series will deal with issues of great contemporary importance. They will examine questions discussed by the Second Vatican Council. As the name implies, ecclesial theology must first concern itself with the Church, what the Church knows herself to be, as expressed in the insights of the new *Constitution on the Church* and with the more significant of the Church's allied concerns: other world religions, American Protestantism, its history, its motivating forces and spirit, and finally the new sacramental theology so enriched by the many magnificent liturgical advances. All of this growth has brought a wider and deeper appreciation of the nature of the Roman Catholic Church and her relationship rooted in understanding and love with the whole world.

The fourth and final section of the series is devoted explicitly to Christian moral response. The editors subscribe to the position that the proper place for the Catholic college or university to examine ethical questions is in a revelational rather than in a purely philosophical context. In addition to the "virtue" divisions of the *Summa* or the classic moral theology text, designed primarily for confessors, there is a need and a place for a "Christian ethics" that reflects the new insights which both biblical and dogmatic theology can provide. These books will strive to be openly Christian in spirit, eclectic in approach, up to date in scholarship, and will address themselves to those ethical problems which are most real to the modern American mind.

Finally, the editors would like to express their thanks to all those whose interest, advice, and cooperation have made this series possible. They are especially grateful to Mr. William May of The Bruce Publishing Company, who not only initiated the project and sustained it through the inevitable disappointments and complications, but contributed so much of his editorial skill to its final shape. To the individual authors who so graciously added to their heavy burden of academic responsibility by undertaking these books, we can only express the hope that their share in the shaping and influencing of the American Catholic community of today and of tomorrow will be far more meaningful to them than any meager thanks of ours.

The Editors,
Rev. J. Frank Devine, S.J., Boston Collge
Rev. Richard W. Rousseau, S.J., Fairfield University

.

Introduction

This text may well be a different kind of presentation of the Church from the one with which college students are generally familiar. It is intended to be a *formally theological* treatment of the Church, and this implies two things: (1) It supposes faith in the reader, but presumes that the reader is also seeking a deeper understanding of his faith. The definition of *theology* given by St. Anselm of Canterbury, "Faith in search of understanding," has been commonly accepted. A formally theological treatment of the Church, therefore, is simply one that accepts the Church in faith but seeks a deeper understanding of this faith. (2) This text will dispense with the impossible task of proving scientifically that which is scientifically unprovable, namely that the Roman Catholic Church is the one true Church of God and must be accepted by all men of sincerity. Many respected apologists of our faith have, especially since the Protestant Reformation, given the impression that they have tried to prove scientifically the Church's claims, and many Catholics have memorized their lines and tried to back nonbelievers into a corner with the muscular cogency of their arguments. Reported successes with this method are, at best, questionable.

Historically, the roots of such an attempt are to be located in the Protestant Reformation, a time of accelerated emotions when both sides of the dispute were carried by the momentum of antagonism into extravagant positions. In the heat of disputation, by a kind of spontaneous combustion, Catholic theologians for the most part seem to have accepted the position that the historical evidence for the claims of the Church is so unrelenting that it forces the decision of faith on the unprejudiced mind. The fact of the matter is that only the grace of God can make a man a believer. The First Vatican Council (1869–1870) has defined this:

> . . . no one can "assent to the gospel preaching," as he must in order to be saved, "without the enlightenment and inspiration of the Holy Spirit, who gives all men their joy in assenting to and in believing the truth." Hence, faith itself is essentially a gift of God . . . by this act man offers to God himself a free obedience inasmuch as he concurs and cooperates with God's grace, when he could resist it (*Denzinger-Schönmetzer* 3010. The citation is from the Council of Orange).

> If anyone says that the assent of Christian faith is not free, but necessarily results from arguments of human reason; or that the grace of God is necessary only for living faith, which works through charity (see Gal 5:6): let him be anathema (DS 3035).

By our act of faith, we believe and accept, according to the same First Vatican Council: ". . . everything that is contained in the written word of God or in Tradition, and that is (also) proposed by the Church as a divinely revealed object of faith, either in a solemn decree or in her ordinary universal magisterium" (DS 3011). One of these truths so revealed by God and so proposed by the Church is the Church herself as the true Church of God. We accept the Church and her claims on us because they have been revealed by God, and because God has given us the gift of faith to accept this revelation.

This is not to deny that there are historico-philosophical proofs for the credibility of the Church and her claims. We can prove that the position of our Catholic faith is the more plausible position. Cardinal Newman, who was himself a convert to Catholicism, once wrote:

> Some hypothesis, this or that, all controversialists, all historians must adopt, if they would treat of Christianity at all. . . . The question is, which of these theories is the simplest, the most natural, the most persuasive.

Faith is not blind. Admittedly, there are very forceful arguments for the credibility or reasonability of accepting the Church. However, even if one were to accept these arguments with his whole heart and mind and strength, it still would not be a supernatural act of faith. The act of faith is not the conclusion of a waterproof syllogism. The man who accepts the apologetic arguments of the Church is simply led to admit this much: the Church and its claims are reasonable. This would be the only legitimate hope of the apologist, that his partner in dialogue will see that it is reasonable to accept the Church. This is the corridor's end for natural, scientific proof. The rest lies with man's cooperation with the grace of God. *No man reasons his way into or out of the faith.*

The only apologetic argument that has been officially defined by the Church is that which is called the "empirical" argument: the existential Church itself. The First Vatican Council has defined:

> If anyone says that it is impossible for external signs to render divine revelation credible and that, therefore, man ought to be impelled towards faith only by each one's internal experience or private inspiration: let him be anathema (DS 3033).

> For all the many marvelous proofs that God has provided to make the credibility of the Christian faith evident point to the Catholic Church alone. Indeed, the Church itself, because of its marvelous propagation, its exalted sanctity, and its inexhaustible fruitfulness in all that is good, be-

cause of its catholic unity and its unshaken stability, is a great and perpetual motive of *credibility* and an irrefutable proof of its own divine mission (DS 3013).

Even this defined apologetic argument may sound like an overstatement to one who has not been exposed to the inner life of the Church, to the compelling beauty of what God has done for man in Christ. Without such a tour of the interior, a recitation of the statistics of conversions, mission stations and canonized saints might sound as hollow as a computer reciting its own epic poetry.

The plan of this text is to propose the Church as the wonderful work of God, unifying and vivifying all things in his Son, Christ Jesus. It will propose the Church as a challenge to confrontation with and submission to God.

We have said that this would be a formally theological work, and that means that we shall travel by the light of faith. It will be a journey of faith in search of understanding. We will study the Church as it has been portrayed in the Scriptures, which describe the living reality of the Church as experienced by the first generation of believers. Beauty, it has been said, is in the eye of the beholder; in this case, it is in the eye of the believer, for the true vision of the Church is open only to the eyes of faith.

Today many college students are wrestling with the act of faith, and there are, as everyone knows, casualties. The more dealings I have with such students who are living with the agony of this struggle, the more I honestly feel that, if faith really means what they think it means, I would reject it too. Faith is not so much an act of acceptance as a way of looking at things, and most especially a way of life. Faith is an experience that engages the total man something like a sunset or a poem. It calls for a response not only of man's mind but also of his whole heart and strength. It is an encounter with a living God. We all must break through the external structures of revelation, each in his own unique way, but ultimately we must encounter a personal God face to face, mind to mind, heart to heart.

There is no doubt a crying need to proclaim the faith effectively, but no matter how effectively it is put *it will be understood only when it is lived,* and this is no easy matter. There is the practice of the virtues, especially the virtue of charity, which always sounds so symphonically sweet to those who do not know the inroads on one's time it will make and the demands on one's energies it will involve. There is faith itself, the vibrant and vital kind of faith that could lead a man like Teilhard de Chardin to remark: "I see and touch God everywhere. Everything means both everything and nothing to me. Everything is God to me;

everything is dust to me."[1] There is fidelity in the encounter of the liturgy and the sacraments, where man meets God in the encounter of love and grace. Ultimately, this engagement of faith will challenge everything in us, and we must be strengthened by this love and grace. It is not easy, yet everything depends on it. And we cannot honestly reject faith unless we have really lived it. As G. K. Chesterton once said: "It isn't that Christianity has failed; it's just that no one has ever tried it."

Each of us must say yes or no to God, must face the *I–Thou* relationship and live it or run from it. The saddest tragedy would be to run from it without ever trying to understand it, which means living it.

If we lived in a State where virtue were profitable, common sense would makes us good, and greed would make us saintly. And we'd live like animals or angels in the happy land that *needs* no heroes. But since in fact we see that avarice, anger, envy, pride, sloth, lust and stupidity commonly profit far beyond humility, chastity, fortitude, justice and thought, and have to choose, to be human at all — why then perhaps we must stand fast a little — even at the risk of being heroes.[2]

[1] Teilhard de Chardin, *The Divine Milieu* (New York: Harper & Row, 1960), p. 120.
[2] Robert Bolt, *A Man for All Seasons* (London: Heineman, 1960), p. 83.

Contents

3. The Messianic Offices of Christ in the Church, 200
4. Religious Life in the Life of the Church, 207
5. Religious Vows and Christian Perfection, 208
6. The Religious as a Witness to Christ, 213

THE MYSTERY OF THE CHURCH

CHAPTER ONE

The Changing Concept
of the Church

> . . . this is the hour in which the Church should deepen its con-
> sciousness of itself, in which it ought to meditate on that mystery
> which is peculiar to it, in which it ought to examine, for its own
> enlightenment and for its own development, a particular doctrine
> which it already knows and which it has formulated and made
> known during the past century. That doctrine concerns the origin
> of the Church, its own nature, its own mission, its own ultimate
> destiny — a doctrine never sufficiently investigated and understood.
> — Pope Paul VI, Ecclesiam Suam, Part 1

Through his Son, God has formed a people of his own, a mystical corporate person. Like every human person in the course of his life, the
corporate person of the Church grows gradually in wisdom, age, and
understanding. Like a human person, it is always seeking self-understanding and a sense of identity. We, who are the Church, must practice
great patience while "we are exiled from the Lord" (2 Cor 5:6),* and
endure many identity-crises.

---

* All citations from the New Testament are taken from the Kleist-Lilly translation;
the Old Testament is cited in the Revised Standard Version.

1

The Church, as the agent of human salvation, is perennially engaged in the vital tension of dialogue with the world into which it is inserted. This dialogue not only affects the seeking, disunited, and swiftly evolving world, but it also has had and will have at the same time an influence on the Church itself. As social beings, each of us must accomplish his own sense of identity through interpersonal relationships with others. It is not surprising that the Church, built of human stones, must live under the same law.

The self-purification and renewal that results in the Church from such a dialogue is not sheer opportunism, but the result of the growing and deepening perception of her own nature and mission in a world that is becoming increasingly conscious of its own nature and problems. Pope Paul makes this quite clear in his encyclical letter, *Ecclesiam Suam:*

> When the Church understands herself more and more clearly, and strives to conform to the ideal that Christ put before her, all that distinguishes her from the human situation in which she lives and with which she engages, will stand out more clearly (par. 19).

However, while there is a call to patience, there is also a right to confidence. The Church proceeds confidently because of its faith in the Love that gave it birth (Jn 3:16), in the Lord that abides in it (Jn 14:23), and in the Spirit of Truth, our Advocate, who will teach the Church all things (Jn 14:26).

1. The Concept of the Church Before the Reformation

Until the late Middle Ages, the Church was regarded by her members as a *reality* to be lived and in which men go to God. Up to this time, however, theologians did not make the Church the object of specific theological treatises. Of course, one can comb through the Fathers and the great theologians of this period and find many passages of illumination, but none of them formulated an entire dogmatic treatise on the Church.

The notion of the Church as a reality to be lived is most vital today. The Church lives in her faithful and the faithful, living the life of the Lord (Gal 2:20), are the Church. This life is not necessarily determined by a reflex knowledge, such as Pope Paul describes in his encyclical:

> . . . this need to consider in a reflex act things that are known, in order to contemplate them in the interior mirror of his own mind, is characteristic of the mentality of modern man. His thought easily turns back

upon itself and finds certitude and fullness in the light of its own conscience (Part I, par. 30).

One might regret this lack of reflection upon the mysterious reality of the Church, but the Church has always lived despite it, and this is the important thing. If the life of the Church depended on its reflex knowledge of its own essence, the life of the Church would have withered long ago.

When theologians did take up the rather serious effort of self-reflection, it was in an attempt to "be ready always to give an answer to everyone who asks you the basis of the hope you cherish" (1 Pet 3:15). It was "faith in search of understanding." The temptation, however, was to see and explain the Church almost exclusively as a visible institution and in terms of its institutional lines. This extrinsicism neglected the deeper divine reality that is the ultimate principle of vitality in the Church. The classic example is Cardinal Bellarmine's definition of the Church: "The one and true Church is the assembly of men, bound together by the profession of the same Christian faith, and by the communion of the same sacraments, under the rule of legitimate pastors, and in particular of the one vicar of Christ on earth, the Roman Pontiff."[1]

Of course, the Church is a visible reality, but it is not totally visible; it is divine in origin, but it is also divine in its very essence. We would rightly expect a description of the Church to embrace this inner divine reality as well as the exterior features that are visible.

But it was, ultimately, when the Church failed to live its own reality as the prolongation of Christ in time and his extension in space that its membership was decimated during the Protestant Reformation.

2. In the Wake of the Reformation: The Juridical Church

Four hundred years ago the Church was shaken in the depths of its being by the forces of reform. The vexatious pressures of Protestantism, and subsequently of Gallicanism and Jansenism, may have forced the Church to take a second look at herself, but they also pushed the Church into a defensive posture, and into an imbalance of identifying herself in terms of that one part of her total reality which was questioned: her authority. Theologians occupied themselves with forging scientific apologetics for the scientifically unprovable claims of the Church. As the well-known French Jesuit theologian, Henri de Lubac, once complained: "We have, since the Protestant Reformation, been learning our theology against someone. It is very bad to learn theology against someone." It is also

---

[1] De Controversiis Christianae Fidei, Vol. II, Bk. 3, Chap. 2 (Naples, 1857), p. 74.

true that it is very bad to learn theology *for* someone. The truths of theology and the truth of the Mystery of the Church seek to be loved for themselves.

The Protestant Reform has led us to teach and learn a polemical theology of the Church, which portrays that Church as a juridical institution. We have, until recently, been seriously overconcerned with converting others to our point of view instead of trying to grow ourselves in understanding. We have rehearsed a less than compelling apologetics which has generated more heat than light, and inspired people to argue rather than marvel.

The tide began to reverse its flow with a German patrologist and historian, Johann Adam Möhler, onetime professor at the University of Tübingen during the latter part of the 18th and the first part of the 19th centuries. It was a time of ebb in the vigor of theology. Möhler's book, which transfused new life into the theology of the Church, was called *Einheitige Kirche* (Unity in the Church). As a patrologist and historian, Möhler portrayed the Church in the spirit of the Fathers of the first three centuries. Although his book suffered from a miscalculation that the author later recognized, it was a work of genius. It resurrected a great many of the patristic themes which gained permanence as the man himself fell into obscurity.

Möhler constructed the Church from the inside out, so that it represented an efflorescence of the presence and activity of the Holy Spirit. Later he redressed the imbalance in a second book, *Symbolik* (Symbolism), in which he realizes that the Incarnate Word is the pattern of the life and structure of the Church, rather than the Holy Spirit.

The momentum of Möhler's thought happily did not die with the man. Two Roman theologians, Clement Schroeder and Jean Baptiste Franzelin, who kept Möhler's thought and vision alive, were what we would call today "theological consultors of the doctrinal commission" for the First Vatican Council. They were, it is thought, largely responsible for the *primum schema de Ecclesia* (the first draft of the Constitution of the Church). Unfortunately, because of the abrupt adjournment of the Council, the schema never reached the conciliar floor for discussion; but it has remained a notable theological source for the last eighty years.[2]

The *schema* describes the Church as the Mystical Body of Christ, a true and visible society, and God's appointed means of salvation. The infallibility and authority of the Church are also treated. The doctrine contained in this *schema* gained further expression and became a part

---

[2] The *primum schema de Ecclesia* can be found in English translation in *The Church Teaches* (Documents of the Church in English Translation) (St. Louis: B. Herder Book Co., 1955), nos. 189–200.

of the official teaching of the Church in two encyclical letters of Pope Leo XIII, *Satis Cognitum*, dealing with the unity of the Church, and *Divinum Illud*, dealing with the presence and activity of the Holy Spirit in the life of the Church and in the life of each of the faithful.

The next notable milestone was the encyclical letter of Pope Pius XII, *Mystici Corporis*, of June 29, 1943. The encyclical has, in the minds of many respected theologians, changed the face of ecclesiology. While it reviews the nature and necessity of authority in the Church, its pervading theme is the inner life of the Church in its most intimate union with Christ, the Lord of the Church, through the animation of the Holy Spirit, the Soul of the Church. It brings the reader inside the Church, and enables him to view it as a tabernacle of divine life. The towering figure of Christ becomes the central point of focus and the meaning of Christian life as a union of life with Christ is presented as the paramount significance of the Church for men.

3. Vatican II and the Church

When the final history of the Church is written, there will no doubt be a chapter reserved for Angelo Giuseppi Roncalli, the peasant-pope, the pope of pastoral concern, the man of warm heart and open arms. But perhaps the future will remember him primarily for the incalculable effects of a single act: the convocation of the Second Vatican Council. Theoretically, this council was to complete the unfinished work of Vatican I, but John made it known that he did not want a mere continuation of the previous council. Astonishingly, this elderly Pontiff, humorously designated in the whispering gallery of Rome as the "penicillin Pope," wanted to open the windows of the Church hoping for a gust of new life and new ideas. He adopted the word, *aggiornamento* (updating), as the council's watchword; he wanted to bring the Church of the twentieth century into confrontation with the problems of the twentieth century. He wanted to accentuate the evangelical nature of the Church and to de-emphasize the exaggerated lines of its juridical, hierarchical nature. He declared:

> It is time to shake off the imperial dust which has accumulated upon the throne of Peter from Constantine onwards.[3]

The principal aim of Vatican II, as projected by John and later by

---

[3] Quoted in Carlo Falconi, *Pope John and the Ecumenical Council* (New York: Hawthorn, 1964), p. 22.

Pope Paul VI in his opening address of the Third Session,[4] was that the Church might gain and express a new awareness of her own inner nature and her universal mission to the world. The council, in its fresh and positive approach to the Church as the people of God and its function in the world, touching on the roles of the hierarchy, the priesthood, the laity and religious, represents a descent from the tower of isolation and re-entry into the world.

Vatican II, in its *Dogmatic Constitution on the Church (Lumen Gentium)*, achieved a masterpiece of the Church's self-understanding. Redressing the imbalance of exaggeration of the juridical, hierarchical elements in the Church, the Fathers of Vatican II present a radically different vision: it is the *plan of God* to unify and vivify all things in his Son, Jesus Christ; the Church is a *community of love*, and as Pope John described it in his opening allocution at the First Session, "the *loving mother of all*," spreading everywhere the fullness of Christian charity; it is the *People of God*, a biblical image which reflects at once the predilection of God and the struggle of weak human beings groping for the truth while on the way to Truth.

Impressive as the *Dogmatic Constitution*[5] is, most theologians have viewed it gratefully as a beginning, "a stepping stone and not a final accomplishment,"[6] "a great breakthrough and every advance can be traced back to it,"[7] because "far from canonizing the past, or even consecrating the present, it prepares for the future."[8] Only the future can provide the full renewal and the answers now sought in anguish. The Church is and always will be an *ecclesia semper reformanda* (a Church in need of constant renewal)[9] but with adequate implementation of *Lumen Gentium* and Vatican II's *Pastoral Constitution on the Church in the Modern World (Gaudium et Spes)*, which calls the Church to put itself vigorously in the service of mankind, the time-lag of the Church in

---

[4] "The principal concern of the Council is to examine the intimate nature of the Church and to express in human language a definition which will reveal the Church's Fundamental constitution and manifest her manifold mission of salvation" (Sept. 30, 1963).

[5] "With something like unanimity it has been hailed as the most momentous achievement of the Council, both because of its important contents and because of its central place among the Council documents." Avery Dulles, *The Documents of Vatican II* (New York: America Press, 1966), p. 10.

[6] Dom Christopher Butler, *Foreword* to the Paulist Press edition of *The Constitution on the Church* (New York: Deus Books, 1965), p. 9.

[7] Charles Davis, "The Parish and Theology," *The Clergy Review* (May, 1964), p. 266.

[8] G. Dejaifve, S.J., "La 'Magna Charta' de Vatican II," *Nouvelle revue théologique* 87 (January, 1965), p. 21.

[9] See Yves Congar, O.P., "Comment l' Église Sainte doit se renouveler sans cesse," *Irénikon*, 34, (1961), pp. 322–345.

achieving self-identity and addressing the contemporary world might well be reduced from centuries to years. The Church cannot, in the words of Karl Rahner, "expect more of this Council than it can reasonably accomplish. Some water will always be poured into the best wine; the essential thing is that we are now on the right road. I am confident that we will make further progress."[10]

In his encyclical, *Ecclesiam Suam*, Paul VI has issued a vigorous call for dialogue with the world on the part of the Church, a summons to address the world in direct confrontation; and he proposes that, at the heart of the reform, lies a *metanoia* (change of mentality) in the total membership of the Church, an interior conversion. And in this encyclical letter, he promises:

> The word, *aggiornamento*, rendered famous by our predecessor of happy memory, John XXIII, should always be kept in mind as our program of action (par. 52).

It may well be that, in the long and arduous work of self-understanding and self-renewal, the Church has arrived at what Cardinal Newman would have called a "Second Spring."

4. *Progress of Understanding Through the Holy Spirit*

In their *Dogmatic Constitution on Divine Revelation*, the Fathers of Vatican II describe the role of the Holy Spirit as the dominant influence in all Christian understanding:

> . . . the Church, in her teaching, life, and worship, perpetuates and hands on to all generations all that she herself is, all that she believes. This tradition which comes from the apostles develops in the Church with the help of the Holy Spirit. . . . For, as the centuries succeed one another, the Church constantly moves toward the fullness of divine truth until the words of God reach their complete fulfillment in her . . . and the Holy Spirit, through whom the living voice of the gospel resounds in the Church, and through her, in the world, leads unto all truth those who believe and makes the word of Christ dwell abundantly in them (cf. Col 3:16).[11]

Sacred Scripture assures us that it is the Spirit of God, "the Spirit who will lead you to the entire truth" (Jn 16:14), who guides this progress of self-understanding in the Church. It is his presence in the Church that

---

[10] Quoted from an interview in *Guide* (January, 1964), p. 17.

[11] Vatican II, *Dogmatic Constitution on Divine Revelation*, no. 8. All citations of the Constitution, Decrees, and Declarations of Vatican II are taken from *The Documents of Vatican II*, edited by Walter Abbott, S.J., and published by the Guild Press, the Association Press, and Herder & Herder. © 1966 by the America Press, and used by permission.

alone can guarantee the paths of human minds and feet as the pilgrim People of God seeks its destiny and identity. "You will know him, because he will make his permanent stay with you and in you" (Jn 14:17)[12]

The Holy Spirit will lead the Church to an ever deepening understanding of the central intuition of its faith, Christ. "He will witness in my behalf" (Jn 15:27). It was he who inaugurated Christian understanding on the great day of light, Pentecost (cf. Acts 2:15-21).

St. Paul urges his colleague, Timothy, to "guard that noble trust [revelation] with the aid of the Holy Spirit who dwells in us" (2 Tim 1:14). And he reminds the Thessalonians: ". . . our preaching . . . was accompanied also with power, with the blessing of the Holy Spirit . . . you welcomed the message and experienced the joy the Holy Spirit imparts" (1 Thess 1:4-6). St. John tells us that it is by the Holy Spirit that we have been purified and redeemed, and that "the Spirit also *continually* bears reliable witness, because the Spirit is Truth" (1 Jn 5:6).

Certainly it is the vivifying and guiding presence of this Holy Spirit, who is in each of us individually and in all of us corporately (1 Cor 6:19), that must endow the Church with self-understanding and self-identity. When Christians cooperate with the gracious guidance of the Spirit of Truth, the life of Christ deepens within them. In Pauline terminology, we "put on Christ" (Eph 4:24), no longer living just for ourselves, but allowing Christ to live in us (Gal 2:20). Through the Holy Spirit we become "a new creature in Christ" (2 Cor 5:17) and our "life is hidden with Christ in God" (Col 3:3). Christians are alive in the Spirit, "if the Spirit of God really dwells in you, whereas no one who is deprived of the Spirit of Christ belongs to Christ" (Rom 8:9).

As this life of Christ is deepened in us by the Holy Spirit, there is created in the Christian "a sense of Christ," a taste and instinctual judgment for the things of God, a deeper perception of God's truth, an increased understanding of God's dispositions and love toward us. This is what Christians must strive to attain individually and corporately; theologians call it Christian *connaturality*. It is like a natural instinct or intuition, but it is not natural, since it results from the supernatural realities of the Divine Indwelling and the impulses of grace. No amount of dialectical or analytical facility, which is purely human, can provide this connatural instinct. It is increased only by the continual nourishment of the life of God that vivifies the Christian.

Consequently, each of us who corporately are the Church is called in his own life to the most thorough Christian commitment and the most

---

[12] Read Jn 16:7-15. Here Christ explains that the Spirit of Truth will come to complete the work of revelation and ultimately lead the faithful to "the entire truth."

deep-rooted engagement with the life of faith. For it is this inner vitality alone, which is the gift of the Spirit, that will lead the Church to understand its treasure, Christ, and its own vocation as his *pleroma* or completion. Paul tells the Romans:

> Whoever are led by the Spirit of God, they are the sons of God (8:14).
>
> The Spirit himself joins his testimony to that of our spirit that we are children of God (8:16).

In the search for self-identity, the Church must rely on the resonance of his voice alone, for the Spirit alone can "teach everything" to us (Jn 14:26); he alone can "conduct us through the whole range of truth" (Jn 16:13). Christ has promised this Spirit to us (Jn 15:26) to tabernacle in us (1 Cor 6:19), to speak through us (Mt 10:19–20).

> I have told you this, that my joy may be yours, and your joy may be perfect (Jn 15:11).
>
> I have told you this, that you may not waver in your faith (Jn 16:1).

Eventually, this Church will attain its "perfect manhood" (Eph 4:13), to the "mature proportions that befit Christ's completion" (Eph 4:13). It will find out that it is the fullness of Christ, which St. Paul compares to the age of maturity; and this, by definition, excludes any further development.[13] Then all things will be restored in Christ (Acts 3:21), and God will "be everything to everyone and everything" (1 Cor 15:28). We know that this hour of Jesus is coming because we have already received "the promised Holy Spirit, which is the guarantee of our inheritance" (Eph 1:14).

> You shall receive power when the Holy Spirit comes upon you, and you shall be my witnesses in Jerusalem and in Judea and Samaria and even to the very ends of the earth (Acts 1:8).

Veni, Sancte Spiritus! — Come, Holy Spirit!

---

[13] See F. Prat, *The Theology of St. Paul* (Westminster, Md.: The Newman Press, 1933), Vol. I, pp. 295–299.

CHAPTER TWO

The Mystery of the Church

I rejoice now in the sufferings I bear for your sake, and what is lacking to the sufferings of Christ I supply in my flesh for the benefit of his body, which is the Church. Of this Church I have been made a minister . . . to proclaim without stint the word of God, the mystery hidden for ages and generations.

(Col 1:24–26)

1. God's Intention to Share His Life and Love With Man

In his first epistle, John defines God simply as "love" (1 Jn 4:16). The whole thrust of this epistle is the point that one must understand love to understand God, and one must abide in love to abide in God. God is, in fact, a community of love, because community connotes a sharing and the three Divine Persons share the divine nature, united in an ecstatic embrace of love. But love is dynamic, restless, eager to give of itself; love asks to give and share that which it possesses. And so, God, who is love, seeks to diffuse his life, his joy, and his love. It is this desire to share that alone can explain creation; it is the motif of God's dealings with man. To share himself, he brings man into being and forms man to his

10

own image and likeness. The divine community of love, Father, Son, and Holy Spirit, forms a community of love on earth, and all human history is in fact a progressive effort of God to achieve this intention.

We use many different words to express God's intentions for man: He would *save* man, *redeem* him, *vivify* him, *sanctify* him. Perhaps the best all-embracing description of God's love-impelled intention is this: He would *unify* him in a community of love, and this unity in such a community is accomplished through his own Son's entrance into this world. The community of these men not only unites them to one another, but in and through his Son, they are united to God himself, present among men in his Son. In this community heaven and earth come together. In the light of this reality, Father Josef Jungmann writes:

> All reality is a cosmos — a single stream that goes out from God and tends back to him — so too the Catholic teaching which sets this cosmos before us should be characterized by unity and order. A simple catechism can, at first glance, give an outsider an overwhelming sense of the cohesion of Catholic doctrine. But Catholic theology is not merely the development of a single concept, even that of God himself. It is rather the presentation of *a way which unites heaven and earth.*[1]

When one looks at history, as directed by the forces and minds and wills of men, it is *human* history; when he looks at the same narration of the past through the eyes of faith, and from the viewpoint of God's unifying action, it is *salvation* history. In this latter view, it is the story of God gradually bringing man to his salvation, which is the sharing of God's own life and love. It is the effort of the heavenly community of love bringing man into an earthly community of love, alive with the presence and life of God, swept into the very embrace of love which unites Father, Son, and Holy Spirit.

This plan of God so to love man is laid open to the eyes of man only gradually, progressively, in a kind of historical unfolding. From the very first chapter of Genesis to the final explosive words of the Apocalypse, the story is told. God is, in the People of Israel, progressively concentrating all men into the one people of his own adoption; from this people God salvages a remnant, and from this remnant he forms a New People of God, covenanted to himself through the blood of his own Son. God draws men into a communion of life with himself through his Son, "whom he appointed the heir of all things, through whom also he created the world" (Heb 1:2).

St. Thomas Aquinas calls this a *reditio in Deum*, a return to God in

---

[1] Josef Jungmann, S.J., *The Good News Yesterday and Today* (New York: W. H. Sadlier, 1962), p. 9.

Christ.[2] God is drawing men, whom he created under the impulse of love, back to that love which is man's alpha and omega, his origin and destiny. St. Paul tells the Ephesians that God chose man for this destiny, "in Christ, before the foundation of the world . . . marking us out beforehand (so his will decreed) to be his own adopted children through Jesus Christ" (Eph 1:4; my translation). This plan of God to form man into a community of love, as his own adopted children, was the divine intention from all eternity.

This was the plan and this the love that Adam, the father of the human race, rejected by his defection. But love refuses to be stifled, and right from the beginning of man's estrangement from God, he is given reason for hope. God tells the serpent of seduction: "I will put enmity between you and the woman, and between your seed and her seed" (Gen 3:15).

The next stage of this eternal design of love is inaugurated in the intervention of God in human history and in the person of Abraham, a simple Semite, who heard God say to him: "I will make of you a great nation . . . by you all the families of the earth shall bless themselves" (Gen 12:1–3). It was a promise framed in paradox, as are all God's dealings with men. Abraham was seventy-five years old, and childless. Yet through this unlikely man the divine architect begins to shape his community of love, the Church. The author of Hebrews writes:

> By faith Abraham obeyed the divine call, and departed for a country which he was to receive as his property; moreover, he departed without knowing where he was going. By faith he sojourned in the Promised Land as in a foreign country, where he lived in tents, as did Isaac and Jacob, heirs with him of the same promise. Why? Because he was awaiting the city with foundations whose architect and builder is God (Heb 11:8–10).

The details of this remote preparation for the community of Love that is the Church, through the People of God that was Israel, will be discussed more fully in a chapter on the Church as the People of God. Here it suffices to say that in these Jewish folk of the Old Testament, God was already shaping man into a unity in love which would reach its ultimate stage in Christ, the Word God uttered into this world, the Word that was his well-beloved Son.

At surface understanding this explosion of God's loving designs for men through his Son looks like a tragedy. The Gospels are quite clear: He was born to die. And his death is far from glorious, at surface understanding. It is a death of shame, mockery, incredible suffering. His loyal followers, with the exception of a few women, desert him in the moment of his agony; and, when his head dropped down on his chest in death,

---

[2] *Summa Theologiae* I, q. 2, prologue.

hope seemed to have no more life than the rocks on Calvary where he died.

But the eyes of faith penetrate surface understanding. Christ's death was not really an end but a beginning, the ultimate achievement of God in his plan of love to unify and divinize man. Under the dismal sky of Jerusalem, at three o'clock in the afternoon, in the birth-pangs of crucifixion, a community of love was born. A new covenant was sealed in God's own blood. The mysterious plan of God is opened to man.

> I rejoice now in the sufferings I bear for your sake, and what is lacking to the sufferings of Christ I supply in my flesh for the benefit of his body, which is the Church. Of this Church I have been made a minister in virtue of the commission given me by God for your benefit, to proclaim without stint the word of God, the mystery hidden for ages and generations, but now clearly shown to his saints. To them God willed to make known how rich in glory is this mystery among the Gentiles — Christ in you, your hope of glory (Col 1:24–27).

2. St. Paul's Term for This Plan of God: "The Mystery"

This plan of God to share his life and joy and love with us, through the formation of a community established by his Son, Paul calls "the mystery hidden for ages and generations" (Col 1:26). The word mysterion is Greek, and in the Greek world there were two sorts of mysteries: religious and literary. The former was a liturgical renovation of an episode in the life of a deity, in which the initiates tried to experience in themselves the sentiments of the deity; the latter was a form of gnosis or esoteric knowledge, reserved to a special, elite group. However, contemporary scholars do not believe that Paul drew his meaning of mysterion from either of these.[3] For Paul, the mysterion is the benevolence of God toward man in sharing his life through his Son; it is God's eternal intention, hidden in God from all eternity, for which man is gradually prepared by repeated divine intrusions into human history. God withdraws the veil concerning his intentions when he sends his Son into the world:

---

[3] Cf. D. Deden, "Le mystère Paulinien," Ephemerides Théologicae Lovanienses (1936), pp. 405–442; Hastings' Dictionary of Christ and the Gospels, under the word "mystery" by B. W. Bacon; Kittel's Theologisches Wörterbuch zum Neuen Testament, II, p. 205; F. Prat, The Theology of St. Paul (Westminster, Md.: Newman Press, 1945), Vol. II, note L; C. Spicq, Les Epîtres Pastorales (Paris, 1947), Excursus V, "Le Mystère Chrétien"; G. Bonsirven, Il Vangelo di Paolo (Rome, 1951). Also see Raymond E. Brown, "The Pre-Christian Concept of 'mystery,'" The Catholic Biblical Quarterly (Oct. 1958), p. 443. A treatment of the whole question, the use of "mystery" in the pagan mystery religions and St. Paul's usage, is found in L. Bouyer's Liturgical Piety (Notre Dame, Ind.: University of Notre Dame Press, 1954), pp. 86–98.

the mystery is *revealed* in Christ and *realized* in us — the community of love on earth, alive with the life and love of God himself. These are the stages of the mystery: (1) hidden in God from all eternity, (2) revealed in Christ, (3) realized in us.

1. **The Mystery as hidden in God.** Paul presents the mystery as the divine plan, conceived under the impulse of love, but hidden from man. It is God's intention to vivify men with his own life, through his Son who will himself enter the world to unite men to his Father by joining a community to himself. In the blood of his Son, God will seal a new covenant with man and take to himself a new people, a community of love.

> We do . . . not [speak] the wisdom of this world. . . . The wisdom we speak is of God, *mysterious, hidden,* which God *foreordained to* our *glory before the world's beginning,* a wisdom which none of this world's rulers knew, because if they had known it, they would never have crucified the Lord to whom belongs all glory. It is the wisdom which, in the words of Scripture (Is 64:4; Jer 3:6), proposes "What no eye has ever seen, what no ear has ever heard, what no human heart has ever thought of, namely, the great blessings that God holds ready for those who love him" (1 Cor 2:7–10).

> Of this Church I have been made a minister in virtue of the commission given me by God for your benefit, to proclaim without stint the word of God, *the mystery hidden for ages and generations,* but now clearly shown to his saints. To them God willed to make known how rich in glory is this mystery among the Gentiles — Christ in you, your hope of glory (Col 1:25–27).

> Out of love he predestined us for himself to become through Jesus Christ his adopted children, conformably to the good pleasure of his will, to the praise of his resplendent grace, with which he had adorned us in his beloved Son. . . . With this grace he has inundated us, by imparting to us all manner of wisdom and practical knowledge, making known to us, in keeping with his good pleasure, *the mystery of his will.* And this good pleasure he decreed to put into effect in Christ *when the designated period of time had elapsed,* namely to gather all creation both in heaven and on earth under one head, Christ (Eph 1:5–10).

> . . . by revelation was made known to me *the mystery* . . . you can perceive how well versed I am in this mystery relative to Christ, *which in former ages was not made known to mankind,* as it has now been revealed by the Spirit to his holy apostles and spokesmen (Eph 3:3–5).

> . . . to me, the very least of all the saints, this grace was given to announce among the Gentiles the Good News of the unfathomable riches of Christ, and to enlighten all men as to what is the wonderful plan, *that mystery which has been hidden from eternity in God,* who created all things (Eph 3:8–10).

Before we take up the second and third stages of the mystery in Paul, the more immediate question seems to be: Why did God not reveal his design for man, the divine community of love forming a human community of love, right from the beginning? The question has apparently occurred to others before us. In fact, one of the first great theologians of the Church, St. Irenaeus (A.D. 130–c 200), Bishop of Lyons, poses the same question.[4] He asks why was man not made perfect right from the beginning, and he answers his own question by saying that God could have given himself to us, but we were much too *puerile* (his word), too worldly to be able to receive such an astonishing revelation. "God certainly was able," he writes, "to give man his perfection right from the beginning, but man was unable to receive it because (morally) he was an infant." So God, the Saint reasons, had to prepare man for his gifts in a gradual process. The same answer is suggested by St. Paul himself in writing to the Galatians, when he says that ". . . the [Mosaic] Law was our attendant (*paedagogus*) on the way to Christ" (Gal 3:24).

In creating us, God taught us his existence; in the covenant with the People of Israel and in Mosaic revelation, he told us of his own transcendent holiness and unity, and began to form man into a community of love. In Christ and Christian revelation, God tells us of his own intimate life of love and invites man to share that life in a human community of love, the people of God's predilection, the Church.[5]

The time-factor has a meaning, and has been pondered from the beginning by theologians. However, theologians would be the first to admit that we are children asking questions that are too precocious for our limited understanding. It is always this way when we are dealing with a God of mystery.[6] However, the God of whom we ask our questions is also our Father, by his own gracious act of adoption, and we can know at least this: his loving intentions are unquestionable. He has graciously and gradually prepared us for the coming of his Son and the intimate union that is possible to us because of and in that Son.

2. **The Mystery as revealed in Christ.** When God uttered his Word into the world, in the Incarnation of his Son, the Mystery was laid before the eyes of man. In his Son, God would gather together a community, the Church, fashioned to his own image and likeness, to the image and

---

[4] St. Irenaeus, *Adversus Haereses* (ca. A.D. 185), Part IV, Chapter 38, "Cur non ab initio perfectus factus est homo?" (Why was man not made perfect from the beginning?)

[5] Cf. Jean Daniélou, *Le Mystère du Salut des nations* (Paris, 1948), esp. Chapter 2. Also Danielou's *Advent* (New York: Sheed and Ward, 1950), and his *Essai sur le mystère de l'histoire* (Paris, 1953).

[6] Cf. Karl Rahner, *Encounters With Silence* (Westminster, Md.: Newman, 1963), Chapter 1: "God of my Life."

likeness of the community of love in heaven. He would give men a share in his own life, bring them into the intimacy of his own love, as his adopted children and his people. St. Paul writes:

> I strive to bring consolation to their hearts, and by strengthening their love, to enrich them with the fullness of understanding and to bring them to the deep knowledge of the divine mystery, Christ. In him are to be found hidden all the treasures of wisdom and knowledge (Col 2:2–3).

> I rejoice now in the sufferings I bear for your sake, and what is lacking to the sufferings of Christ I supply in my flesh for the benefit of his body, which is the Church. Of this Church I have been made a minister . . . to proclaim without stint the word of God, the mystery hidden for ages and generations (Col 1:24–26).

> This preaching [which heralds Jesus, the Messiah], reveals the mystery which has been kept hidden through eternal ages, but which is now made known by the prophetical writings and proclaimed, by the command of the eternal God, to the Gentiles, so as to bring about their submission to the faith. Yes, to God who alone is wise, be glory through Jesus Christ forever and ever. Amen (Rom 16:25–27).

> . . . how rich in glory is this mystery — Christ in you, your hope of glory (Col 1:27).

> At the same time pray for us, too, that God may give us an opportunity to preach and announce the mystery of Christ, for which I am indeed a prisoner. Then I shall make it known as it is my duty to do (Col 4:3–4).

> In many fragmentary and various utterances, God spoke of old to our ancestors through the prophets; at the present time, the final epoch [the ultimate divine economy of grace and salvation], he has spoken to us through his Son, whom he has appointed heir of the universe (Heb 1:1–2).

3. The Mystery as realized in us, the community of love, sharing the life of God. Paul tells the Colossians (1:25) that the mystery is "Christ in you." From the context it is clear that he is talking about the Church because he writes: "I supply in my flesh for the benefit of his body, which is the Church. . . . Of this Church I have been made a minister . . . to proclaim . . . the mystery known to his saints [those received into the Church] . . . Christ in you" (Col 1:24–27). "Christ in you" means that the members of the Church, having been incorporated into Christ by baptism, receive of his fullness the grace to be the sons of God. This final stage of the mystery, in which the union of God and man is achieved through Christ, is therefore contemporaneous with the entire history of mankind from Christ onwards. It is "the final epoch," in which the Church, as the complement and extension of Christ, will be the assumed mystical humanity through which Christ himself continues to live, redeem, vivify, and unite men in himself, the center and source of the community of love on earth.

We will discuss the Church as the Body of Christ in the next chapter, but it should be noted here that all the Body of Christ texts in the Pauline letters are pertinent here.[7] The "Christ in you" of Colossians is spelled out in a variety of ways under the image of the Church as the Body of Christ. In Gal 3:28, Paul insists: "You are all one in Christ Jesus." In Eph 5:21-33, Paul speaks of the union of Christ and the Church as comparable to that of a man and his wife, and concludes: "This is the great mystery — I mean in regard to Christ and the Church" (Eph 5:32). Paul tells the Romans that we are "one body in Christ, and individually related to another as part to part" (Rom 12:4-6). In speaking of baptism, he tells the Roman church that in this sacrament we die (to sin) with Christ, and rise "alive to God in Christ Jesus" (Rom 6:11). Finally, in the letter to the Ephesians, Paul describes the Church as "the complement of him who fills all the members with all graces" (Eph 1:23).

The three stages of the Mystery in Ephesians.[8] In discussing the mystery of God's love for men, it has been pointed out that all three stages of this mystery are found in the letter of St. Paul to the Church at Ephesus.[9]

The intention of God from all eternity:

These blessings correspond to his choice of us in Christ before the foundation of the world, that we should be holy and without blemish in his sight. Out of love he predestined us for himself to become through Jesus Christ his adopted children, conformably to the good pleasure of his will, to the praise of his resplendent grace, with which he has adorned us in his beloved Son (Eph 1:4-6).

The enactment of this plan in time:

In him [Christ] we have our redemption through his blood, the remission of our transgressions, in keeping with the riches of his grace. With this grace he has inundated us, by imparting to us all manner of wisdom and practical knowledge, making known to us, in keeping with his good pleasure, the mystery of his will. And this good pleasure he decreed to put into effect in Christ when the designated period of time had elapsed, namely to gather all creation both in heaven and on earth under one head, Christ. In him we have also been constituted a Chosen People, since, in keeping with the decree of him who carries out everything according to the designs of his will, we have been predestined to be devoted to the praise of his glory — we who before Christ's coming had hoped in him (Eph 1:7-12).

---

[7] Cf. F. Prat, *The Theology of St. Paul*, Vol. II, pp. 283-284.

[8] The first to point this out was H. Coppieters, in "La Doxologie de la Lettre aux Ephésiens," *Revue Biblique* (1909), pp. 74-88.

[9] Cf. the *Prologue*, Chapter 1, verses 4-14.

The mystery in relation to men:

> You, too [were joined to the chosen people], after you heard the message of truth, the Good News proclaiming your salvation, and had believed in it, and had been sealed with the promised Holy Spirit, who is the first installment of our inheritance [as God's children by baptism]. The final purpose of thus being sealed is our redemption as God's possession to the praise of his glory (Eph 1:13–14).

The final term or stage, then, of the mysteries hidden in God, revealed in Christ and realized in us is our life in and through him. Paul uses the phrase "in Christ Jesus" 164 times in his letters.[10] It is a paraphrase and equivalent of "Christ in us." We are somehow grafted onto Christ. Paul says that we "put on" the person of Christ (Gal 3:27). Christ becomes our atmosphere and environment. We "are in Christ" and thus we "possess Christ" (cf. 2 Cor 1:12). We are incorporated into him as his "members" (1 Cor 6:15), integral parts of "his body, which is the Church" (Eph 1:23). This gift of incorporation is the profound reality of Christian life, our participation in the life and love of God through membership in Christ. By the very fact that a man is a Christian, he has a new nature; Peter says that we become "partakers of the divine nature" (2 Pet 1:4). Paul refers to our "former nature" (Rom 6:6) and of "forming anew our body into his image" (Phil 3:21). This "new nature" (2 Cor 6:17) is the source of a new supernatural life, given not to individuals as individuals, but which, because it is shared in common by many, forms a new race, a new people, a new Israel. (Cf. Acts 15:14; Rom 9:25; Tit 2:14; Heb 4:9; 1 Pet 2:9 ff.)

The mystery in its final stage is the Church, and this has many aspects and ramifications; but the central fact is that God is sharing his life with man, divinizing man, through his Son, to whom men are engrafted, thus forming a community of love. It is the union of heaven and earth, time and eternity, God and man. Father Emile Mersch writes:

> This is the most astounding mystery of all. Christ is God; hence to be one with him means necessarily to be one with God. Thus St. Paul's teaching on incorporation in Christ includes a doctrine on the divinization of men in Christ. It is this doctrine that fully explains the mystery and shows how that mystery which has eternity for its source, likewise has eternity for its term.[11]

The Church, the mystery of God realized in man, is the "unfathomable riches of Christ . . . the wonderful plan . . . hidden from eternity in God . . . realized in Christ Jesus, our Lord" (Eph 3:8–11). It is God's

---

[10] F. Prat, *The Theology of St. Paul*, Vol. II, note M, p. 391.

[11] Emile Mersch, *The Whole Christ* (Milwaukee: The Bruce Publishing Co., 1938), p. 140.

plan or design to unify all men and vivify them with a sharing in his own divine life; God fathers a new life in men whom he adopts as his own sons (Eph 1:5). The Church is a re-gathering of mankind in Christ (Jn 11:53), and the means God uses to redeem man (Eph 1:7) and reconcile them to himself. It is a mystery of praise and glorification (Eph 1:6, 12, 14).

Therefore, when we consider the Church as a mystery, manifested in Christ and realized in the Church, the connotation is not hiddenness, reserve or inaccessibility, but, in a sense, just the opposite. It is the benevolent love of God, who is Love, for mankind; it is the admission of man into the knowledge, life and love of God. Because the Church is the means by which God communicates to his children and his people this knowledge of himself, his life and love, it has been called the ur-sakrament, the primordial or fontal sacrament; the external sign which both signifies the presence of God's love and grace, and channels these gifts to man. It is to this plan,[12] concretized in the Church, that each of us must witness "in Jerusalem and in all Judea and Samaria and even to the very ends of the earth" (Acts 1:8).

3. The Life-Theme in St. John[13]

By the fact of creation, we belong to God as his creatures. To be adopted as his own children, however, means much more. To be taken into the divine community of love, there has to be some elevation of human nature. If we are to call our God "Father," he must somehow share his own divine life with us, "divinize" us. The implications of true sonship mean more than merely trusting and loving God and feeling safe in his protection, great though these gifts are. To be taken into the divine familial intimacy means to be received through grace into an almost incredible relationship with God. We become by adoption what Christ, the Incarnate Word, was by nature. Through our union with Christ we share this gift of sonship. "Of his fullness we have all received" (Jn 1:16).

This is the apex of what Paul calls "the mystery," that man is empowered not only to know God and experience his goodness, but to share his life. When John says that we have all received from the fullness of

---

[12] See A. Becker, "God's Great Design: The Church," Lumen Vitae (1953), pp. 449–466.

[13] For a fuller treatment, see Dom Jacques Dupont, Essais sur la Christologie de Saint Jean (Bruges, 1951), esp. pp. 163–231; Emile Mersch, The Whole Christ, pp. 178–181; J. B. Frey, "Le concept de 'vie' dans l' Evangile de St. Jean," Biblica (1920), pp. 37–58; 211–239.

the divine life which graced and divinized the human soul of Christ by
our incorporation into him (Jn 1:16), he is echoing the words of Christ
himself who proclaimed the reason for his coming: "I have come so that
men may have life, and have it in abundance" (Jn 10:10). This life is,
of course, the life of God's grace, which elevates us to the status of God's
children. God is father of this new life in man.

> But to as many as welcomed him [by the spiritual rebirth of baptism], he
> gave the right to become children of God . . . who were born not of
> blood, or of carnal desire, or of man's will; no, they were born of God"
> (Jn 1:12–13).

Of course, this life is visible only to the eyes of faith and its value can
be glimpsed only by such eyes. Only in the acceptance of Christ by faith
is a man called into this new life of divine intimacy. In John we find
the following:

> Yes, I tell you frankly: he who heeds my message and believes him whose
> ambassador I am, is in possession of eternal life, and is not liable to judg-
> ment [condemnation]. On the contrary, he has once for all passed out of
> the realm of death into that of life. It is the truth when I tell you that
> a time is coming, in fact, it is already here, when the dead [spiritually
> dead] will hear the voice of the Son of God, and those who heed it will
> have life. Just as the Father is the source of life, so too, has he given the
> Son the power to be a source of life; and . . . after all, I am not seeking
> to do my will, but the will of him who sent me (Jn 5:24–30).

Jesus solemnly proclaims that whoever believes in him shall have this
life of divine intimacy forever (Jn 6:40) because he is "the resurrection
and the life" (Jn 11:25). In his prayer to the Father at the Last Supper,
Jesus prayed:

> Father, the hour is come! Glorify your Son, that your Son may glorify
> you. You have given him authority over all mankind, that he might give
> eternal life to all you have entrusted to him. And this is the sum of
> eternal life — their knowing you, the only true God,[14] and your ambassador,
> Jesus Christ (Jn 17:1–3).

We have seen, in the writings of Paul, that this life is a people-forming
life, the community of love that is God sharing his life with a community of believers of this earth. This is the mystery of God in its terminal
stage and the kingdom of God in its earthly stage. This is the implication
of our Lord to Nicodemus, who questions the meaning of "rebirth":

> I must be frank with you: if one is not born anew, he cannot see the
> kingdom of God. . . . I am telling you the plain truth: unless a man is
> born again of water and the Spirit [baptism], he cannot have entrance into

---

[14] We know God by faith in this world; by vision in the next.

the kingdom of God! What is born of the flesh is flesh, and what is born of the Spirit is spirit . . . we speak what we know, and we testify what we have seen; but you all refuse to accept our testimony! (Jn 3:3–13.)

In his First Epistle, John says simply that Christ is the only source of this divine life:

> Now this testimony is to the effect that God has given us eternal life, and that the Son has this life. He, then, who partakes of the Son partakes of that life; he who does not partake of the Son does not participate in that life (Jn 5:11–12).

However, because of our union with Christ in faith and baptism, we do become the children of God in name as well as in fact (1 Jn 3:1); we are the "seed of God" (1 Jn 5:1), and can address him as a child speaks to his father (1 Jn 3:1). This life, given in baptism (Jn 3:5), is nourished in us by the Eucharistic Body of Christ (Jn 6, 56–58): "He who eats my flesh and drinks my blood is united with me, and I am united with him. As the living Father has appointed me to be his ambassador, and I live because of the Father, so too, he who eats me will have life because of me. This is the bread that has come down from heaven."

It is by reason of this divine life, shared by men, that all who are united in Christ are as branches of a vine, in a way comparable to the union of the Three Persons of the Holy Trinity. It is the gift by which the community of love in heaven creates a community of love on earth: "That they may be one as You, Father, in me and I in you" (Jn 17:21).

4. On the Irrelevance of Theology

Theologians have come more and more to face the danger of irrelevance. There is always the Scylla of making theological truth sound too noetic or exclusively intellectual and the Charybdis of making it sound too heaven-swept and wonderful. Theological truth is sterile unless it is incarnated in human lives and experience. Admittedly the way each of us will experience and incarnate the truth of the mystery of the Church will be as individual and personal as our individual acts of faith.

Between the truths of theology and our living them out there are many obstacles. The first is that of understanding. Just as food benefits us only to the extent that we have digested it, so will truth become incarnational in my life only to the extent that I have wrestled with it, digested it, and made it a part of myself. It is not simply a matter of God's grace, but of my willingness to be involved. The truths that we have been discussing in this chapter on the mystery of the Church ask involvement of me, involvement in God's plan to unify and vivify all men in his Son. I cannot begrudge the labor of consideration. Not only my own personal life and destiny are involved but the lives and destinies of many depend on my involvement and commitment as a witness to Christ. My baptism is not really a past event, but a perennial commitment, which I cannot fail without serious ingratitude.

The second problem is the surrender of my self-interest. The center of gravity is strongly within myself; I need a Copernican revolution, which locates the God of love and his designs for mankind at the center of my life. I need to pass from the infantile *I* to the *WE* of Christian maturity. My Christian faith asks this surrender of me: "I live now, no longer I, but Christ lives in me" (Gal 2:20). I must be in labor until Christ be formed in me, until I achieve the stature of Christ, until the divine life bestowed upon me is brought to full growth.

The one thing theological truth is not is irrelevant.

CHAPTER THREE

A Biblical Image of the Church: The Body of Christ

> In the Old Testament the revelation of the kingdom had often been conveyed by figures of speech. In the same way the inner nature of the Church was now to be made known to us through various images.
>
> By communicating His Spirit to His brothers, called together from all peoples, Christ made them mystically into His own body.
> — Vatican II, Lumen Gentium, nos. 6 and 7

The Church can be called a mystery in two senses. We have already discussed the mystery of the Church in the Pauline sense. The Church is also a mystery in that it is such a profound divine reality that, without revelation, we could not have known its existence, and, even after reve-lation, we cannot fully comprehend it. As Pope Paul VI said in his open-ing allocution at the second session of the Vatican Council: "The Church is a mystery. It is a reality imbued with the hidden presence of God. It

23

lies, therefore, within the very nature of the Church to be always open to new and greater exploration."[1]

Consequently, the Church cannot be adequately defined. The sacred writers of the New Testament never attempted such a definition, but tried to express the wonder, depth, and beauty of the mystery of the Church in metaphors or images, each of which is meant to depict some aspect of the vast mystery of the Church. It is something like the viewing of a magnificent piece of sculpture; one must look at it from various positions, moving slowly around the statue, and discovering in each new view a new wealth of beauty.

1. The Meaning of Biblical Images

A biblical image is basically the use of a metaphor, which is a figure of speech in which one thing is likened to another, different thing by being spoken of as if it were that other. However, in metaphorical usage, there is usually one point of implied comparison. For example, if I say that "This man is a lion," I mean that he is courageous; I do not mean that he has four legs or shaggy hair. Similarly, each image of the Church expresses one aspect of the reality of the Church. Not everything which is true of the image used is true of the reality which it is intended to expose.

Let us take the example of the Church as a "sheepfold."[2] The general connotation of this image is that the Church is "ceaselessly led and nourished by Christ Himself, the Good Shepherd and the Prince of Shepherds (cf. Jn 10:11; 1 Pet 5:4), who gave His life for the sheep (cf. Jn 10:11–15)."[3] It does not relegate Christians, who are creatures of intelligence and choice, to the status of brute animals.

And this is precisely the problem with biblical images. Their connotation is open to discussion and debate. Very often professional biblical scholars see different nuances of meaning expressed in these figures, and the Church has officially taught very little by way of clarification.

The difficulty is complicated by what we might call "the time element." The images or metaphors of the New Testament were written in an age very different from our own. In fact, the penchant of the Semitic mind for such images seems exaggerated to us.[4] With the Jews

---

[1] September 28, 1963. See *Documents of Vatican II*, edited by Walter Abbott, S.J. (New York: Guild Press, 1966), p. 14, note, 1.
[2] Cf. Ps 23:1–4; Jn 10:1–18; Lk 12:32; 1 Pet 5:2 f.; Jn 21:15 ff.
[3] *Lumen Gentium*, no. 6.
[4] Note that the great announcement of Christ, in Mt 16:16 and Jn 21:15, is made in metaphorical language.

and in their world of two thousand years ago, this priority of metaphorical language was not merely a matter of preference, but one of apperception and reflection. Conceptual language challenges the intellect, but metaphorical language simultaneously enlists the help of, and activates, the imagination and emotions.

It is basically an epistemological problem, the always great gulf between the reality as it exists outside the mind and the expression of the objective reality in the mind through a concept or idea. Concepts cannot embrace the whole of reality, cannot include all the accidental modifications of reality; they frequently seem to be less effective in this respect than concrete, metaphorical language.

The many images of the Church in the New Testament[5] are helpful to us in trying to understand the reality of the Church because they stir the imagination, which is so vital to the perception of mysterious reality. Without some awakening of the imagination, these mysterious realities of God will very often seem drained of vitality and dynamism.

Karl Rahner speaks of the writings of the New Testament as "a genuine self-expression of the primitive Church," depicting its process of becoming.[6] In the images of the Church in the New Testament, we might say that the Church is attempting to achieve self-expression, trying to express all that she is in an authentic self-portrait.

Maud Bodkin writes:

> We see that the mediating process necessary before living experience can come to awareness is the linking of such experience with actions and objects that affect the senses and can be contemplated, and with words that recall these in all their variety of human experience.

> When a poet uses the stories that have taken shape in the fantasy of the community, it is not his individual sensibility alone that he objectifies. Responding with unusual sensitiveness to the words and images which already express the emotional experience of the community, the poet arranges these so as to utilize to the full their evocative power. Thus he attains for himself vision and possession of the experience engendered between his own Soul and the life around him, and communicates that experience, at once individual and collective, to others.[7]

So it is that the images of the sacred writers of the New Testament, in trying to describe the mysterious reality of the Church, are drawn from a communal imagination. They are hardly the original achievements of

---

[5] The most complete study is that of Paul S. Minear, *Images of the Church in the New Testament* (Philadelphia: Westminster, 1960).

[6] Karl Rahner, *Inspiration in the Bible* (New York: Herder and Herder, 1961), pp. 65–66.

[7] Maud Bodkin, *Archetypal Patterns in Poetry; Psychological Studies of Imagination* (New York: Vintage Books, 1958), pp. 7–8. Reprinted by permission of the Viking Press.

the individual authors, but, like all images, were the outgrowth of a common stock of images used by the communities in which they lived, moved, and had their being.

2. The Value of Biblical Imagery Today

There are many problems involved in our trying to grasp the reality of the Church through biblical imagery. We have already alluded to the "time element," and to the fact that these images were drawn from a communal imagination whose stock of images is not our own. There is also the problem of interpretation or translation of meaning in discovering the precise point of comparison; trying to express this same meaning in conceptual terms is futile, precisely because the meaning of an image is the image itself, since its force of communication lies largely in the realm of imagination.

Still there is a growing tendency in the proclamation of the Church today to revert to biblical language and image as the most effective expression of the mystery of the Church. Conceptual expressions and scientific definitions have left the faithful cold; they have not engaged the whole of man with all his powers. And the whole raison d'être of the Church lies in the radical imperative of her Lord to reach and save all men.

Furthermore, the Church today must express herself to men of all nations and cultures, to the opulent and starving, to the educated and uneducated, to the free and the imprisoned. She must tell them the good news as a living fullness rather than a dissected and dessicated series of formulae, which sound neither good nor like news.

So the Church today and the fathers of Vatican II have returned to the original and inspired expression of the Church's self-awareness as found in New Testament imagery. Lumen Gentium portrays the Church as "a kind of Sacrament" (no. 1), "the kingdom of Christ now present in mystery" (no. 3), "the edifice of God" (no. 6), "the holy city" (no. 6), "the new Jerusalem" (no. 6), "the Body of Christ" (no. 7), "the Bride of Christ" (no. 7), and "the People of God" (no. 9). These, and the other images recalled by the Dogmatic Constitution on the Church, are intended not only to challenge the minds of the faithful in search of understanding, but to evoke a total human response in the living and dynamic process that is salvation history. It is a vision of the Church in terms of the primitive and essential things that have great power to touch the heart of the beholder.

3. The Church as the Body of Christ: Human Unity in Christ

We have said that, in each of the biblical images of the Church, there is one implied point of comparison, and in the image of the Church as the Body of Christ, it is clearly *human unity in Christ*.

The gospel of existentialism according to men like Jean-Paul Sartre is one of aloneness and of the meaninglessness of life. "No man can count on anyone but himself," writes Sartre; "he is alone, abandoned on earth in the midst of his infinite responsibilities, without help, with no other aim than the one he sets himself, with no other destiny than the one he forges for himself on this earth." Such pessimism strikes hard at the heart of man, who fears such alienation from others, and who, in his deepest human instincts, knows with the metaphysical poet, John Donne, that "no man is an island."

Dostoevski, in his *The Brothers Karamazov*, asks God why he did not forcibly coerce man into unity, why he did not provide "some means of uniting all in one unanimous and harmonious ant-heap, for the craving for universal unity is the third and last anguish of man."

On June 29, 1943, Pope Pius XII spoke reassuringly to a war-torn world, to a lonely and shattered world, in his encyclical on "The Mystical Body of Christ."

> Moreover, We trust that the following exposition of the doctrine of the Mystical Body of Christ will be acceptable and useful to those also who are outside the fold of the Church. We are inspired to this hope not only because their good will toward the Church seems to grow from day to day, but also because, while before their eyes today nation rises up against nation, kingdom against kingdom, and discord is sown everywhere and the seeds of envy and hatred, if they turn their gaze to the Church, if they contemplate her divinely given unity — by which all men of every race are united to Christ in the bond of brotherhood — they will be brought to admire this fellowship in charity, and with the guidance and assistance of divine grace will long to share in the same union and charity.[8]

In the same encyclical, Pope Pius also spoke reassuringly to the heart of man, afflicted by a sense of life's meaninglessness. Summarizing the Catholic theology of redemption, the Pope spoke of man's role in the great drama of human salvation, of the corporate effort of the faithful of Christ to communicate the fruits of Christ's life and death.

> . . . Jesus crucified not only satisfied for our sakes the violated justice of the eternal Father, but merited for us as His blood-relations an indescribable abundance of grace. He would have been able to bestow this on the whole human race by Himself; but He wished to do that through the means of a visible Church, in which men would be bound together so that they

---

[8] Pope Pius XII, *Mystici Corporis*, America Press Edition, no. 6.

might cooperate with Him and thereby communicate mutually the divine fruits of the Redemption. Just as in fact the Word of God wished to take on our nature so that He might redeem men with His sufferings and torments, in a way almost the same He is served by the Church down through the centuries in the perennial continuation of the work which He initiated.[9]

Because of this divinely-chosen manner of redemption, man is not alone and his life cannot be meaningless. Around a splintered world of national rivalries and irreconcilable ideologies there are the supranational, encircling bonds of charity, community, and responsibility "in Christ Jesus."

4. Human Unity in Christ According to St. Paul

The revealed doctrine of the Mystical Body which Pope Pius proclaimed in his Encyclical, is largely drawn from the writings of St. Paul, whose letters are charged with this message of our unity in Christ. It was six or seven years after Pentecost when Paul, who was then Saul of Tarsus, a young Jewish Pharisee, was riding hard toward the Syrian city of Damascus to terrorize those "belonging to the Way"[10] (Acts 9:2). As he approached Damascus, he was blinded by a sudden flash of light, and was astonished by a sudden thundering question: "Saoul, Saoul, why do you persecute me?" "Who are you Lord?" Jesus replied, "I am Jesus whom you are persecuting. Arise now and go into the city, and you will be told what you must do . . ." (Acts 9:2–6).

And so Saul the Pharisee became Paul the Christian apostle. It was a rather dramatic introduction to the mystery of human unity in Christ,[11] and perhaps no one grasped the depth and universality of this mystery better than the Apostle to the Gentiles. In our chapter on "The Mystery of the Church," we have seen that Paul expresses this mystery in terms of our being "one in Christ Jesus" (Gal 3:28). It is the dominant theme in all of Paul's writings. He invents new metaphors and employs others which were more common; he uses phrases like *buried with* Christ, *risen-with* Christ, *joint-heirs with* Christ. It has been pointed out that "our English translations fail to convey here the strength of the original Greek. In each case St. Paul has coined a single word to depict the indescribably intimate and multiform union of the Christian with his Savior

[9] *Ibid.*, no. 16.
[10] Because Christianity directs man's whole life toward God, it was simply called "The Way." (Cf. Acts 9:2; 11:9, 23; 22:4; 24:14, 22.)
[11] Cf. St. Augustine, *Explanation of Psalm 30*, S. 1:3; he maintains that it is only the intimate union of Christ and the Church that explains Christ's question to Saul.

in the very mysteries of redemption."[12] We have pointed out that the phrase "in Christ Jesus" occurs 164 times in his letters and more than thirty-five times in Ephesians alone. Both Catholic and Protestant Scripture scholars see in it Paul's way of expressing the "closest conceivable union between the Christian and Christ, the triumphant spiritual Lord."[13]

To express this bond of human unity in Christ, the image of a body seems to have arisen spontaneously in the mind of Paul. It builds up in his letters, from the earlier period of Galatians, 1 Corinthians and Romans, and reaches its fullest development in his so-called "Captivity Epistles" to the Colossians and Ephesians. We will attempt to trace the use of the metaphor in Paul according to the chronology of his Epistles, but it should be mentioned first, that some theologians believe that Paul had not yet reached the notion of a "mystical body" in his earlier epistles. Cerfaux maintains that, prior to the Captivity Epistles, Paul's references to the Body of Christ refer to the Eucharist, the physical body of Christ, as the source of Christian unity.[14] For an example, Paul writes to the Corinthians:

> Does not the chalice of blessings which we bless bring us into union with Christ through his blood, and does not the bread which we break bring us into union with Christ through his body? Because the bread is one, we, the many who all partake of that one bread, form one body (1 Cor 10:16–17).

The more traditional interpretation of these earlier epistles is that Paul is already proposing the reality of the mystical body of Christ, which St. Augustine called "the whole Christ, head and members,"[15] Cerfaux and Huby, in defense of the minority opinion, maintain that "the body of Christ" in the earlier epistles always refers to the natural body of Christ, which, according to the Hebraic way of thinking, would mean the person of Christ.

This ambiguity is reflected in theological references to the body of Christ for twelve centuries. Paul obviously uses it in Ephesians and Colossians to designate the Church.[16] In Patristic literature, both the expression and the meaning are frequently found. Among the Fathers, some describe the Church as the "spiritual body," or "the mystical temple," "the mystical people," "the mystical head and members," but strangely enough the expression "the mystical body of Christ" is not found in

---

[12] Cf. Frank Norris, God's Own People (Baltimore: Helicon, 1962), p. 78.

[13] A. Wikenhauser, Pauline Mysticism: Christ in the Mystical Teaching of St. Paul (St. Louis: Herder, 1960), p. 22.

[14] Lucien Cerfaux, The Church in the Theology of St. Paul (New York: Herder & Herder, 1959), p. 265 ff.

[15] Cf. Mystici Corporis, no. 82.   [16] Cf. Eph 1:23; 5:23; Col 1:18; 1:24.

Patristic literature. Among theologians from the ninth to the twelfth centuries the expression "mystical body" seems to have been used frequently, but always of the Eucharist and never of the Church. In the twelfth century, the Eucharist was designated as "the true body of Christ," corpus Christi verum, and the "mystical body," signified by this Sacrament, was the Church. After this time, the expression "mystical body of Christ" has been reserved to mean the Church.[17]

5. The Development of the "Body of Christ" Doctrine in St. Paul

The Letter to the Galatians. This letter, composed about A.D. 56, was written in anger. From it we gather that some misguided and ill-intentioned Jewish converts had told Paul's poor, gullible Galatians that the apostle who founded their Church was not really an apostle, that he had not even seen Christ or heard his doctrine. So, in the letter, Paul establishes his credentials as an apostle, and then proceeds to summarize his doctrine. He insists that the Mosaic Law, though from God, was intended only as a temporary economy that would eventually lead men to Christ. True justification (holiness) can come only with faith in Christ, accompanied by baptism and fidelity to Christian teaching. And this means unity in Christ.

> You are in fact all children of God through faith in Jesus Christ, since all of you who have come to Christ by baptism have clothed yourselves with Christ. No longer is there Jew or Greek; no longer is there slave or freeman; no longer is there male or female. You are all one in Christ Jesus (Gal 3:26–28).

Here Paul stresses that the unity of men in Christ is that of adoption. Through and in Christ, we become adopted sons of God and heirs of God's infinite riches:

> God sent his Son . . . that we might receive the adoption. And because you are sons, God sent the Spirit of his Son into your hearts, crying, "Abba, Father." You are, then, no longer a slave but a son; and if a son, an heir also through God's grace (Gal 4:4–7).

The First Letter to the Corinthians. When Paul left Corinth, between A.D. 50 and 52, after about a year and a half spent in residence there, his newly founded church of Corinth was among his most flourishing foundations. It continued in prosperity for about five years, and then thorns began to show through the roses. Visitors from Corinth came

---

[17] Cf. S. Tromp, Corpus Christi quod est Ecclesia (ed. 2a, Roma), pp. 98–102; also Henri de Lubac, Corpus Mysticum, (ed. 2a), pp. 116–135; F. Norris, op. cit., p. 79, no. 3.

to him at Ephesus with disheartening news about cliques, some professing allegiance to Paul, others to Apollos, and still others to Peter. Thus, the theme of his letter to the troubled church was our unity in Christ. There were other problems, including a scandalous case of immorality involving a Christian living in open concubinage with his stepmother, which the Christian community seemed to accept with nonchalance. Christian chastity was not easily preserved in the atmosphere of Corinth, celebrated in the ancient world as a center of immoral life. In the year A.D. 57, Paul wrote:

> Make no mistake; no fornicator, no idolater, no adulterer, no pervert, no homosexualist, no thief, no slave of avarice, no drunkard, no addict of abusive language, no miser will inherit the kingdom of God. That is precisely what some of you were (1 Cor 6:9–11).

> Are you not aware that your bodies are members of Christ's body? Shall I then take the members of Christ and make them the members of a prostitute? Never! Are you not aware that he who unites himself to a prostitute becomes one body with her? . . . Are you not aware that your body is the temple of the Holy Spirit? Him you have received from God! You are not your own masters. You have been bought, and at a great price! So, then, glorify God in your body (1 Cor 6:15–20).

Later, in the same letter, he warns them about participating in the pagan sacrifices. Again, he appeals to the lofty motive of membership and unity in Christ. We are "one in Christ" and when we receive the Lord in the Eucharist our union with him and with one another is deepened.

> This is why, my dearly beloved, you should flee from idol worship. I address you as sensible people: judge for yourselves what I should say. Does not the chalice of blessings which we bless bring us into union with Christ through his blood, and does not the bread which we break bring us into union with Christ through his body? Because the bread is one, we, the many who all partake of that one bread, form one body (1 Cor 10:14–17).

In the first part of Chapter 12, Paul explains that the Holy Spirit has given each member of the Church a role to play and a contribution to make. Here Paul explicitly compares the Church to a body, and explains at great length the meaning of his metaphor or image:

> For example, just as the body is a unit, although it has many members, and all the members of the body, many though they are, form but one body, so too is the Christ.[18] In fact, by a single Spirit all of us, whether Jews or

[18] "(Christ) so sustains the Church, and so in a certain sense lives in the Church that it is, as it were, another Christ. The doctor of the gentiles in his letter to the Corinthians affirms this when, without further qualification, he called the Church 'Christ,' following no doubt the example of his Master, who called out to him from on high when he was attacking the Church: "Saul, Saul, why do you persecute me?" *Mystici Corporis*, no. 66.

Greeks, slaves or free men, were introduced into the one body through baptism, and all were given to drink of a single Spirit. The body, I repeat, is not formed of one but of many members. . . . God has put the members, every last one of them in the body, as he wished. Now if they were all one member, where would the body be? But, as it is, there are certainly many members, but a unified body. The eye cannot say to the hand, "I have no need of you." . . . In case one member is in pain, all the members share it. In case one member is honored, all the members share its satisfaction. You are Christ's body and individually its members (1 Cor 12:12–27).

Paul is demanding an absolute abdication of self-interest and competitive conduct. He seems astounded at the thought that Christians could be haggling over petty issues, when they form but one body of Christ.

The Letter to the Romans. Chronologically, Paul's next letter was to the Romans. Ostensibly, the letter is written to the Romans to tell them of his intended visit, but he uses the occasion to seize upon the theme that had dominated his thinking for twelve years of feverish missionary activity: unity in Christ. To Paul this was the most fundamental issue in the Church of his day, and his greatest fear was a split between Jewish and Gentile Christians.

Do you not know that all of us who have been baptized into union with Christ Jesus have been baptized into union with his death? Yes, we were buried in death with him by means of baptism, in order that, just as Christ was raised from the dead by the glorious power of the Father, so we also may conduct ourselves by a new principle of life. . . . But if we have died with Christ, we believe that we shall also live with him. . . . Thus you too must consider yourselves dead to sin, but alive to God in Christ Jesus (Rom 6:3–11).

The divine life and inheritance, forfeited by Adam, is re-offered to man in Christ; and Christ presents this new dispensation of grace as a second birth, a regeneration. Christ, acting through the sacrament of baptism, begets this new life, communicates his life of grace to those who have died (to sin) with him; and by this communication of grace incorporates into himself a new people, his Mystical Body. Of this Pope Pius writes:

It was by His blood shed on the cross that God's anger was removed and that all the heavenly gifts, especially the spiritual graces of the New and Eternal Testament, could then flow from the fountains of the Savior for the salvation of men. . . . It was on the tree of the cross, finally, that He entered into possession of His Church, that is, all the members of His Mystical Body; for they would not have been united to this Mystical Body through the waters of baptism except by the salutary virtue of the cross, by which they had already been brought under the complete sway of Christ.[19]

---

[19] *Mystici Corporis*, no. 37.

Later, in the letter to the Romans, Paul tells them that there is no longer any condemnation against those "who are in Christ Jesus" (8:1), and speaks of the norm which directs "my life in Christ Jesus" (1:2). Again, as with the Corinthians, he urges as the motive of upright moral conduct the unity of the Christian with Christ:

> You are not sensual but spiritual, if the Spirit of God really dwells in you, whereas no one who is deprived of the Spirit of Christ belongs to Christ. But if Christ is in you, the body, it is true, is destined to death because of sin, but the spirit has life because of its holiness (Rom 8:9–10).

A short while later, Paul urges confidence in the love of God, which is manifest in the union he has offered Christians through incorporation into Christ:

> Now we know that God causes all things to work together for the good of those who love him, who according to his purpose are called because those whom he has foreknown he has also predestined to be conformed to the image of his Son, so that this Son should be the first-born among many brothers (Rom 8:28–29).

Near the conclusion of his lengthy letter, Paul asks that each of the members of the Roman church accept his place in the Church, again using the metaphor of a living body to illustrate the unity of Christians in Christ.

> Let no one esteem himself more than he ought, but let him esteem himself in moderation according to the degree of faith which God has apportioned to each one. For just as in one body we have many organs, yet not all the organs have the same function, so we, the aggregate, are one body in Christ, but individually to one another we stand in the relation of part to part. We have gifts differing according to the grace that has been given us (Rom 12:3–6).

The Letter to the Colossians. Colossians is the first of Paul's "Captivity Epistles," so called because he wrote them from prison.[20] Actually, at the time he wrote Colossians, between A.D. 61 and 63, he was in Rome, waiting for his case to be tried and in the custody of a Roman soldier. Paul had not personally founded the church at Colossae, about 110 miles east of Ephesus, but he had converted one Epaphras, and quite likely commissioned him to found a church in his home town, Colossae. When Epaphras found the situation in the newly-founded church more than he could handle, he came to Rome and briefed St. Paul. The result was the letter to the Colossians. The peril which seems to have menaced this young community was a tendency to compromise with certain Jewish beliefs and practices, which were strangely blended with certain pagan

---

[20] See Eph 3:1; 4:1; 6:20; Col 4:3; Phil 1:7; Acts 21:17–26, 32.

notions. Paul's intent in the letter is to describe the absolute supremacy of Christ over all creation.

> He is the image of the invisible God, begotten before every creature, because in him were created all creatures in the heavens and on the earth, both visible and invisible, . . . All have been created through him and for him. He exists prior to all creatures, and in him they are all preserved in being. Further, he is the head of his body, the Church, in that he is the beginning, the first to rise from the dead, so that he may have pre-eminence over every creature. For it pleased God the Father that in him all fullness should dwell, and that through him God should reconcile to himself every being, and make peace both on earth and in heaven through the blood shed on the cross (Col 1:15–20).

> I rejoice now in the sufferings I bear for your sake, and what is lacking to the sufferings of Christ I supply in my flesh for the benefit of his body, which is the Church. Of this Church I have been made a minister in virtue of the commission given me by God for your benefit, to proclaim without stint the word of God, the mystery hidden for ages and generation, but now clearly shown to his saints. To them God willed to make known how rich in glory is this mystery among the Gentiles — Christ in you, your hope of glory (Col 1:24–27).

In decrying the influence of the false teachers, who had apparently influenced the church at Colossae, Paul writes:

> Such men fail to hold fast to the head from whom the whole body is supplied with nourishment and strength by the joints and ligaments, thus growing with a growth that is divine (Col 2:19).

And he asserts that, because we are all united in Christ, we are remolded in his image:

> Here there is no Gentile, no Jew, no circumcised, no uncircumcised, no barbarian, no Scythian, no slave, no free man, but Christ is everything in each of us (Col 3:11).

> Let the ruling principle of your hearts be the peace of Christ, to which you were called as members of one body; and be thankful (Col 3:15).

The Letter to the Ephesians. Although this letter is identified as "the letter to the Ephesians," there is considerable doubt that it was actually written for the church at Ephesus.[21] The most common solution today is that it was sent by Paul as a sort of encyclical to all the churches of the province of Asia; it has all the characteristic impersonality of an encyclical, but remains one of Paul's richest legacies to the Church. In the letter, he reiterates the dominant theme of Colossians, the absolute

---

[21] The two most ancient complete manuscripts (fourth century) do not contain the words "at Ephesus," as also the Chester Beatty Papyrus (p. 46). It has been proposed that the letter was written to the Laodiceans (see Col 4:15–16), or is a common letter to the churches of Asia.

supremacy of Christ, but fills it out in terms of Christ's supremacy in the Church, the Mystical Body of which he is the dynamic head, as opposed to the cosmic supremacy of Christ.[22]

It is true that all human history finds its fullest meaning in Christ. Because of his material body and human soul, hypostatically joined to his divine nature, he joins in himself all of created being to the Uncreated Being, the divine nature, which Christ possessed. In this letter, however, Paul emphasizes that, just as all creation is joined to Christ, in an even more intimate way all the baptized become one in him and with him. The reality of this union is so deep and intimate that Paul likens it, metaphorically, to the union of a living body, which forms one entity. The doctrine of our human unity in Christ is the pervasive, though not exclusive, theme of this letter. The following citations summarize his doctrine, which reaches its fullest development in this letter to the Ephesians:

In him [Christ] we have our redemption . . . the mystery of his will. And this good pleasure he decreed to put into effect in Christ when the designated period of time had elapsed, namely to gather all creation both in heaven and on earth under one head, Christ (Eph 1:10).

You, too, were joined to the Chosen People, after you had heard the message of truth, the Good News proclaiming your salvation, and had believed in it, and had been sealed with the promised Holy Spirit, who is the first installment of our inheritance.[23] The final purpose of thus being sealed is that we may be his possession by right of purchase to the praise of his glory (Eph 1:13–14).

He has subjected every single thing to his authority and has appointed him as universal head of the Church, which is truly his body, the complement of him who fills all the members with all graces[24] (Eph 1:22–23).

[22] Cf. Eph 1:3–14, which deals with this cosmic supremacy. Cf. A. Robert, Dictionaire de la Bible, Supplément, "Médiation dans l' A.T.," Vol. V, Cols. 997–1020; C. Spicq, "Médiation dans le N.T.," Ibid., Cols. 1020–1083.

[23] Pope Leo XIII wrote in Divinum Illud: "The Church which, already conceived, came forth from the side of the Second Adam in his sleep on the cross, first showed herself before the eyes of men on the great day of Pentecost." See Rom 5:5, where the Holy Spirit is depicted as the divine bond that joins us to Christ and the Father by giving us a share in their life and love: "God's love is poured forth in our hearts by the Holy Spirit who has been given to us."

[24] This is one of the few places where Paul uses the word ekklēsia to denote the universal Church, which he identifies in the next verse as Christ's Body. The notion of plērōma (complement) is that, while Christ is the total source of life and holiness in the Church, the Church is the completion of Christ, as the body completes the head. The Church is the "fullness" of Christ. Cf. St. Thomas, Summa Theologiae, III, q. 8, also Havet, "Christ collectif ou Christ individual," Ephemerides Theologicae Lovanienses (1947), pp. 499–520; P. Benoit, Revue Biblique 47 (1938), pp. 115–119. Cf. also Mt 28:18; 1 Cor 15:27; Col 1:18–24; 1 Cor 12:12. The most complete investigation of the Church as the fullness of Christ in recent journalistic writing is the articles of A. Feuillet, "L' Eglise plérome du Christ, d' aprés Ephés. 1, 23," Nouvelle Revue Théologique 78 (1956), pp. 449–472; 593–610.

For he himself is our peace; he it is who has made both Jews and Gentiles one, and has broken down the partition wall of hostility which separated them. The Law with its commandments and decrees he abolished through his human nature, that of the two races he might create in himself one new being, so making peace and reconciling both in one body to God by the cross, since he had killed that hostility (Eph 2:14–16).

For this reason on bended knees, I beseech the Father . . . that he may grant you, in keeping with his glorious riches, to be strengthened with power through the Spirit for the development of your inner selves, and to have Christ dwelling through faith in your hearts, and to be rooted and grounded in love. Thus will you have the power to grasp fully, together with all the saints, what is the breadth and length and height and depth of this mystery, and to know Christ's love which surpasses knowing, in order that you may be perfected and bring to realization God's complement . . . to him be glory in the Church and in Christ Jesus down through all generations for ever and ever (Eph 3:14–21).

Strive anxiously to preserve harmony of mind by means of the bond which effects peace. There is one body and one Spirit. . . . He who descended is the same one who also ascended above all the heavens, that he might fully impart all graces. He established some men as apostles, and some as inspired spokesmen, others again as evangelists, and others as pastors and teachers, thus organizing the saints for the work of the ministry, which consists in building up the body of Christ, until we all attain to unity in faith and deep knowledge of the Son of God. Thus we attain to perfect manhood, to the mature proportions that befit Christ's complement. Thus we shall no longer be children tossed to and fro and carried about by every wind of doctrine. . . . Rather by professing the truth, let us grow up in every respect in love and bring about union with Christ who is the head. The whole body is dependent on him. Harmoniously joined and knit together, it derives its energy in the measure each part needs only through contact with the source of supply. In this way the body grows and builds itself up through love (Eph 4:3–16).

Near the end of the epistle Paul reaches the final development of his thought on the Church as the Body of Christ, where he compares the union of Christ and the Church to the union between man and wife, which he is treating explicitly. This conjugal union is to be patterned on the union of the Lord with his Church; and here the apostle joins the body-image to the bride-image of the Church, which suggests the deepest intimacy and love. Christ bathes and heals and transforms his Bride in the waters of baptism; the Church is his Bride, radiant with his own life.[25]

---

[25] Cf. also Mk 2:19–20; Jn 3:29; 2 Cor 11:2–3; Apoc 19:7–8; 21:1–9; 22:17. Also see J. H. Darby, "The King and His Bride," *Irish Ecclesiastical Review* (1959), pp. 248–255.

Be subject to one another out of reverence for Christ. Let wives be subject to their husbands who are representatives of the Lord, because the husband is head of the wife just as Christ is the head of the Church and also the savior of that body. Thus, just as the Church is subject to Christ, so also let wives be subject to their husbands in all things.

Husbands, love your wives, just as Christ loved the Church, and delivered himself for her, that he might sanctify her by cleansing her in the bath of water with the accompanying word, in order to present to himself the Church in all her glory, devoid of blemish or wrinkle or anything of the kind, but that she may be holy and flawless. Even so ought husbands to love their wives as their own bodies. He who loves his wife, loves himself. Now no one ever hates his own flesh; on the contrary, he nourishes and cherishes it, as Christ does the Church, because we are members of his Body. "For this cause a man shall leave his father and mother, and cling to his wife; and the two shall become one flesh." (Gen 2:24)

This is a great mystery — I mean in regard to Christ and the Church (Eph 5:21–32).

6. Human Unity in Christ: A Summary

Ernest Mura, whose recent book on the Mystical Body is one of the most complete works on the subject,[26] writes that:

The analogy of the Mystical Body is the most perfect of those used by the Apostle of the Gentiles, and it contains all the preceding ones in an eminent way. It is also the most complete expression of many supernatural realities that constitute our union with Jesus.[27]

Father Mura summarizes the doctrine of the Mystical Body, as culled from Paul's Epistles, under these headings: (1) There is a total or whole Christ, which is Jesus Christ, the Son of God made man, the Head of redeemed and sanctified humanity, which is the fulfillment or pleroma of Christ. The members of the Church are the members of Christ. (2) These members are men called to incorporation into the body of Christ the Redeemer, to form one single, supernatural organism in union with him. (3) This organism, the Mystical Body of Christ, is the Church, the extension of Christ in space, the prolongation of Christ in time, the completion of Christ in the redemptive act of God. (4) Christ is the source of the total life and the needed graces in the sustenance of this integral organism. Mura says that these facts make up St. Paul's doctrine of salvation through Jesus Christ, and his doctrine of our union with him.[28] They also delineate the privilege and responsibility of Christians.

---

[26] Ernest Mura, R.S.V., *The Nature of the Mystical Body* (St. Louis: Herder, 1963).
[27] *Ibid.*, pp. 18–19.
[28] *Ibid.*, p. 59.

St. Augustine gives a more lyric summary-expression to the reality of human unity in Christ, when he writes:

> Let us rejoice, therefore, and give thanks, not only that we have become Christians, but that we have become Christ! Do you grasp this, my brothers? Do you understand the enormous grace God has given us? Stand in awe and rejoice: — we have become Christ! For if he is the Head, we are the members; the whole man — he and we. The fullness of Christ, therefore, is Head and members. What is this "Head and Members"? It is Christ and the Church![29]

We have explained that a biblical image, such as the Body of Christ, is a metaphor, an implied comparison. Some authors[30] seem to insist that the image of the Mystical Body is "far more than a mere metaphor." It would seem that these authors think that the metaphorical usage, by which the society of the Church is likened by analogy to a human, physical, and living body, denies the reality of the interior, spiritual bonds of union that join the members of the Mystical Body to one another and to Christ. Of course, this is out of the question. There is a reality, realized in the Church, by which the members of Christ are joined not only by external, social bonds but also by the internal life of faith and grace. Since it is a unique reality, Paul conceives it as though (by an implied comparison) it were a living, human body. This is, strictly speaking, a metaphor, but the metaphor is intended to illustrate the deepest and most intimate reality: the union of the members of Christ with Christ himself.

7. The Holy Spirit Is the "Soul" of the Mystical Body

"A human body" suggests an organic whole. There is a oneness, a unity, which is also capable of diversity (diverse members), and this body or organism is living, which implies the presence of a single source of life, which, in the integral, human composite, we call a "soul." In a living human being, the rational, human soul makes the body human; of itself the body would simply be an aggregation of atoms and molecules. What makes it a oneness or unity is the human soul. The human body is, furthermore, capable of a variety of activities, including human actions, all of which arise from the one principle of all life, namely the soul. By

---

[29] *Treatise on the Gospel of St. John*, 21:8.

[30] Norris, op. cit. p. 79: ". . . as it is used by the Apostle it is far more than a mere metaphor." Note that Pope Pius XII, in *Mystici Corporis*, says: "We have thus far seen that the Church has been so constituted that it may be likened to a body" (*ita constitutam esse Ecclesiam, ut corpori adsimulari queat*), America Press Edition, no. 32.

an extension of the analogy between the Body of Christ and the living, human body, we call the Holy Spirit the *soul* of the Mystical Body.

In his encyclical letter on the Mystical Body, Pope Pius quotes his predecessor, Leo XIII:[31] "Let it suffice to say that, as Christ is the Head of the Church, so is the Holy Spirit her soul."

Although St. Paul frequently alludes to the Holy Spirit in describing the unity of the members of Christ, he never explicitly speaks of the Spirit as the "soul" of the Body of Christ. But the Fathers of the Church did in fact make this extension of the metaphor, and almost unanimously taught that the internal principle of all vital activity in the Church is the Holy Spirit.[32] St. Augustine especially evolved this notion, and St. Thomas Aquinas frequently describes the Holy Spirit as "soul" of the Body of Christ.[33] It is found also in the Catechism of the Council of Trent,[34] and St. Robert Bellarmine speaks of the Holy Spirit as the soul of the Mystical Body insofar as he is the principle of vital operation in the Church.[35]

The classical passage in Paul, in which the Holy Spirit is portrayed as the soul or vital principle of all supernatural life and movement in the Church is 1 Cor 12:4-11. Here Paul proclaims that the Holy Spirit distributes the gifts in the Body of Christ, according to the role that each is to play; the Holy Spirit is the giver of gifts, activating all the supernatural potential of the members of Christ, "acting in all these gifts, which he distributes as he wishes."

In fact, the whole New Testament is rich with this thought of the lifegiving role of the Holy Spirit. In the Acts of the Apostles, the Spirit of Jesus (16:7) is borne in the persons of the Apostles (5:3); he descends upon them in "tongues of fire" and fills them with the gifts of understanding and expression (Ch. 2); he presides over the choice of the Apostles in filling up the ministry (13:2), and he places the bishops in office, who are to rule the Church (20:28).[36]

In St. Paul, the Holy Spirit is the Spirit of the Son whom God has sent (Gal 4:6), and it is this Spirit who warms hearts with divine love (Rom 5:5), and who produces by his own profound activity all virtues (Gal 5:22). He sanctifies and regenerates the children of God in baptism

---

[31] Pius XII, Mystici Corporis, no. 69, quoting from Pope Leo's encyclical *Divinum Illud*. See J. Beumer, "Der Heilige Geist, die Seele der Kirche," *Theologie und Glaube* 39 (1949), pp. 249–267.

[32] Cf. S. Tromp, *De Spiritu Sancto anima Corporis Christi Mystici; Testimonia Selecta e Patribus graecis; Testimonia Selecta e Patribus latinis, Textus et Documenta* (ed. 2a, Roma), Vols. 1 and 7.

[33] See places indicated in Tromp's edition of Encylical, note to no. 55.

[34] Part I, Chapter 10, question 12.

[35] *De Ecclesia Militante*, Chapter 9.

[36] Also see Acts 9:31.

(Tit 3:5), and infuses into them the filial sense by which they appeal to God as their Father (Gal 4:6; Rom 8:15). To belong to Christ, one must possess this Spirit (Rom 8:9). He is the Spirit of divine life (Rom 8:2); he gives life to the soul and resurrects the body (Rom 8:11). Every supernatural activity among the members of Christ is his work; he is even the hidden source of all power in prayer (Rom 8:26–27). He is the source of the interior life within men, and of all supernatural understanding of Christ (Eph 3:14–21). Through him we walk from glory to glory in our progressive configuration or assimilation to Christ (2 Cor 3:18). Through the impulse of the Holy Spirit the Church yearns for its ultimate and perfect union with Christ (Rom 8:23).[37]

While the explicit extension of the metaphor is not in Paul, the reality is certainly there and in the other inspired writers. As we have said, the Fathers of the Church do explicitly use this metaphor. Augustine, for example, writes:

> What our spirit, that is our soul, is to our members, the Holy Spirit is to the members of Christ, to the Body of Christ, which is the Church.[38]

> If you want to have the Holy Spirit, listen to this, my Brothers. Our Spirit, the one by which each man possesses life, is called the soul . . . It sees through the eyes, hears through the ears, smells through the nose, speaks through the tongue; through the hands it works, and through the feet it walks. It is present in all the members, giving life to all, and giving each its proper function. The same is true of the Church of God. In certain saints she works miracles, in others she preaches the truth; in some she preserves virginity, in others she observes conjugal sanctity. In some she accomplishes one thing, in others, something else. Each of the members has his own work, but the life of all is the same. What the soul is to the body, the Holy Spirit is to the Body of Christ which is the Church. The Holy Spirit accomplishes in the Church as a whole what the soul accomplishes in the diverse members of a single body.[39]

The Holy Spirit is the universal and primary principle of all supernatural life and activity in the Church. He structures the Church, appointing each to a given role in the life of Christ's Body, supplying the charismata by which each of us is enabled to discharge his responsibilities. Pope Pius XII summarizes the doctrine of the vivifying role of the Holy Spirit in the Body of Christ as follows:

> To this Spirit of Christ, too, as to an invisible principle, is to be ascribed the fact that all the parts of the Body are joined one with the other and with their exalted Head; for He is entire in the Head, entire in the Body and entire in each of the members. To the members He is present and

---

[37] Cf. these texts, already cited: Gal 4:6–7; 1 Cor 3:16–17; 6:19–20; 12: 4–31; Eph 3:14–21; 4:3–6.

[38] Sermon 268, no. 2.

[39] Sermon 267.

assists them in proportion to their various tasks and offices and the greater or lesser degree of spiritual health which they enjoy. It is He who through His heavenly grace is the principle of every supernatural act in all parts of the Body. It is He who, while He is personally present and divinely active in all the members, also acts in the inferior members through the ministry of the higher members. Finally, while with His grace He provides for the constant growth of the Church, He yet refuses to dwell with sanctifying grace in members that are wholly severed from the Body. This presence and activity of the Spirit of Jesus Christ is tersely and vigorously described by Our predecessor of immortal memory, Leo XII, in his encyclical letter *Divinum Illud* in these words: "Let it suffice to say that, as Christ is the Head of the Church, so is the Holy Spirit her soul."[40]

8. Membership in the Church: Who Are the Members of the Mystical Body?

In the revised schema on the Church, presented for debate at the second session of Vatican II, the first and most prominent image proposed to elucidate the true nature of the Church was that of the Mystical Body. However, in the final draft of the Constitution, although a rather long section on the Body image is retained, prominence is given to the image of the People of God. We shall discuss the reasons for this prominence in the next chapter, but one advantage was that the complex and hotly controverted question of membership in the Church, connected with the Mystical Body image, was painlessly bypassed.

Pope Pius XII, in his encyclical *Mystici Corporis*, had authoritatively, though not infallibly, taught that the "actual members" of the Body of Christ, which is the Church, are those and only those who are (1) validly baptized, (2) profess the true faith, (3) and have not been separated from body-unity by heresy or excommunication.[41]

Such qualifications for membership in the Body of Christ would, in the judgment of many theologians, exclude from actual membership all Protestant and Orthodox Eastern Christians. As the mysterious Xavier Rynne has pointed out:

> The concern of a rather large number of speakers with what may be called the ecumenical implications of the schema on the Church indicated that there was a kind of general consensus on this point which may be summed up by saying that what was most desired was a thoroughly biblical definition of the Church, based on such scriptural images as the People of God or the Kingdom of God, one that would be meaningful to Protestants, Orthodox and even non-Christians, and as free as possible, therefore, from the traditional post-biblical terminology — largely

[40] *Mystici Corporis*, no. 69.
[41] *Mystici Corporis*, no. 29.

of a juridical inspiration — which has characterized Catholic speculation on the nature of the Church in recent centuries.[42]

In a memorable contribution to the discussion of this topic, and in a speech which many felt set the tone for the whole debate on the Church, during the second session, Cardinal Lercaro clearly portrayed the need to avoid misunderstanding concerning the use of such terms as "society," "church," and "mystical body." He qualified the statement of Cardinal Ruffini, made a few days earlier, identifying the visible Roman Catholic Church with the Mystical Body of Christ. He contended that true membership in the Church through baptism is not an empty ecumenical gesture but a traditional theological truth:

> . . . the doctrine according to which baptism validly received incorporates once and for all in the Church as a visible society has always been Catholic doctrine.[43]

Very early in the discussion of this question, Cardinal Frings had suggested that the Council should not seek a definitive solution of this question; in fact, he suggested that it could not be solved or decided at this moment's stage of enlightenment, and the final document, *Lumen Gentium*, seems to reflect this view. The description of the Church as the Mystical Body, while largely consonant with Pius' teaching, does not ambition a declarative statement about membership in the Church.

> Basing itself upon Sacred Scripture and Tradition, it [This Sacred Council] teaches that the Church, now sojourning on earth as an exile, is necessary for salvation. Christ, present to us in His Body, which is the Church, is the one Mediator and the unique way of salvation. In explicit terms He Himself affirmed the necessity of faith and baptism (cf. Mk 16:16; Jn 3:5), and thereby affirmed also the necessity of the Church. Whosoever, therefore, knowing that the Catholic Church was made necessary by Christ, would refuse to enter it or to remain in it, could not be saved.

> They are fully incorporated in the society of the Church who, possessing the Spirit of Christ, accept her entire system and all the means of salvation given to her, and are united with her as part of her visible bodily structure and through her with Christ, who rules her through the Supreme Pontiff and the Bishops. The Bonds which bind men to the Church in a visible way are profession of faith, the sacraments, and ecclesiastical government and communion.[44]

After affirming this, however, the Council Fathers continue:

> The Church recognizes that in many ways she is linked with those who, being baptized, are honored with the name of Christian, though they do

---

[42] Xavier Rynne, *The Second Session. The Debates and Decrees of Vatican II, September 29 to December 4, 1963* (New York: Farrar Straus, 1964), p. 61.

[43] *Ibid.*, p. 63.

[44] *Lumen Gentium*, no. 14.

not profess the faith in its entirety or do not preserve unity of communion with the successor of Peter. [The Council here enumerates the sources of this union]. . . . In all of Christ's disciples the Spirit arouses the desire to be peacefully united, in the manner determined by Christ, as one flock under one shepherd, and he prompts them to pursue this end.[45]

Perhaps the clearest statement by the Fathers of Vatican II that ecclesial reality reaches far beyond the visible bounds of the Roman Catholic Church is to be found in the *Decree on Ecumenism*. In that epochal document the bishops assembled in Council acknowledged quite clearly that the term "Church" can, indeed must, be used to describe Christian communities separated from Rome, that they are genuinely "ecclesial communities," not "sects" or "denominations." The following statements are of major importance here:

All those justified by faith through baptism are incorporated into Christ. They therefore have a right to be honored by the title of Christian, and are properly regarded as brothers in the Lord by the sons of the Catholic Church.

Moreover some, even very many, of the most significant elements or endowments which together go to build up and give life to the Church herself can exist outside the boundaries of the Catholic Church: the written word of God; the life of grace; faith, hope, and charity, along with other interior gifts of the Holy Spirit and visible elements. All of these, which come from Christ and lead back to Him, belong by right to the one Church of Christ.

It follows that these separated Churches and Communities . . . have by no means been deprived of significance and importance in the mystery of salvation.[46]

---

[45] *Lumen Gentium*, no. 15.
[46] *Decree on Ecumenism*, no. 3.

CHAPTER FOUR

A Second Biblical Image of the Church: The People of God

For you are a people holy to the Lord your God; the Lord your God has chosen you to be a people for his own possession, out of all the peoples that are on the face of the earth. It was not because you were more in number than any other people that the Lord set his love upon you and chose you, for you were the fewest of all peoples; but it is because the Lord loves you. . . (Dt 7:6–8).

Behold, the days are coming, says the Lord, when I will make a new covenant with the house of Israel and the house of Judah. . . . I will put my law within them, and I will write it upon their hearts; and I will be their God, and they shall be my people
(Jer 31:31, 33).

1. The New Self-Understanding of the Church

We have seen that, in the wake of the Protestant Reformation, the theologizing of ecclesiology degenerated into a polemical apologetics, which presented the Church as a desiccated, juridical structure. This imbalance of vision and stress tended to identify the Church with her external, hierarchical aspects, and tended to lose all realization of the divine, inner life of the Church. The rediscovery of this inner life and unity was actually inaugurated at the beginning of the nineteenth century by Möhler at Tübingen, and was kept alive by Franzelin, Schroeder, Scheeben, and Newman. These men were seminal thinkers, but the fruits of the harvest did not begin to nourish the general life of the Church until the beginning of this century.

The first World War was the shattering reality that rattled the minds of men, and drove them to look for something more meaningful. In the years of uneasy peace that followed the war, theologians began to present the mystery of the Church in deeper and more richly supernatural accounts. Great men like Karl Adam and Romano Guardini emerged to usher in the first period of the general rediscovery of the Church. It has been characterized as "the Mystical Body phase,"[1] which ran from about 1920 until 1943, when Pope Pius wrote his famous encyclical letter, *Mystici Corporis*. It was an immensely valuable time in the life of the Church, in which the new nourishment deepened the Christian lives of many, increased the number of lay apostles, and gave a much needed impulse to the liturgical movement.[2]

In the new and present phase of self-understanding in the Church, all the wealth of realization resulting from the image of the Body of Christ has been incorporated into a more total vision of the Church, characterized by the Church as the People of God, the messianic community of Christ. It is the opinion of many theologians[3] that this image allows a fuller, better balanced presentation of the Church than exclusive concentration on the Church as the Body of Christ.

On October 17, 1963, in an allocution to the Observers at Vatican II, Pope Paul said: "Your hope that 'a theology' will be developed 'that is both concrete and historical' and 'centered on salvation history,' is one which we gladly support. We believe that this suggestion deserves to be studied in depth." It is interesting to note that a special intervention was made by the Coordinating Commission of the Council, which resulted in what is now the second chapter of the Constitution on the Church: "On the People of God."

---

[1] See Charles Davis, "Past Trends and Present Tensions," *The Clergy Review* (July, 1963) pp. 417–436, esp. p. 421.

[2] Another strong impulse was a later encyclical of Pope Pius, *Mediator Dei*, published on November 20, 1947.

[3] See Cerfaux, *The Theology of the Church in St. Paul* (New York: Herder & Herder, 1959). He holds that "The People of God" is the primitive and fundamental idea which dominates Paul's theology of the Church.

Yves Congar explains this revision as follows.[4] The first chapter of the Constitution, entitled "The Mystery of the Church," shows the divine causes of the Church, the love of the Trinity, and the Incarnation of the Son of God. It is this chapter that incorporates the vision of the Church as the Mystical Body of Christ. It was thought that there should be a second chapter, following immediately, to show this Church also in another aspect, in the process of fulfilling itself in human history; to show the Church expanding and diffusing among men the fullness of the life that is in Christ and of which the Church is the witness and sign of sacrament. Such a presentation or image of the Church would also explain the common dignity of Christian existence, shared by all the members of the People of God, prior to the distinctions of office and state, which are taken up in subsequent chapters of the Constitution.

It should be noted, too, that the original *schema* on the Church was rejected by the Council Fathers and sent back to the committee for revision, because, as Bishop De Smedt of Bruges said in expressing his discontent: it opens the way to the triple temptation of *legalism, clericalism,* and *triumphalism.*[5] The Bishop felt that, before a study of the hierarchy and laity, one should proclaim the Church as a single family, a brotherhood; prior to any division into groups it is one in faith and baptism. This is effectively brought out by the presentation of the Church as the People of God.[6]

2. The General Import of the Image, "The People of God"

As we have seen, each of the metaphorical expressions or biblical images of the Church brings out an individual aspect of the depth and beauty of the Church. "The People of God," as the predominating image in current ecclesiological literature, views the Church in its temporal and social dimensions. It considers the mystery of Christ and his perennial saving-presence in the Church, a community of men, gathered together into unity by God's benevolent design, advancing historically, with the continuing help of God, toward a destiny of kingdom and fulfillment. It illuminates the human element in the Church, its inadequacies, and the need for reform that is constantly before the Church during its pilgrimage

[4] Yves Congar, "The Church: The People of God," *Concilium*, Vol. 1 (New York: Paulist Press, 1964), p. 11.

[5] See William H. Shannon, "The Council, the Liturgy and Christian Formation," In *Guide* (Jan., 1965), p. 8. A deeper understanding of the Bishop's views can be gained from reading his well-known pastoral letter, *The Priesthood of the Faithful* (New York: Paulist Press, 1962).

[6] See Gregory Baum, "Pope and Bishops," *The Commonweal* (Nov. 8, 1963).

on earth. The Church is always *in via* on the great journey from Pentecost to Parousia. It is easier for us to feel a part of such a mystery, to feel challenged by such a presentation of the Church. Many other images of the Church, which stress the sanctity of God's community, can seem to turn us away on the grounds of unworthiness; we can place the Church on such an enormous pedestal that few of us would feel equipped to risk the thin air of its presence. There is little risk of this in approaching the Church as the People of God.

We will now consider this presentation of the Church in the specific connotations of the image of the Church as the People of God.

3. The Historical Implications of the "People of God"

More and more the Church is realizing that faith is a total response of man,[7] and the doctrinal "instructions" of recent memory have given way to a presentation of God's salvific interventions in human history. It is the dramatization of the mystery, God's plan to unify and vivify all men through his Son. As we view this dramatization, each of us realizes his involvement; each of us has a special role to play. The dramatic element is captured in the presentation of God making human history salvation history, revealing himself and his plan to share his life with man only gradually. "Doctrine," as we know it, is a development which grows out of the reflection on these events in salvation history. Even the New Testament, the earliest doctrinal expression of the Church, represents the reflection of the Church on the events of the first century. The New Testament is basically an announcement of the Christ-event, the person of Christ and the events of his life, death, and resurrection. These early Christians were converted by the person and events, and only later spoke in doctrinal terms when they had been thoroughly permeated with the person and events. The Christian today is no different: only in exposure to the person and events of Christianity will he make the wholehearted response of a Christian.

God's mercy to men did not begin with Christ and is not confined to Christians. God's love and mercy have been operative from the beginning of human history. In fact, the coming of Christ is presented in Scripture as the climax of a long series of mercies, and a continuation of the mercy announced to Israel.

The Church may be called the new People of God because of her

---

[7] Cf. Bruce Vawter, "The Biblical Idea of Faith," in *Worship* (Aug.–Sept., 1960). Father Vawter describes justifying faith as a wholehearted commitment which is the beginning of a new way of life.

regeneration in the Spirit, but at the same time she is the fulfillment of Israel, the continuation of God's first chosen people. The pilgrim People of God has its roots in Israel, and God's dealings with Israel are continued in the Church today. He still scourges and purifies, forgives and blesses us as he did with Israel, which is alive within us. Paul sees the New Israel as grafted on the Old Israel,[8] ". . . they are most dear in virtue of the divine choice. For God does not revoke his gifts and call" (Rom 11:29). In the New Testament, God pronounces his perfect Word of love and reconciliation; in his Son he brought to a close the period of preparation, fulfilled his promises, and said the last word of his self-revelation.

This was the preaching of the early Church, as we know from the sermons in Acts.[9] In these sermons the emphasis is placed upon God's dealings with his People, upon his mighty deeds recorded in their Sacred History. Jesus the Messiah is presented as the culminating act of God's mercy, of which all of his previous mercies are a type and foreshadowing.

Father Bernard Cooke writes:

> In this understanding of the Church as something dynamic, something growing and developing, precisely because it is a community of persons in history, the whole notion of salvation history seems increasingly important. If the Church is a reality in history, a reality essentially historical in its being, then somehow or another historical methods must be utilized in providing this sort of insight. If the Church is to be considered an outgrowth of the history of salvation which preceded and which is itself a continuing mystery of God's workings in the midst of mankind, then salvation history must be considered a reality which is not just of the past but which continues through the present into the future. To teach the Church in this way means that one must teach it in its roots and in its present existence, but also in its movement toward the future, toward its eschatological realization.[10]

The *Constitution on the Church* of Vatican II sees the dealings of God with man in salvation history as summarized and recapitulated in the image of the People of God. In the second chapter of the *Constitution*, entitled "On the People of God," we read:

> God, however, does not make men holy and save them merely as individuals, without bond or link between one another. Rather has it pleased Him to bring men together as one people, a people which acknowledges Him in truth and serves Him in holiness. He therefore chose the race of Israel as a people unto Himself. With it He set up a covenant. Step by step He

---

[8] Rom 11:11-36.

[9] Cf. Henry St. John, "Presenting the Christian Message," *Life of the Spirit:* editorial in issue of Oct. 1958.

[10] See Bernard Cooke, "Theology and Catechetical Renewal," in *Pastoral Catechetics,* edited by Hofinger and Stone (New York: Herder and Herder, 1964), p. 99.

⊬⊬809

taught and prepared His people, making known in its history both Himself and the decree of His will and by making it holy unto Himself. All these things, however, were done by way of preparation and as a figure of that new and perfect covenant which was to be ratified in Christ, and of that more luminous revelation which was to be given through God's very Word made flesh.

"Behold the days shall come, saith the Lord, and I will make a new covenant with the house of Israel, and with the house of Juda. . . . I will give my law in their bowels, and I will write it in their heart: and I will be their God, and they shall be my people. . . . For all shall know me, from the least of them even to the greatest, saith the Lord" (Jer 31:31–34). Christ instituted this new covenant, that is to say, the new testament, in His blood (cf. Cor 11:25), by calling together a people made up of Jew and Gentile, making them one, not according to the flesh but in the Spirit. This was to be the new people of God.[11]

There is needed, if we are to understand the continuity of God's salvific action in history and the continuity between Israel and the Church, some familiarity of God's meeting with Abram (Gen 12:1–8; 17:1–8) and the promise which Abram received with such docile faith (Gen 15:6). Yahweh repeats his promises and gradually reveals himself more and more to the man he had claimed for his own (Gen 15:1–20; 17:1–22). The relation between God and Abram is called a "covenant" (Gen 17:7), and God changes his name from Abram to Abraham as a symbol of his own lordship and Abraham's new destiny. Paul calls Abraham the father of believers, because all believers in some sense are called upon to accept God's invitation and journey to destinations unknown at his word (Gen 15:1–12).

God repeats his invitations to Abraham's son and grandson, Isaac and Jacob (Gen 26:1–6; 23–25; 28:10–12). Some five hundred years later, he keeps the promise he made to Abraham to "make a great nation" of him and to make his "name great" and his person a source of blessings for "all the nations on the earth" (Gen 12:1–3). The man he works through is Moses, the greatest of Yahweh's prophets in the Old Testament (Ex 3:1–22). He is the appointed liberator of God's People (Ex 6:1–9; 11:4–8; 12:29–36), and his People recall God's favor in the memorial service of the Passover (Ex 12:1–28).[12]

After many vicissitudes of the exodus (going out) from Egypt, God's People, Israel, arrives at Mt. Sinai in the Arabian desert, where God reveals the promised land (Ex 19:1–8) and the terms of covenant (Ex 20:1–20). Israel seals its covenant with Yahweh (Ex 24:3–8) with the blood of a victim animal and a banquet of celebration. The rest of the

[11] No. 9.
[12] So-called because Yahweh's punishing angel "passed over" the Israelite homes and struck only the Egyptians.

Old Testament records the struggles and disasters of God's People, armed with the covenant, moving toward its destiny.[13]

The Messianic expectation, seen growing in this people from the time of the covenant at Sinai, is a difficult concept. It has many senses and connotations, many strata of understanding. In its broadest sense, it was Israel's conviction that, by Yahweh's predilection, it possessed a divinely appointed destiny as a priestly people. In its strictest sense it was the expectation of an extraordinarily endowed individual who would lead them to the perfect fulfillment of that destiny. They cherished the hope that Yahweh would lead them to the *eschaton*, the final and ultimate historical condition of supremacy and fulfillment. A kingdom, rather than a king, preoccupied their desire.

This was the People of God: pressing on to a dramatic and extraordinary destiny, and, for all its human weakness, consistently conscious of its vocation. They could not have dreamed that their fulfillment would be the entrance of Yahweh's own Son into this world. But this he did, and all the hopes of Israel and the fulfillment of destiny were achieved in this moment and in this coming. The "new covenant" prophesied by Jeremiah (31:31-34) was to be fulfilled in Jesus. In the Incarnation the movement of salvation history toward a healing redemption reaches its apex.

The New Testament is filled with this conviction, that Jesus is the fulfillment of Israel's hope.[14] The title of "Savior" is attributed both to God[15] and more frequently to Jesus.[16] Salvation is seen, not as a national liberation, but as a freedom from sin, and a deliverance from God's wrath and condemnation.[17] Positively, salvation in the New Testament is "life": — to be transferred from the kingdom of death to the kingdom of life.[18]

Paul sees the New Covenant, which forms the new People of God, as ratified in the blood of Christ.[19] The Old Covenant could only make slaves,[20] whereas the New Covenant makes us the children of God,[21] who enjoy the freedom effected through Christ.[22] Paul's basis for distinc-

---

[13] There is no need here to recapitulate all of God's actions with Israel. Suggested as excellent: Robert Dyson and Alexander Jones, *The Kingdom of Promise, Its Preparation, Foreshadowing and Fulfillment* (Westminster, Md.: Newman, 1955); Neal Flanagan, *Salvation History* (New York: Sheed and Ward, 1964); Augustine Stock, *Lamb of God* (New York: Herder and Herder, 1963).

[14] Lk 2:29-32; Acts 4:11-12.

[15] Lk 1:47; 1 Tim 1:1; 2:3; 4:10; Tit 1:3, etc.

[16] Lk 2:11; Jn 4:42; Acts 5:31; 13:23; Eph 5:23; Phil 3:20, etc.

[17] Mt 1:21; Lk 1:77; 7:49-50; 1 Tim 1:15; Rom 5:9; Jn 12:47; 1 Cor 5:5.

[18] E.g. Eph 2:5.

[19] 1 Cor 11:25.

[20] Gal 4:22-31.

[21] Rom 8:14; Gal 4:6.

[22] Rom 8: 1-4.

tion between the Old and New Covenants is the conferring of the
Spirit.[23] The redeeming death of Christ has established an entirely new
relationship between God and his people.[24] The New Covenant surpasses
the Old just as the life-giving spirit surpasses the letter-of-the-law which
kills.[25] In Hebrews, most of the letter is dedicated to the superiority of
the New over the Old Covenant. In this letter, too, we find repeated
allusions to Christ as the fulfillment promised to Israel. Christ is called
"the high priest of messianic blessings,"[26] and the Law is portrayed as
incomplete because "it possesses only the shadow of messianic blessings
. . . the full expression of their reality" being found only in the efficacy
of Christ's one sacrifice.[27]

The Church in the New Testament is, therefore, presented as the
continuation and the messianic fulfillment of the Chosen People of God,
the heir of Israel's promises. Matthew begins his gospel by saying that it
is "A record of the life of Jesus Christ, the Son of David, the Son of
Abraham."[28] The Church of the Gentiles is grafted onto the people of
Israel, but it is the total Israel that will be saved and reach fulfillment.[29]

At the same time we must balance this spiritual *continuity* with Israel
with a *new* covenant and a *new* entity, the Church, constituted as the
People of God in the blood of Jesus.

> The Law with its commandments and decrees he abolished through his
> human nature, that of the two races he might create in himself one *new*
> being, so making peace and reconciling both in one body to God by the
> cross, since he had killed that hostility (Eph 2:15–16).

There cannot be any exaggeration of this continuity which would minimize the fact that the Church represents a new economy of grace and
salvation in Jesus.[30] Still the Church is the eschatological Israel, elevated
to cosmic dimensions, and it is an anticipation of the heavenly Jerusalem.
Without this vision, the history of salvation is fragmented, and the continuous cultivation of his vineyard by the loving Yahweh is lost from
our sight. And this is precisely what the image of the Church as the
People of God keeps in focus; it summons to mind the whole history
of God's execution of his mystery, his loving design for man. It is a
history permeated and dominated by God's patient love for man. Through
his continuous and gracious interventions, man is led step by step toward

---

[23] 2 Cor 3:6; Rom 7:6; cf. Ezek 37:14–28.
[24] Rom 3:21–25.
[25] 2 Cor 3:6–13.
[26] Heb 9:11.
[27] Heb 10:1–10.
[28] Mt 1:1.
[29] Rom 9:6–29.
[30] See J. Jocz, A Theology of Election: Israel and the Church (London, 1958).

his destiny over the roads of this earth and the roads of history, not as an individual but as the People of God.[31]

So the Church is not simply the People of Israel having received its Messiah. The intervention of God, in making a personal entrance into this world and into human history, is such an enormous and loving act that it transcends all of the promises made to Israel, and, while continuing the notion and motion of the ancient Israel, at the same time it results in a new creation: The People of God in Christ Jesus, which is the Church.

> If then any man is in Christ, he is a new creation; the old state of things has gone; wonderful to tell, it has been made over, absolutely new. All this comes from the action of God, who has reconciled us to himself through Christ . . . (2 Cor 5:17–18).

4. The People of God and the Human Element in the Church

Rare is the Catholic who does not know of defections from the Church, occasioned by the ill-temper of a priest, the supposed deceitfulness or narrowness of a Sister, or even the suspicion of general hypocrisy among Catholics. It is a stereotype story of shattered ideals and a whole gamut of resultant emotions: disappointment, outrage, bitterness, and a disdain that prefers protective isolation. Whatever truth lies under the angry words of accusation, there is always sadness both for the weakness of the person who has gone and for the weakness that may have occasioned his departure.

No less real is the despondency that grows out of the realization that, true and honest as my own ideals are, they are always beyond my powers of realization. I confront, in moments of truth, my own ill-temper, my own deceitfulness, my own hypocrisy. There is another law warring in my members. I am confused by a spiritual schizophrenia that splits my sense of integrity.

My rearing in the faith had led me to expect that the Church is a spotlessly holy reality, a thing of stained-glass windows and angelic saints with heaven-swept eyes, a part of heaven's incorruptibility descended upon this earth. Then, as it had to, there came a day of disillusion; a sudden traumatic insight or an agonizing conclusion to a long submerged thought process.

The world of incense and flowers is usually exposed during adolescence as a phantasy world; it does not stand the probing questions of young adult minds. The whole utopian world can suddenly look like a world of

---

[31] *Lumen Gentium*, no. 9, quoted *supra*, pp. 48–49.

slums and ghettos. The celebrities on the pedestal of public admiration are found to have the clay feet of impostors; the dynasty of pornography capitalizes on the concupiscence of man, and all the grandiloquent lessons about the Christian social order seem like a distant and naïve thought. The "good news" of the gospel is neither good nor news in this world.

If the young Christian huddles more closely to the Church in search of warmth and light, pours himself into the Church's channels of actions, he will see the stark humanity of the Church exposed in all its ugly nakedness: politicking, power struggles, obduracy and obstructionism, the preeminence of the financial, scandal and sin. One is sometimes tempted to wonder if the Church hears her own sermons and, if so, how seriously she takes them. The world groans for redemption "While the True Church remains below / Wrapt in the old miasmal mist."[32]

No matter how stirring we find the love and salvific will of God concretized and personalized in the Church, and no matter how consoling we find the realities that lie under the biblical images of the Church as Christ's Body and Bride, her weakness — of which my personal weakness is part — is ever before us. We are the struggling People of God wandering in the desert toward the promised land of a distant, heavenly Jerusalem. The Church is a bleeding Church in need of hands to bandage her wounds. The Church is not only an *object* of faith; it is also a *test* of faith.

In its historical connotations, the People of God suggests these sorrows. The whole history of Israel is marked with a stumbling infidelity. Somehow God holds it intact, but almost in spite of itself. And the whole history of the New Israel is likewise a scarred narrative with many sad chapters. There is always great need for God's help and God's mercy, the need for graces of fidelity and perseverance.[33] The journey from Pentecost to Parousia is like that from Egypt to the Promised land; a time of struggles and failures. This is why reform and renewal must always be a part of the program of the Church in living out its covenant and vocation.

The image of the People of God also reminds us forcefully that the Church, while it is a divine institution, is a society of men. It is not a temple into which come worshipers; it is rather a living temple, a temple of men corporately working out their salvation. It is a living organism forever engaged in the process of growing and healing, moving unendingly if unevenly toward its consummation.

---

[32] From *The Hippopotamus*, by T. S. Eliot.

[33] See Paul Simon, *The Human Element in the Church of Christ* (Westminster, Md.: Newman, 1954); it is this aspect of the Church which is stressed in Dom Anscar Vonier's, *The People of God* (London, 1937).

This apparent weakness in the Church can be a source of temptation to us.[34] God, whose ways are not our ways, seems to ask us to see his presence in human disfigurement. But it is not surprising. God once asked men to look upon a man, scourged to rawness and writhing on a cross, and to believe that this man was really God. In fact, God seems to have expected that it would be precisely at this moment of physical disfiguration that his Son would be recognized.

When you have lifted up [crucified] the Son of Man, then you will know that I am he (Jn 8:28).

And I, if I be lifted up [crucified] from the earth, will draw all things to myself (Jn 12:32).

God's will is that the eyes of faith recognize his power in weakness. Christ on the cross portrayed a picture of utter dereliction and weakness; yet it was really the manifestation and revelation of God's power. Paul tells the Corinthians how he implored God to relieve him of "a thorn for the flesh, a messenger of Satan to buffet me."

Concerning this I three times besought the Lord that it might leave me. And he said to me, "My grace is sufficient for you, for *my power is made perfectly evident in your weakness*" (2 Cor 12:8–9).

In the first letter to the Corinthians, Paul had already explained this "power in weakness" theme:

Why, there is more wisdom in the "absurdity" of God than in all the "wisdom" of men and more might in the "weakness" that God has made his own than in all the might of men. . . . But God chose what the world holds foolish, to put to shame the wise, and what the world holds weak God chose to put to shame the mighty, and what the world holds ignoble and despicable, and what counts for nothing God chose to bring to nothing the things that count. Lest any weak mortal should pride himself in God's sight (1 Cor 1:25–29).

God seems to have willed to show his power through the weakness of men. One is reminded of the dialogue recorded in the life of St. Margaret Mary Alacoque, the cloistered Visitation Nun, when she was commissioned to proclaim the love of the Sacred Heart of Jesus to the whole world. The poor Sister, it seems, had some trouble believing that God had come to the right person, protesting her inability as a cloistered and insignificant nun to tell the world of the love that blazes in the heart of Christ. It is said that the Lord reassured her in a way that is almost as paradoxical as the choice of his People: "It is precisely because of your weakness and insignificance that I have chosen you, so that, when the

---

[34] See Henri de Lubac, "Our Temptations Concerning the Church," in *The Splendor of the Church* (New York: Sheed and Ward, 1956).

message is proclaimed, the world will know that it is my message and my work, not yours."[35]

In an ancient liturgy of the Church there was a preface for the Feasts of Saints Peter and Paul, which runs:

> Therefore it should be proclaimed that it depends not upon the resources of man [i.e., the life of the Church], but on the gifts of God. It should be comprehended how all the apparent greatness of this world is but foolishness without you, O God. It should be taught how all folly will be lifted up through you, for so has your providential will ordained.[36]

Just as his Son, hanging on a cross, was God's sign of salvation, so is this poor pilgrim People, the Church, "a sign raised up among the peoples of the earth, an invitation to all those who do not yet believe."[37] The People of God is destined to be a sign to be contradicted, hanged upon the gallows of history, and yet, in the appearance of dereliction, a sign of salvation.

Down through two millenia and into our own day, the Messiah remains in the world he came to save; in his complement, the Church, he "bears all things, believes all things, hopes all things, endures all things" (1 Cor 13:7). He comes to men in new appearances of shame and dereliction, and once more asks men to find in crippled ugliness immortal beauty, in human limitations the presence of an infinite God.

> Probably there is much in the Church that betrays the weaknesses of our human nature. Her divine Founder, however, endures these weaknesses. He endures them even in the higher members of his Mystical Body, for this reason, so that in this way the strength of the virtuousness of the flock and the shepherds will be tested, and that the merits of faith should grow in each of them. Christ would wish all to know that even sinners are not shut out of this community. Therefore, the fact that many members suffer from spiritual infirmity is no reason for us to have less love for the Church; rather it is an occasion for us to feel deeper sympathy with her members.[38]

St. Ambrose recalls the "theophany" of the Burning Bush (Ex 3:5-6), in which Yahweh spoke to Moses, the first of his prophets and his intermediary in the establishment of the Covenant of Sinai, and finds it a type of the Church:

> For so speaks our Lord: In this Church I appear to you as once I appeared in a bush of thorns. You are the thornbush; I am the fire. I am the fire in

---

[35] Cf. Dt 7:6-7: "It was not because you were more in number than any other people that the Lord set his love upon you and chose you, for you were the fewest of all peoples."

[36] *Sacramentarium Leonianum*, Muratori I, 333; PL 55, 51 BC.

[37] Vatican I, DS 3013.

[38] *Mystici Corporis*, no. 80.

the thornbush in your flesh. I am the fire to illuminate you, to burn away the thorns of your sinfulness, to give you the favor of my grace.[39]

The People of God, which is the Church, is a Church of flames and thorns, of humanity and divinity, of trial and joy, of ugliness and beauty, of unfaithfulness and fidelity, of struggle and glory.

"For my power is made perfectly evident in your weakness." . . . For this reason I take delight, for Christ's sake, in infirmities, in insults, in hardships, in persecutions, in distresses. For when I am weak, then am I strong (2 Cor 12:9–10).

Our reluctance to accept the People of God with all its manifest human weakness is very often, in its unexposed roots, a form of triumphalism, a poorly disguised form of snobbery. Pope John explicitly apologized to our separated Christian brothers for this sin. Triumphalism is basically the urge to be associated or identified with power, either in a person or an organization. It is usually a tacit admission of personal inadequacy, and so the triumphalist wants to see the Church equated with the honor, preference, and deference shown to her and her representatives. When this honor, esteem, and glory starts into descendancy, the triumphalist is gripped with the ostensible fear that the Church is losing her influence, and he feels a great sense of loss. He is no longer identified with an honored organization which is exempted from criticism and accusation. His own sense of loss may lead him to be "scandalized" with the Church.

Another root of this reluctance is the psychological phenomenon of "displacement." Men often take to criticism of a system — a Church, government, or organization — for failing to live up to their cherished ideals for that system; it is an easy refuge from self-scrutiny and the admission that one personally falls very short of his own ideals. It can often be true that we use our disappointment in the People of God to avoid being disappointed in ourselves. This would be the most difficult source of temptation concerning the People of God for a man to face, for, if he faces it, he would suddenly be facing himself.

Finally, it might also be true that a man, here or there, is uncomfortable in the Church. He would like very much to find a reasonable pretext for divorcing her and breaking the bonds that hold him to the Church. He becomes a detective in his efforts to uncover that sufficiency of evil and hypocrisy in the Church which will justify his renouncing the system that stifles him and restricts his activities. He is like a married man with an eye for another woman. This, too, is a difficult form of temptation to cope with, for who would be willing to admit that he is becoming more and more indignant with the bride that is the Church because he wants to leave her?

---

[39] *Epistle* 63, PL 16, 1200 CD.

5. The People of God: A Pilgrim People of Destiny

The seventh chapter of the *Constitution on the Church* is entitled "The Eschatological Nature of the Pilgrim Church and Her Union with the Heavenly Church." Firmly grounded in the theology of the New Testament, it presents the eschatological or final consummation of the Church as a gift for which the People of God waits vigilantly but also as a present reality. The destiny of the People of God will be achieved in its "full perfection only in the glory of heaven . . . the time of the restoration of all things."[40] This full perfection will be attained only when all things are "perfectly re-established in Christ."[41]

However, the Constitution reminds us that this "promised restoration which we are awaiting has already begun in Christ, is carried forward in the mission of the Holy Spirit, and through him continues in the Church."[42] It is only through an understanding of this meaning of eschatology, the theology of *what is now* and *what is not yet*, that we can understand that Christianity presents a *hope* both for man and for this material world. Father Congar writes:

> The idea of the People of God, therefore, introduces something dynamic into the concept of the Church. This People possesses life and is advancing toward an end established for it by God. Chosen, established, consecrated by God to be his servant and his witness, the People of God is, in the world, the sacrament of salvation offered to the world. . . . The People of God formed by revelation and by all the institutions and the sacraments of the new and definitive Dispensation of the covenant, is in the midst of the world and is for the world, the sign and, as it were, the sacrament of salvation offered to all men.[43]

Theologians of the Judeo-Christian religion see three phases or stages in the history of salvation: (1) *The Age of Preparation*, as depicted in the Old Testament, (2) *The Age of Christ's sojourn on earth*, and the inauguration of "the final epoch of world history" in the drama of Good Friday and the victory of Easter Sunday, (3) *The Age of the Church*, extending from the time of Christ's ascension into heaven until the Parousia or second coming of Christ at the end of the World.[44] The concept of the Church as the People of God focuses on what God is achieving through man in this third and final stage of salvation history; it is the Church *in via* between Pentecost and the Parousia, in

---

[40] *Lumen Gentium*, no. 48. Cf. Acts 3:21.
[41] *Ibid.*; cf. Eph 1:10; Col 1:20; 2 Pet 3:10–13.
[42] *Ibid.*
[43] Congar, *op. cit.*, pp. 20–21.
[44] See André Feuillet, "Le temps de l'Église d'après le quatrième Évangile et l'Apocalypse," *La Maison-Dieu*, 65 (1961), pp. 60–79.

possession of its identity (what is now) and moving toward its destiny (what is not yet). It is the period of purification of the bride, which, as St. Augustine acknowledged, "is not yet completely holy,"[45] so that Christ can "present to himself the Church in all her glory, devoid of blemish or wrinkle or anything of the kind . . ." (Eph 5:27).

God has already revealed and realized his plan (mystery) in his Son. We are living in eschatological times, in "the final epoch of world history." Through the Incarnation God has given us a participation in his own divine life, but the plan of salvation is not yet fully realized because it calls for the union of all men in Christ and the restoration of all things in Christ.[46] This is the destiny and mission of the People of God, and this is the reality that gives time and history theological significance.[47]

Father Congar calls it the theology of Alpha and Omega, the Paschal and the Parousiacal states of the Redemption.[48] In the Paschal stage — the second age of salvation history, as described above — Christ is all, does all, all by himself for us. The Parousiacal stage represents complete achievement, when Christ will gather his elect to himself. Both Congar and Cullmann[49] refer to the period in between as "the interval" (l'entre-deux). This is the era of the Church, the interval in which the People of God must contribute positively to the final result of redemption. By reason of its election by and covenant with God, the People of God is called not only to privilege but to service and mission, to witness to and glorify the God who has made men a "People of acquisition" (1 Pet 2:9).

The Bible sees man's dignity and greatness in the fact that he has entered into dialogue with God, in fact into a dialogue of covenant. In the era or age of the Church, this dialogue is typified in three points, the relation of the People of God to each of the three divine persons: (1) the efficacious presence of the risen Christ in his Church, (2) the solicitude of the Father for the Church, and (3) the enlightenment and fortification of the Church through the Holy Spirit.

The Presence of Christ.   In the Gospel of St. John, we hear the Lord telling his apostles that he is going to leave them and that they shall miss him (Jn 13:33). He is going away to prepare a place for them, but he will return and take them home with him (Jn 14:2–3). The apostles are assured that they will not be left orphans (Jn 14:18). Jesus will be with them even though the unbelieving world will not detect his presence:

---

[45] Retract., II, 18: PL 32, 637–638.

[46] Cf. 1 Cor 15:22–23; Eph 1:22–23; Col 1:16; 2:15; Phil 2:9.

[47] Cf. J. Daniélou, "The Conception of History in Christian Tradition," Journal of Religion (1950), pp. 171–179.

[48] Cf. Congar's Lay People in the Church (Westminster, Md.: Newman, 1957).

[49] Cf. O. Cullmann, Christ and Time (Philadelphia: Westminster, 1955).

"I am coming back to you. Yet a little while, and the world sees me no longer; but you will see me, because I live, and you, too, shall live" (Jn 14:18–19). The assurance of Christ's presence will be a joy that "no one can take away from you" (Jn 16:22) because it is the "joy made perfect" of Christ's victory (Jn 17:13). In answer to Judas' question as to why Jesus would manifest himself to the faithful and not to the unbelieving world, Jesus assures them that he will come to everyone who loves him and treasures his message: ". . . and my Father will love him and we shall visit him and make our home with him" (Jn 14:23). It is because of this presence of Christ that He could tell them, "I am the vine and you are the branches" (Jn 15:5). And he is quite clear that all their apostolic efforts will depend on this union: ". . . severed from me, you can do nothing" (Jn 15:5).

Paul, as we have seen, expresses this presence of Christ under the image of the Body of Christ, and he proclaims that the mystery, revealed in Christ and realized in the Church is precisely this: "Christ in you!" (Col 1:27.)

The Solicitude of the Father. The action and being of the Son are inseparable from the action and being of the Father. Therefore, when the believer finds Christ, he finds the Father (Jn 14:9–11). Loving Jesus and keeping his word will assure the believer of the love and presence of the Father (Jn 14:23), who will protect us because of the love we show for his glorified Son (Jn 16:26–28). The Father will hear the prayers of those who are to continue Christ's mission (Jn 14:13–14) and through these prayers they will be able to do even greater deeds than Christ did during his earthly life (Jn 14:12). When the Risen Christ says to Mary Magdalen, "Go to my brothers and say to them, 'I ascend to my Father and your Father, to my God and your God'" (Jn 20:17), he is really saying by implication that the cross and resurrection have established a new covenant, extending to all believers the privilege of divine sonship. Christ has become our brother and his Father has become our Father. We can ask him for anything and he will give it to us (Jn 16:23).

The Enlightenment and Fortification of the Holy Spirit. St. John makes it clear that the departure and glorification of Jesus coincide with the giving of the Spirit, who will come to the Church as an intercessor or advocate (Jn 14:16). The Spirit will be permanently with the Church and in it (Jn 14:17). He will teach them all things and give men a deeper understanding of the Son of God made flesh, of his heavenly Father and of Christ his brother, forming with man a family (Jn 14:26). The Spirit will give witness to Christ in an unbelieving world (Jn 15:26–27), and he will show Christians that Christ's apparent defeat is really a glorious victory, the pattern of all Christian lives: triumph-in-defeat (Jn 16:5–15).

The Synoptics stress the universal love that all Christians should display for all fellow human beings, enemies included. St. John reiterates this, of course, but his unique stress is on the special reciprocal love that should unite all Christians — the love of communion to be found among God's Chosen People. It is not a ghetto mentality, but a new love which would be characteristic of this new People during the age of their separation from Christ: "Little children, yet a little while I am with you. . . . Where I go you cannot come. A new commandment I give you, that as I have loved you, you also love one another" (Jn 13:33–34). The reality that underlies this love is a communal sharing in the bond of love which unites the Father with his Son: "That the love with which you have loved me may be in them, and I in them" (Jn 17:26). This love does not make the People of God a closed society, but is in fact its principal means of expansion. It is the most eloquent form of Christian witness.

Consequently, as the People of God moves to its fulfillment and destiny, it is the sign or sacrament principally and primarily of the presence in history of the risen Christ. The summit of salvation history has already been reached in Christ's victory. We are "conformed to the image" of the risen and triumphant Christ (Rom 8:29). "We were buried with him by means of baptism into death, in order that, just as Christ has risen from the dead through the glory of the Father, so we also may walk in newness of life, . . . dead to sin, but alive to God in Christ Jesus" (Rom 6:4, 11).

All of this is the *what is now*. But the Christian cannot forget the *what is not yet*. The passage of the pilgrim People will continue until the whole People is together with Christ in heaven's glory. This People is truly conformed to Christ, but the old tendencies to sin remain and menace the image and likeness of God in his People. The People of God follows after Christ, who has been called "the first, great emigrant of the New Covenant," experiencing "the power of his resurrection and the fellowship of his sufferings" (Phil 3:10), but optimistic in the certain knowledge that the exodus will end, as that of Jesus, in the fullness of glorious life with the Father.

Now the People of God is in the "little while" that separates the two comings of its Lord and Spouse (Jn 16:16), waiting in anticipation through its exodus of purification to be presented to the Lord "without blemish or wrinkle or anything of the kind" (Eph 5:27). In its Eucharistic celebrations this People is proclaiming "the death of the Lord, until he come" (1 Cor 11:26). John describes that which will be:

> No longer will any person or thing deserving of execration be found there, but the throne of God and of the Lamb shall be established in that city,

and his servants will minister to him. They will see his face, and his name will be on their foreheads. Night will be no more, and so they will have no need of the light of lamp or of the sun, because the Lord will shine on them, and they will reign forever and ever (Apoc 22:3–5).

It was this anticipation that was captured in the moving words of the early liturgy of the Church: "Maranatha! — Come, Lord Jesus!" As is evident from the letters of Paul, the early Christians were filled with this anticipation; it was the Parousia of Christ: his Presence or Coming.

It is "the day" when the Messiah will be manifested in all his glory, "in the glory of his father and with his angels" (Mt 16:27), ". . . as lightning comes out of the east and appears even in the west . . ." (Mt 24:27), "And he will send forth his angels sounding a mighty trumpet, and they will assemble his elect from the four winds, from one edge of the horizon to the other" (Mt 24:31).

At this moment the People of God will attain its destiny fully and all things will be subjected to Christ; Christ the redeemer will offer "his own" to the Father as the trophy of his victory, the result of the mission which the Father gave him to accomplish in his own humanity and in his pleroma, the Church.

Once everything has been brought into subjection to him, then the Son himself, in order that God may be everything to everyone, will be brought into subjection to the Father who subjected everything to him, in order that God may be everything to everyone and everything (1 Cor 15:28).

CHAPTER FIVE

The Church as the Primordial Sacrament

By her relationship with Christ, the Church is a kind of sacrament
or sign of intimate union with God, and of the unity of all mankind.

Christ, the one Mediator, established and ceaselessly sustains here
on earth His holy Church, the community of faith, hope, and
charity, as a visible structure. Through her He communicates truth
and grace to all. But the society furnished with hierarchical agencies and the Mystical Body of Christ are not to be considered as
two realities, nor are the visible assembly and the spiritual community, nor the earthly Church and the Church enriched with
heavenly things. Rather they form one interlocked reality which is
comprised of a divine and a human element.
                                        —Lumen Gentium, No. 1 and 8

1. The Sacramentality of the Church

Through the words which God put into the mouth of his prophets in
Israel, he revealed only a vague foreshadowing of the ultimate invitation
to divine unity which would be definitively extended to men in the Word

made flesh. St. John says that "In this has the love of God been shown in our case, that God has sent his only-begotten Son into the world that we may live through him" (1 Jn 4:9). In this Word God reveals the mystery of personal encounter between himself and man; in this Word God effects the new and eternal covenant of salvation, because Jesus is both the realization of God's invitation and the response of man. He is sent from God to call men to salvation and he is the elected representative of called man.

In accordance with the human, composite condition of body and soul, the invisible riches of the kingdom of God are offered to man in earthly, visible garments. In his visible human nature, Christ reveals God's invitation to redemption and salvation and simultaneously, in the same visible human nature, he is the one who accepts the invitation. In him the alliance of the new covenant is definitively concluded and the divine economy of grace and salvation achieves perfect, human visibility, for he is both God's visible invitation and our visible response. The friendship and life of God can be attained by man in this world only by man's participation in the life, death and resurrection of Christ, who is the new Head of mankind (Col 2:18–19; Eph 4:15–16), the cornerstone in whom "all things hold together" (Col 1:17), "the one mediator between God and men" (1 Tim 2:5) and the one "mediator of a new covenant" (Heb 9:15).

A sacrament is essentially a *sign*, an external and visible sign in and through which an invisible, divine reality receives expression and so to speak visibility. Consequently, it is fitting to see Christ as *the* sacrament of God's saving grace, because in his historical existence he is both the external, visible sign as well as the very invisible, divine reality of that grace. God's word is a sacramental word, a word that both signifies and effects God's mercy for men. Rahner calls Christ "the historical Real Presence in the world of the eschatologically victorious mercy of God."[1]

However, Christ in his sacramental humanity is not our contemporary, and this poses a problem: How can men today attain divine life through encounter with Christ? It would seem that it could only be a spiritual encounter, and for man, composed of body and soul, this is impossible.

God continues to speak our language, to provide the possibility of a corporeal encounter with the glorified Christ, and in him with the Trinity, through the sacramental Church which is the earthly, visible, redemptive instrument of the invisible Lord. The Church is the continuation and enduring presence of God's mercy in Christ. It, too, effects what it signifies: God's grace to men. We have become accustomed to

---

[1] Karl Rahner, *The Church and the Sacraments* (New York: Herder and Herder, 1963), p. 15 and *passim*.

think of the particular sacraments as the channels of this grace, but the Church is truly the *Ur-Sakrament* in that it is the originating source of the particular sacraments.

If we understand the sacramentality of the Church properly, there is no danger of belittling the external, juridical, and sociological aspects of the Church. In fact, the external aspects of the Church will emerge more clearly as the institution of Christ because only Christ can institute a sacramental reality, i.e., only Christ can guarantee the efficacy of an external sign as the source of God's grace. In fact, only he who understands this sacramentality of the Church as an intermediary institution of Christ will take the external, visible Church seriously. He will see the visible sign or sacrament of the Church as the visible expression of God's community of grace. It is the bodily expression of redemption and salvation. Both Rahner and Semmelroth stress that this view of the Church gives a fuller intelligibility to the dogma of the Church as the necessary means of salvation. The Church is the continuing presence of Christ's salvific function in history, made visible to men.

God's grace cannot be gained independently of the Church any more than it can be received independently of Christ. God's revealed economy of grace is that this grace is possessed by belonging to the community which *is* the grace of God in space and time, made externally visible in history. We can apply to the Church as the primordial sacrament what Trent has said of every particular sacrament: It is "a symbol of a sacred thing and a visible form of invisible grace" (DS 1639). Symbol, here, does not connote some kind of evolution but simply the reality of God's grace visibly embodied in space and time, and made available to men who are creatures of bodiliness.

At the same time, viewing the Church as the primordial sacrament relieves us of overemphasis on the external, juridical aspects of the Church. The visibility of any sacrament is not for the sake of visibility as such, but as a means of apprehending the inner reality, the union with God through grace, the presence of grace in space and time. Likewise, the visibility of the Church, so often misrepresented in polemical apologetics, is not for the sake of visibility but for the recognition of Christ's redemptive presence and grace.

There are two extremes to be avoided in thinking correctly of the Church: legalism and spiritualism. Both imply an illegitimate separation of the visible and invisible elements of the one reality that is the Church. The image of the Church as the *Ur-Sakrament* seems to insure against this possibility of error, since it construes the Church as the visible sign of an invisible reality; it blends the external and internal, the human and the divine, into an inseparable unity and harmonious perspective.

2. The Primordial Sacrament and the Seven Sacraments

What we have been saying is not to imply that there are eight sacraments instituted by Christ. Trent has clearly defined that there are seven and only seven (DS 1601). The Church is a sacrament in a different manner and dimension than the seven sacraments of the New Law. The seven sacraments are *actions* which, once performed, perdure only in their effects. Only the Eucharist can be seen as a perduring sacrament, and in this sense will help us to see the sacramental nature of the Church. The Church is not a transitory action but a perennial institution. Semmelroth construes it as a permanent power or potency whose supernatural vital principle gives supernatural strength and life, especially through its principal actions, the seven sacraments. And these sacraments are not to be understood in isolation from the Church, but as actions proceeding from the Church.

Rahner makes the point that the image of the Church as the primordial sacrament does not derive from the teaching of the Church on the seven sacraments but from Christology. As is Christ so too is the Church the one and continuing, signifying, incarnationally structured presence of definitive salvation. The Church unites the sign and the reality signified just as Christ unites the human and divine natures. The Church is made flesh in its social structure, and that which is enfleshed is the life or grace of God. Rahner further believes that such an understanding of the Church will lead to a better understanding of the seven sacraments.

In Rahner's theory, the Church is the essential symbol freely chosen by which God's victorious grace presents itself. The seven sacraments are the actualizations of the Church in the case of individuals; they are also inner symbols that make present certain definite offers of grace by God. In these acts (the seven sacraments) the inner reality of the Church which is God's grace is achieved by reaching the level of occurrence and effectiveness. Thus the sacramental sign is the cause of grace, since grace gives itself by signifying itself. Thus the signifying presence of grace in the sacraments is the actualization of the Church itself, since the Church is the visible presence of grace. Grace has incarnated itself in the Church, and the Church acts through these signs or particular sacraments, and realizes itself in these actions.

3. The Ur-Sakrament: A Unified Concept of the Church

The Council of Trent has defined the following concerning the sacraments in general:

If anyone says that the sacraments of the New Law do not contain the grace that they signify or that they do not confer that grace upon those who do not place obstacles in the way — saying that they are only external signs of the grace or justice received through faith and certain marks of a Christain profession by which men distinguish the faithful from infidels. . . .

If anyone says that, as far as God's part is concerned, grace is not given through these sacraments always and to everybody, even if they receive the sacraments correctly, but only sometimes and to some people. . . .

If anyone says that through the sacraments of the New Law grace is not conferred from the rite itself (ex opere operato) but that faith alone in the divine promises is sufficient to obtain grace . . . let him be anathema (DS 1606, 1607, 1608).

We may distinguish three elements which are essential to every sacrament: (1) an external sign which is somehow perceptible by the senses; (2) this sign effects what it signifies, i.e., the sacramental sign guarantees and causes the very grace which it signifies; (3) there must be a certain disposition in the one who would receive a sacrament, which implies that he puts no obstacle to such a reception, but also indicates the disposition of *faith* as a condition for sacramental reception. We find these three elements not only in the seven particular sacraments, but also in the "sacramental Church."

1. **The external sign perceptible by the senses.** Man can "see" the Church, can experience its reality in its sociological structure and constitution and in his submission to the societal laws of the Church. The Church is God's People, a visible society, hierarchically structured. It is in this sense that the Church is a sign and the great sign. The visible Church becomes the meeting place between God and man through grace. Here and here alone man has the "guarantee" that he will be heard and respected by God, because God has willed that man should meet him here. Semmelroth calls the Church the legitimate and juridical expression of this divine guarantee.

The external sign in a sacrament has to be instituted by Christ because this external sign indicates the presence of an invisible divine reality communicated under the sacramental sign. Furthermore, this external sign should somehow indicate what kind of sacramental reality and grace is communicated. The believer needs to know this. Trent says that the sacraments are symbols of that which is communicated to man: "the sacraments contain that grace which they signify [point to]" (DS 1606).

2. **The same can be said of the Church. It effects what it signifies.** That which the Church communicates or effects is salvation, and so, according to the sacramental principle, the Church must somehow be a

sign of salvation. As we consider Christ and the Church in salvation history, this is quite clear.

Christ, the Son of God, is sent by the Father. He is the Word which the Father speaks to mankind to call men into a new dialogue with himself and into a new community which is his People. Mankind heard this Word in faith and received it in submission, in the beginning with the fiat of Mary. Through Mary's submission to God, the Word arrived at its destination, the first phase of the new dialogue. The second phase is the response to God of the Word himself. This is the answer Christ makes on the cross, becoming "obedient unto death; yes, to death on a cross" (Phil 2:8). Christ has already answered for man, given the response of perfect submission, but men are not dispensed from their own personal decision. The response of submission given by Christ must continue. Men must join Christ in his divine sacrifice. He is now for all of us the sacrificial gift, and his sacrificial act becomes our sacrificial act in the Mass. The Council of Trent, and Pope Pius XII in *Mediator Dei*, stress this idea of one priest (Christ), one gift (Christ). Consequently, our salvation rests in our encounter and union with Christ the mediator, who came from the Father to men and who has gone from men to the Father bringing with him all who have received him (as our Lady did) in faith and obedience and who join him in his act of sacrifice.

The Church is the sacramental sign of this redemptive work, and the life of the Church is the ever renewed meeting of Christ and Mary. The life of the Church is to receive its Lord in faith and submission. Christ has given the Church that polarity which is essential for this encounter, in the hierarchical structure of the Church. We meet and receive Christ in the authority of the hierarchy which bears the person of Christ in teaching, ruling, and sanctifying. This hierarchy must preach to us, preach Christ in his coming, death, and redeeming work; and we must be listening and receive the word in faith and obedience. We also receive Christ in faith and obedience in the Mass, the Eucharist, and the other sacraments.

In the submission of the community in faith and in its unity in cult we see that the sacramental Church in its act of signifying actually brings about what it signifies: unity in Christ. Beyond this visible unity there is that dimension of Christian unity which is in no respect human or natural. The grace of God penetrates the whole human effort, symbolized externally by the Church, effecting the unity of the Mystical Body of Christ. Under the visible organism of this Body lies the deeper, non-sensible, unexperienceable reality. The Church is not merely a dispositive agent; by the union of its visible membership, the twofold reality of every sacrament, the sacramental sign and the grace signified, is already fulfilled in a kind of ex opere operato causality.

3. Human Disposition. The realization of a sacrament demands more than the external recognition of the sign. The minister of the sacrament has to supply the sacramental sign together with his own intention, and the recipient has to have the proper disposition of faith and freedom from impediment (DS 1606). Thus the external sacramental sign is the expression of a bipolar internal reality: (a) on the one hand, the sacrament expresses the divine guarantee that God has really given the grace indicated and symbolized in the sacrament (the ex opere operato causality); (b) on the other hand, the recipient must have the dispositions required, the expression of his own personal willingness and openness. In its treatment of justification, Trent says that "each one of us receives within himself his own justice, according to the measure the Holy Spirit imparts . . . and according to the disposition and cooperation of each" (DS 1529).

The sacramental sign is an expression of the encounter between God and man; both are doing and giving something which must be expressed and contained in the sacramental sign. This is true for each of the seven sacraments; but because they have their roots of existence in the sacramental Church, this Church must be filled with this twofold internal reality: the gift of God and the gift of man. Semmelroth points out that God's gift to the Church makes it the Mystical Body of Christ, and that which men give in giving themselves makes the Church the bride of Christ who encounters her Lord in love.

4. Conclusion

Those who have proposed this image of the Church believe that it is the image which embraces the interior and exterior aspects of the Church and consequently presents a unified concept of the Church. It further illustrates how all salvation is fundamentally sacramental in structure: God gives us his grace in visible vessels and under visible signs.

First of all, Christ is the visible sign (in his humanity) and the reality (salvation); he is the one mediator in that he brings God's invitation to the dialogue of salvation to men and in his humanity, in our name, gives the perfect response of obedience.

The Church is the continuing presence of this sign (the visible society) and reality (the graces of salvation); it renders salvation contemporaneously visible to all men by rendering Christ's perfect response contemporaneously visible in the Mass, the Magisterium, Sacred Scripture and Tradition, and inviting all men to join Christ in this perfect response through personal submission in faith and obedience.

Through the particular sacraments which it ministers the Church, which is the sign and reality of salvation, is actualized in history.

The sacramental nature of the Church or the Church under the image of *Ur-Sakrament* adequately brings out the interiority of the Church, emphasized by the Mystical Body image: the Church effects what it signifies, human unity with God through Christ. It likewise brings out the important exterior features of the Church, dramatized under the image of the People of God, in that the Church is the sacramental sign, the external, visible sign of salvation. Finally, it stresses the personal disposition, the response to God's invitation which is illuminated by the image of the Church as the Bride of Christ. Although the sacraments are efficacious *ex opere operato*, their effect is still conditioned by human cooperation. In the concept of the Church as the *Ur-Sakrament*, this human cooperation is the personal response of faith and love in submitting to Christ, present in the liturgy and exercising his messianic offices through the hierarchy.

In this sense Christ is *the* Sacrament and *only* sacrament of the Church, the sign and reality of salvation; in the particular sacraments he comes to us that we might be joined with him in his perfect response to the Father.

It should be mentioned here that the effort of penetrating various images and concepts of the Church is ultimately an effort to understand the reality. When we consider the sacramental nature of the Church, we encounter the same problem of understanding any symbolism which is infused with a spiritual meaning. This meaning or reality which lies under the bodily shapes of sacramental signs is open only to the eyes of faith. This faith regards the sacrament of the Church and the sacraments of the Church as our means of access to Christ, and it is in this encounter that we can experience his saving power.

All sacraments are intended to offer us an affective experience of our faith, helping us to understand the realities in which we believe by engaging not only our intellects but also our imaginations and emotions. We are bodily persons, and our response of faith is meant to be a total response of our person.

Unfortunately, sacramental symbols are usually explained noetically; our teachers address us as though we were disengaged intellects, and because the words of explanation are difficult to follow, there is little room for emotional overtones or imaginative impact. There is no challenge to a total response, and the strain is often too great for those whose faith is adolescent. The institutional Church in which we live very often fails to grip our imaginations and emotions; its symbolism is often alien to our times and our daily experiences. The visibility of the Church often clashes with the present sensibility and affectivity of the contemporary Christian.

There is no easy solution, but we cannot afford to miss the point that the sacramental Church and its sacraments are places of encounter, of union and interaction, which in any personal contact involves feeling as well as understanding. Faith, which alone can see the realities under the symbols, cannot be divorced from feeling. As we know from our experience in getting to know another, this initial emotional awareness leads us to seek a deeper understanding of the other; it is the starting point of the process that ends with reflective understanding and love. Faith is certainly an interpersonal affair which demands this total response which will lead to a total commitment. The problem is not so much to gain an intellectual understanding but to experience the presence of God under his earthen vessels and symbolic veils.

CHAPTER SIX

Encounter With Christ
in the Church and in the World

*The conditions of this age lend special urgency to the Church's
task of bringing all men to full union with Christ, since mankind
today is joined together more closely than ever before by social,
technical, and cultural bonds.*

— Lumen Gentium, no. 1.

1. "Encounter" in Psychology and Theology

During the past few decades we have witnessed an increasing concern
and interest in the phenomena of interpersonal processes, particularly in
the form of encounter. More and more psychiatrists are coming to recognize that mental disorders are the result of a loneliness resulting from
an isolation from others. This is the thesis of Franz Alexander, Thomas
M. French, *et al.* in *Psychoanalytic Therapy* (1946), of Erich Fromm, in
Escape From Freedom (1941), and of Karen Horney in *Our Inner
Conflicts* (1945). Perhaps the greatest contribution to this new wealth
of literature of interpersonal psychiatry has been made by Harry Stack
Sullivan, a prominent psychiatrist. Especially notable is his article on

the study of interpersonal relations as the most important factor in mental hygiene.[1] Frieda Fromm-Reichmann, in her *Principles of Intensive Psychotherapy* (1950), describes in vivid detail the role of interpersonal relations in the genesis of psychological disorders and the importance of healthy relationships for successful therapy.

Smiley Blanton, a psychiatrist who entitled his major work *Love or Perish*, looks back over more than forty years in psychiatric practice to discover that man's most aching need is to love and be loved. Erich Fromm, in *The Art of Loving*, proclaims in the introduction to that book that "love is the only satisfactory answer to the problem of human existence."

Philosophers, especially those of existential orientation, have contributed important studies of the question. The early classic was that of the Jewish philosopher, Martin Buber, in his *I and Thou*. Recent important philosophical works would include Remi Kwant's *Encounter* (1960) and William Luijpen's *Existential Phenomenology* (1960) and Kenneth Gallagher's *The Philosophy of Gabriel Marcel* (1962).

The general insistence of these psychiatrists, psychologists, and philosophers is that for man *to-be* is *to-be-with-others*. It is the we of interpersonal encounter that creates the I. Life, without the encounter of love, is a disunited existence. Man, in isolation, is incomplete. Erich Fromm maintains logically that it is separateness, the experience of isolation, that is the source of all anxiety.[2] It is frightening but true that others hold my human maturity in their power.

The second insistence of psychology is extremely paradoxical. It is the underlying theme of Adrian Van Kaam's *Religion and Personality*: If I seek my own fulfillment and happiness in the being loved by others, I will never find them. If ever I do find my own fulfillment and happiness, it will be because I have forgotten myself to work for the fulfillment and happiness of others. The French lay-Catholic philosopher, Gustave Thibon, in his *Love at the Crossroads* puts it this way: There is one thing that man finds by never seeking it: himself. C. S. Lewis, in *The Four Loves*, speaks of ". . . those pathetic people who simply 'want friends' can never make any."[3] In other words, if I seek the love of others, the convergence on self that this implies will condemn me to the concern for self that isolates self and induces loneliness. I am caught in a vicious circle: loneliness, in seeking relief in the love of others,

---

[1] Harry Stack Sullivan, "A Note on the Implications of Psychiatry, the Study of Interpersonal Relations, for Investigations in the Social Sciences," in *American Journal of Sociology*, 42 (1937), pp. 848–861.

[2] Erich Fromm, *The Art of Loving* (New York: Bantam Books, 1963), p. 7.

[3] C. S. Lewis, *The Four Loves* (New York: Harcourt, Brace, 1960), p. 98.

multiplies its own agonies. Gabriel Marcel says that ". . . my love is the more authentic according as I love less for my own sake, that is, for what I can hope to obtain from another, and more for the sake of the other."[4]

The final insistence of contemporary psychology is that the interpersonal encounter must, for all human beings, be a "bodily" encounter, one which is somehow perceptible to the senses. This aspect of encounter occupies much of Ortega y Gasset's well-known work, Man and People.[5] Alfred Schutz says that it is ". . . in the face-to-face situation that the conscious life of my fellow-man becomes accessible to me by a maximum of vivid indications. . . . I observe his movements, gestures, and facial expressions, I hear the intonation and the rhythm of his utterances. Each phase of my consciousness is coordinated with a phase of my partner's."[6]

If I were to give up my body, I would no longer be human. My body embodies me, incarnates me, manifests me to the world. My body is my very mode of presence to the world I live in and the personal vehicle by which I have contact and confrontation with the world. In this sense the body is the medium or means of all interpersonal relationships; it is a constant source of contact with other persons, in what we call "intersubjectivity." Body is a given of human existence; it is the means by which I enter the life of another, by which I reveal myself to him and become personally available to others. It is through my sensibly perceptible words, gestures, facial, and oral expressions that I convey that which I am, my person. Father Schillebeeckx writes:

> The human body is not only the appearance and countenance of the human person who reveals himself, it is also that in which and by which the soul develops into a full-fledged person. To join both ideas together: in and through the body the soul externalizes the process of becoming a person. By going out into the world, the human person gains self-consciousness. It is only in incarnation, becoming-flesh that personal activity is completed. Thus, embodiment serves as the sign, although a sign that also veils the most intimate personal activity.[7]

In passing now from the consensus of psychology to the incorporation of this consensus into theology, we might profitably cite one of the most eminent psychiatrists of the last century, Carl G. Jung, a founder of the Zurich school of analytic psychology. He reported that most of his clients have been people in middle and late life — from thirty-five onward — who have lost their religious faith. Jung writes:

---

[4] Gabriel Marcel, The Mystery of Being (Chicago: Regnery, 1951), Vol. 2, p. 109.

[5] J. Ortega y Gasset, Man and People (New York: William Norton and Co., 1957).

[6] Alfred Schutz, "Studies and Social Theory" Collected Papers, II (The Hague: Nijhoff, 1964), p. 29.

[7] From "The Sacraments: An Encounter with God" by E. Schillebeeckx, O.P. from Christianity Divided edited by Callahan, Oberman, and O'Hanlon. Sheed and Ward Inc., ©1961.

I am now convinced that I have never had a case that did not originate in a spiritual unrest. Most of my patients have gone through some form of psychotherapeutic treatment, usually with partial or negative results. Almost a third of my cases are suffering from no clinically definable neurosis, but from the senselessness and emptiness of their lives. It seems to me, however, that this can well be described as the general neurosis of our time. . . . Among all my patients in the second half of life — that is to say, over thirty-five — there has not been one whose problem in the last resort was not that of finding a religious outlook on life. It is safe to say that every one of them fell ill because he lost that which the living religions of every age have given to their followers, and none of them has been really healed who did not regain his religious outlook. . . . The psychologist must also remember that certain religious convictions not founded on reason are a necessity of life for many persons.[8]

In the light of these reflections of psychology, the Incarnation of Christ assumes a new freshness and has been given a diffusion of insights in current theology. The Incarnation is viewed, in the new incarnational theology, as the great saving event, the Christ event. God comes to encounter man in the most humanly meaningful and powerful terms: The divine initiative is prompted by love — "God so loved the world that he gave his only-begotten Son . . . that the world might be saved by him" (Jn 3:16–17). "And the Word was made flesh" (Jn 1:14). Christ is the visible, bodily-present "image of the invisible God" (Col 1:15). "Being God by nature, he thought it [his divine majesty] was not something to be clung to, and so he emptied himself, taking on the nature of a slave" (Phil 2:6). In Christ, his Son, God manifested himself and his redeeming love for sinful man, from within the human situation. God initiates the encounter of love by coming to man clothed in human flesh; he draws men into union with himself in bodily, human terms.

In so doing, God has opened a totally new dimension for interpersonal contact with himself. He allows men entrée into his own life and love.[9] For the contemporaries of Christ, the encounter was startling and unique. John wrote of this encounter:

We proclaim what was from the beginning, what we have heard, what we have seen with our own eyes, what we have gazed upon, and what we have embraced with our own hands. I refer to the Word who is and who imparts life. Indeed, this life has manifested himself. We ourselves have seen and testify and proclaim that Eternal Life which was with the Father and has manifested himself. To you we proclaim what we have seen and heard, that you may share our treasure with us. That treasure is union with the Father

---

[8] Carl G. Jung, *Modern Man in Search of a Soul* (New York: Harcourt, Brace, 1939), pp. 70, 224, 264. See also Henry C. Link, *The Return to Religion* (New York: Macmillan, 1936).

[9] See Henri Rondet, "La divinization du Chrétien," *Nouvelle Revue Théologique* 71 (1949), pp. 449–476.

and his Son, Jesus Christ. I write this to you that we may have joy in the fullest measure (1 Jn 1:1–4).

Notice the emphasis upon the bodily fashion of this contact with Christ.[10] It is through this bodily encounter that the contemporaries of Christ had access to his divine person; their eventual faith, expressed memorably by Peter "You are the Christ, the Son of the living God" (Mt 16:16), was inseparable from the sign of the visible humanity which they encountered.

2. The Problem: Christ Is Not My Contemporary

God's dispensation of grace and salvation clearly involves union with his Son, who is the "one mediator" (1 Tim 2:5); all knowledge of God is to be gained through Christ, for "no one knows who the Father is but the Son, and those to whom the Son chooses to reveal his Father" (Lk 10:22). "Whoever has seen me," Christ said, "has seen the Father" (Jn 14:9), and "no one comes to the Father except through me" (Jn 14:6). In Christ, man has a visible avenue to encounter with the Father.

The problem is that Christ is not my contemporary. God uttered his Word, the Word made flesh. But this was some two thousand years ago, and the contemporary world is not contemporary with this intrusion of God into human history. Contemporary man cannot touch and see and hear him, and we know that all personal faith must somehow be radicated in the earthly condition of man, in the bodily existence of man with all its wondrous unwieldiness. It points up the seemingly absurd element in faith: to affirm that man, in this bodily state, can encounter a *wholly other* God. It seems preposterous, and yet, if it is not true, it is an incalculably terrible error for the believer. The psychological presumption of encounter remains: for man to-believe, just as for man to-be, is to believe-in-a-body.

In the encounter of love with God man can experience the most interpersonally creative moments of his life on this earth. Such an encounter gives man the opportunity to be more fully, but only at the price of his own self-giving. Still, as Father Schillebeeckx puts it:

> It is in the body the soul presents itself to another. What we in encounter call body is that through which we situate ourselves, and make ourselves known; in short, the form of man's being-in-the-world. The person we encounter has this form, but he also is this form. It is through the body and in the body that human encounter takes place. In virtue of this, human relationships of a spiritual nature, no matter how independent they

10 See also Mt 13:11 ff.: ". . . eyes to see."

are in themselves of bodily encounter, nevertheless do attain their high points in such an encounter because in it the spiritual interrelationship is made fully present.[11]

And Christ is *not* my contemporary.

3. *Encounter With the Contemporary Christ in the Church*

In our study of the Church as the Mystical Body of Christ and the People of God, we have already viewed the reality of the Church as the prolongation of Christ in time and the extension of Christ in space. In the chapter on the Church as the Primordial Sacrament, we have seen the Church as the visible sign of what Karl Rahner has called "the official presence of the grace of Christ in the public history of the one human race." Father Rahner summarizes his thought on this point:

> The Church is the official presence of the grace of Christ in the public history of the one human race. In its socially organized form the People of God, as in fact redeemed by Christ, receives his permanent presence throughout history. And when we examine what this one reality implies, it means a presence, as it were an incarnation, of the truth of Christ in the Church through Scripture, tradition, and the magisterium; a similar embodiment and presence of Christ will be in the Church's teaching when it announces Christ's precepts in her pastoral office and her constitution; and a presence and embodiment, again analogous to the Incarnation, of the grace of Christ, for the individual as such, through the Sacraments. Viewed in relation to Christ, the Church is the abiding promulgation of his grace — giving presence [to Christ] in the world. Viewed in relation to the Sacraments, the Church is the primordial and fundamental sacrament.[12]

Rahner stresses the presence of Christ in his truth, as contained in the revelation in Sacred Scripture and Tradition and presented by the magisterium or teaching office of the Church. René Latourelle has, following the distinction originally made by Karl Buhler, emphasized three distinct aspects of this revelation: (1) It has *content;* it signifies or represents something. (2) It is a *summons* addressed to someone and tending to elicit a response from him. (3) It is an *uncovering* of the divine personality, a manifestation of God's interior attitude and dispositions.[13]

This revelation sets up a summons-response circuit, says Father Latourelle, which develops into a dialogue, which can take various forms: command-obedience, prayer-concession, promise-trust, explanation-

---

[11] Schillebeeckx, *op. cit.*

[12] Rahner, *The Church and the Sacraments* (New York: Herder and Herder, 1963), p. 19. Also see pp. 9–24.

[13] René Latourelle, "La révélation comme parole, témoignage et rencontre," *Gregorianum* 43 (1962), pp. 39–54.

attention, testimony-faith. On a higher level, this revelation is the self-expression of God's person, a communication intended to initiate dialogue, a reciprocal opening up, a mutual revelation founded on mutual trust, utter availability, and friendship.

God's revelation, visible to us in the Church through Scripture, Tradition, and the Magisterium, is God's "I" calling to the "Thou" of man. It summons man to the obedience of faith with a view to sharing life. But God's revelation does not only inform but it effects what it signifies; it changes the status of man, whom God invites to become his sons and heirs. It invites the specific affirmative response of man, which we call faith.

In the New Testament, Christ is the unique source of revelation and its witness par *excellence*. He tells of what he has seen and heard in the bosom of the Father, and we are invited to the obedience of faith. He establishes a body of witnesses to testify to his life and teaching, and who call other men to believe. They are the visible representation of Christ, who continues to give his witness in them.

This personal response of faith takes on its fullest depth only when understood in terms of personal encounter. Jean Mouroux has beautifully described the fundamental insight that faith is specified in its entirety by Christ, is a very participation in the life of a divine person made flesh, in the mystery of his death and resurrection and the sharing of the life by which he lives, the trinitarian life of love.[14]

In faith we must seek and meet a person. True faith can never be, in the last analysis, faith in words or formulae or external material things. It is ultimately and always belief in the person behind the things and in the person beyond the words. Faith must truly be an interpersonal relationship, an encounter with Christ. And it is an encounter of love because God, in his revelation or speaking to man, is uncovering his personality, unveiling his heart; he is saying to man: "I love you." This he says in the superlative expression of the Incarnation. It is a summons not only to the response of submission in faith, but invites the response of an answering love on the part of man. In his humanity Christ makes this response, the perfect response of his own life, obedient unto death. It is for the Christian, in his individual act of faith, to join himself to Christ in this perfect response.

And this brings us to the encounter of the sacraments. Those who believe are incorporated into the perfect response of Christ by baptism; they become members of God's people and Christ's Body in this sacramental moment. They become alive with the life of Christ, and his

---

[14] See Jean Mouroux, *I Believe: The Personal Structure of Faith* (New York: Sheed and Ward, 1959).

witnesses. In faith man encounters a personal God in his word, in the sacraments he encounters this God in his life.

> Yes, we were buried in death with him by means of baptism, in order that, just as Christ was raised from the dead by the glorious power of the Father, so we also may conduct ourselves by a new principle of life. . . . Thus, too, you must consider yourselves dead to sin, but alive to God in Christ Jesus (Rom 6:4–11).

Father Schillebeeckx writes of the sacramental encounter:

> The Sacraments bring about the encounter with Christ in exactly those seven instances in which, on account of the demands of a special situation of Christian life, a man experiences a special and urgent need of communion with Him. They are the divine act of redemption itself, manifest in the sacred environment of the living Church, making a concrete appeal to man and taking hold of him in a living way, as really as does the embrace of a mother for her child. And it is not enough for the child merely to know that its mother loves it; it needs the actual embrace to perfect the experience of love.[15]

The sacraments are the acts of Christ, not only because he instituted them, but because they draw their efficacy to give grace from the redemptive work of Christ, who is the "one mediator between God and men" (1 Tim 2:5). Pope Pius XII says in the encyclical *Mediator Dei* that "Christ acts each day to save us, in the sacraments and in His holy sacrifice." The encounter with Christ in the sacraments, entrusted to the Church, is the means God has chosen by which Christ continues to exercise his priesthood and to effect the sanctification of men.

The Church is the custodian of these sacraments. They are the acts of Christ, but they can come into being only through the representative function of the Church to which Christ confided his messianic mission and powers. Those who dispense the sacraments in the Church are simply donating their humanities to Christ so that He can continue his mission on earth. It is Christ, as Pope Pius XII wrote in *Mystici Corporis*, who administers the sacraments, who baptizes, confirms, consecrates, etc.[16] It is notable that when the priest consecrates at Mass, his words are not "This is the Body of Christ," but "This is my Body."

The sacraments are all essential acts of the Church, and each of them expresses the nature of the Church. Baptism incorporates us into the Church, which is the Body of Christ; it illuminates the Church as a mother who gives birth to the adopted sons of God, who begets a community of redeemed children. The Eucharist indicates the social nature of the Church, the People and Family of God gathered around the

---

[15] From *Christ the Sacrament of the Encounter with God* by Edw. Schillebeeckx, O.P., Sheed and Ward Ltd., 1963. Published by Sheed and Ward Inc., New York.
[16] Pius XII, *Mystici Corporis*, America Press edition, par. 67.

common table of nourishment, eating together. Sacred Orders manifests the Church as a hierarchical society in which certain persons are deputed to give the common spiritual treasures to the whole community. All of the sacraments together identify the Church as a worshiping and sanctifying community in Christ, and all of the sacraments are privileged places of encounter for the Christian with Christ.

These sacramental encounters are the highpoints of Christian existence; they are the valid if veiled contacts through which man enters the life of God and God enters the life of man. They are the constant, visible proof of Christ's constant readiness and desire to be with us, the ever-present offering of himself, made by Christ to the members of his People. Their effect is partially conditioned by the response of openness in the recipient. They achieve their effect by virtue of the sacramental rite itself (ex opere operato), but the force of this effect depends upon the response of the recipient's realization and love (ex opere operantis). Consequently, this encounter, as in human encounters, requires preparation and subsequent reflection.

According to the psychological principles of encounter, which we have discussed, I become and am my relations with others. Through this sacramental encounter I somehow but truly become and am Christ and he is me; the interior elements of mutual openness and affection are here given their fully human and personal character through the concrete bodily expression of the physical, sacramental sign.

In a sense it can be said that all human contact and encounter within the People of God is encounter with Christ, present in all his members. "And in explanation the King will say to them: 'I tell you the plain truth, inasmuch as you did this to one of these least brethren of mine, you did it to me'" (Mt 26:40). In the context of faith every encounter with another takes on a new dimension, a new sacramentality for the Christian. Consequently, in all our actions we can, at least in principle, make the sharing of our human lives and selves with others a simultaneous presence of the saving influence of Christ. The Christ who saves is present in all who are incorporated into him; in them he is made present in a visible form, and the possibility for encounter is present in all its presuppositions.

Being and encountering Christ in the Christian is not a challenge to imagination; that would be foolish. In fact, I must encounter another as he is in himself, a unique, embodied person. He is, as a mystically assumed humanity, a unique sign of Christ's presence to me as I am to him. Otherwise, the encounter is not authentic. In each person whom I grow to love and with whom I experience interpersonal encounter, I must find through faith a sign that reveals to me the saving Christ; and, bearing Christ's person, I must offer such a sign. "There is but one **Lord**, one faith, one baptism, one God and Father of all, who is above all, pervades us all, and is within us all" (Eph 4:5–6).

Sometimes we pretend to ourselves that the Church is an obstacle to the divine encounter, in moments when our overheated emotions need ventilation or some other Christian has wronged us, but, in the end, this Church, of holiness and human weakness, provides the only avenue by which man goes to the encounter with God. It is, in Kierkegaard's phrase, "the absolute paradox."

When a person, infant or adult, is brought to the threshold of the Church for the rite of baptism, which incorporates him into the Body of Christ, he is asked: "(Name), what do you ask of the Church of God?" The response is: "Faith." And if faith is, as we have seen, a personal encounter with God in his Son, then it is only this Church, the sacramental sign of Christ's presence and grace, that can give him the faith he seeks.

For it is this Church that prolongs Christ's saving presence in time and extends it in space to the ends of the world. This Church is the site of encounter, where Christ is perennially present and available, acting and sanctifying in the Mass and Sacraments, teaching in the voice of the Magisterium, living in members he has assumed mystically to complete the redemption of the world. The presence of God's Son, once available to men under the sign of an assumed nature in Palestine, is now available to men under the sacramental veils, the liturgical, biblical, and magisterial signs; and what God's Son did in Palestine under the veil of historical happenings is now being continued by the humanity of the Church which he has mystically assumed as his completion. It is in and through the person of Christ, present in these ways in the Church, that he acts on me and I open to him; he is present to me and I am present to him. The Church is the place of encounter, for this is what is meant by encounter.

If a person finds himself unable to accept this identification of Christ and his Church, he will certainly never understand the thundering question of Christ to a man named Saul, whose chief preoccupation at the time was to destroy the Church: "Saoul, Saoul, why do you persecute ME?" (Acts 9:4).

4. The Mission of the Church to the World

Prior to its consideration as a theme of ecclesiology, the mission of the Church to the world must be considered as a charismatic fact in the

Church.[17] In his desire for a new Pentecost in the Church, Pope John XXIII clearly summoned the Church to readdress itself to the profound dimensions of the Church's mission to proclaim the gospel by rethinking its relationship to "others" (Christians, believers, and non-believers). He called upon the faithful to be aware of the enormous changes taking place in the world.

As far back as 1929, Pope Pius XI attempted to reassert the place of the mission of the Church into ecclesiology. "Catholic Action," he said, "does not differ from the divine mission entrusted to the Church nor from its apostolate."[18] He asserted the final end of the Church in these terms: "Men are not created for the Church, but the Church is created for men."[19]

Pope Pius XII, in addressing the International Congress of Historical Science, touched upon one of his favorite themes in saying:

> The Church knows also that its mission, while pertaining by its nature and proper ends to the religious and moral domains, situated in the beyond and in eternity, nevertheless penetrates the full heart of human history. Always and everywhere, in adapting itself without ceasing to the circumstances of place and time, it seeks to model, after the law of Christ, human persons, individuals, and, in so far as possible, all individuals, attaining in this way the moral foundations of human society. . . . We would add: In the present century as in the past, in which the problems of the family, of society, of the State, of the social order have acquired an ever-increasing and even capital importance, the Church has made every effort to contribute to the solution of these questions, and, we believe with some success.[20]

Still Pope John demanded a new *opening to the world*, as is evident from his opening address to the Fathers of Vatican II. While recording the Johannine vision of the world as radically divided between light and darkness, he is careful not to oppose the Church and the world. Rather he betrays a perceptive acknowledgment of the world and its growth, which he calls upon the Church to respect, value, and profit from. He links the salvific mission of the Church to the world in unmistakably clear terms:

> Uniting the best energies of the Church, trying to have the news of salvation made more favorably received by men, it prepares somewhat . . . and

---

[17] See Marie-Joseph Le Guillou, "Mission as an Ecclesiological Theme," *Concilium*, Vol. 13 (Glen Rock, N.J.: Paulist Press, 1966), pp. 81–130.

[18] Pius XI, *Quae Nobis*, Nov. 13, 1928, in *Documenta Catholica* (1929), cols. 390–393.

[19] Address to Lenten Preachers of Rome, Feb. 28, 1927.

[20] Pius XII, *Discorsi e Radiomessaggi di Sua Santità, Pio XII*, Tipografia Poliglotta Vaticana, Vol. 17, p. 214.

shapes the path for that uniting of the human race which is basic and indispensable, so that the earthly city may resemble the heavenly city.[21]

Pope John felt that the mission of the Church involves a serious effort to prepare the way for the unity of the human race, by giving men "an awareness of what they truly are."[22] Only a few months before his election to the Papacy, as the successor of Pope John, Pope Paul VI said in an address at Milan: "When the Church opens herself to the world, she defines herself. . . . When the Church seeks herself, the Church seeks the world."[23] He repeated this theme in his encyclical letter, *Ecclesiam Suam*.[24]

In 1935, Yves Congar followed up the investigation of *La Vie Intellectuelle* concerning unbelief with a theological conclusion. Previous articles had called for considering unbelief as a phenomenon of conscience and for looking at the Church with the unbeliever, not in order to refute him but in order to understand and sympathize with him. In his theological conclusion, Congar contended that contemporary lack of faith is a consequence of "the narrowness of the Church turned in on herself, which conspired to make Catholicism appear a part of the world, a sect, a party."[25] He further insisted that "Neither the Church nor faith radiate in their totality upon life,"[26] and that "Our world must be filled again with signs of God."[27]

In a recent article, Congar returns to his theme of the relationship between the Church and the world:

> . . . the Church says, "I recognize this world, I love this world, and accept it as it is." This is what is new and very important. "It is this world which God has given me to love," says the Church, "having first of all himself given it his Son. I accept it and wish to enter into dialogue with it. . . . Faced by its hopes and projects, I shall not adopt a critical, grumbling, negative attitude. I shall go out to meet it as it is." And in fact, it is the actual substance of the world that makes a dialogue with it possible. Basically the Church and the world are the same thing, but each in a different way and possessing different resources. The world exploits its own immense, terrestrial but limited resources; the Church mediates God's light and grace . . . it offers the world not a relative future, however great, but an absolute future.[28]

---

[21] Oct. 11, 1962, Documenta Catholica (1962), cols. 1380–1384.

[22] Ecclesiam Christi Lumen Gentium, "Message au monde," Sept. 11, 1962; Documenta Catholica, 59 (1962), col. 1219.

[23] March, 1963, in "Quest. Italia," p. 57.

[24] See Documenta Catholica, cols. 1057–1093.

[25] Y. Congar, "A Theological Conclusion to the Investigation of the reasons for Contemporary Lack of Belief," La Vie Intellectuelle, 37 (1935), p. 249.

[26] Ibid., p. 247.

[27] Ibid., 36 (June 25, 1935), see pp. 357–389.

[28] Yves Congar, "A New Church/World Relationship?" Pax Romana Journal, 1966, p. 3.

Congar goes on to cite the two grounds for dialogue between the Church and the world: (1) The Church must proclaim its message of salvation to the world; and (2) The Church must dialogue with the world about man himself and the problems of the world itself.[29]

In recent centuries, the Church has tried with unofficial anathemas to segregate itself from this world. Words like *secularism*, *worldliness*, and *profanity* were frightening words of accusation. Only when the world became increasingly deaf to the proclamation of the gospel by the Church did the Church turn to reassess its too godly, separatist spirituality. It returned to God's original affirmation that the world is good and charged with God's own presence, but wondering if it may be too late.

In our own times the "radical theology" has redirected the Church to the secular, to see the world as God sees it. A non-radical Episcopalian theologian has written recently:

> What we need is to look at the world again with the eyes of a great delight. And only God's eyes will do for that. God's eyes, and ours, in His image, looking out gladly on the goodness of being. Matter *matters* before it *means*. Its *being* must be loved before its *use* can be discovered. Omit the delight of God from creation and the world will soon look as if it had been left in the custody of a pack of trolls.[30]

Whatever we say about this mission of the Church to the world, we must recall that it is all part of God's mystery and a part of God's action. The Church participates in God's plan to unify and vivify all of this world's inhabitants in himself. This is the very *raison d'être* of the Church.[31]

God himself inaugurates this mission because he loves the world so much. He sends his only Son into the world on this mission, and the mission is not to condemn the world but to save it (Jn 3:16 f.). Jesus is the lamb who takes away the sin of the world (Jn 1:29), and he offers himself as a propitiation for this world (1 Jn 2:2) by giving his life to and for it (Jn 6:33). God has made known the mystery of his plan to "sum up all things in Christ" (Eph 1:10). He has determined to unite all men with himself and with one another.

But this plan also means, "since Christ is not only fully God but also perfect man, the enabling of men to be fully human, and so it includes the enabling of natural life to be its true self as communion with God."[32] The Church, therefore, which is involved, as the sign giving Christ presence in the world, in the action of God in this world, is involved

---

[29] *Ibid.*

[30] Robert Farrar Capon, "The Secular and the Sacred," *America*, March 4, 1967, p. 309.

[31] O. G. Myklebust, *The Study of Missions in Theological Education*, II, 1957, p. 301.

[32] J. G. Davies, "The Meaning of Mission," *Cross Currents* 16 (1966), p. 418.

in a work of reconciliation and unification and not one of alienation. And if God has determined to unite all men in Christ to himself, then Christians must be concerned with all human concerns, with the things that divide men and the things that unite them.

In communion with Christ, her Lord, the Church is immersed in his mission as servant of the Father and of all mankind. The Church, like Christ, is primarily the servant of the Father's will but for that very reason the servant of all men. Like Christ, whose priesthood of mediation the whole Church shares (1 Pet 2:4), the whole Church must experience the *kenosis* of Christ (Phil 2:5-9), literally empty of all personal ambition, living a life of total and free transparency, open to the Father and utterly ready to live no longer for itself but for God and the world that God desires to draw to himself.

> The Church is not set up to seek earthly glory, but to proclaim humility and self-sacrifice, even by her own example. She (the Church) recognizes in the poor and the suffering the likeness of her poor and suffering Founder. She does all she can to relieve their need and in them she strives to serve Christ.[33]

The Church must manifest to the world that the Father does care, does have a fatherly concern for all his children. The Church must be the sacrament of God's love and God's mystery, the plan to unite all men with himself and with one another. Beyond as well as within the boundaries of the institutional Church God is constantly active in and through his Son.

> The Church, therefore, will appear as a sign among men, actually drawing and inviting them, only when the love of her members for humankind becomes concretely and historically visible here and now, and is no longer confined to those particular climactic moments in which at present Christ places his grace in a concentrated manner. . . . In the Church's confrontation with mankind in history her members must be living examples and "types" of this overflowing love and manifest their willingness to give up their personal lives in the service of others. . . . Our whole immersion in the world of men and things penetrates also into our communion with God, not as mere distraction, but essentially. We cannot tell God that we love or desire to love him except with words, concepts and pictures taken from our human environment. Moreover, our communion with God is not individualism, for our prayer would be insincere — not prayer at all — if we did not pray: "Our Father . . . " or if in our prayer we forgot God's kingdom and our fellowmen.

> Christianity means not only communion with God in the concrete milieu of Christ in his Church, but also *working* with the living God, with the Father "who is ever active" (Jn 5:17) both in the Church and in the world. Religion is primarily personal encounter with God — the living God,

---

33 *Lumen Gentium*, no. 8.

who is the Creator of men and things, all of which he offers to us for humanization. Therefore, our living relationship with our neighbor and with the world is not only cultural but also religious. . . . In Christ alone do we learn the proper meaning of "being a man for the sake of others," although secular and human experience will teach us how we must express this fellowship in concrete situations.[34]

When we talk about the mission of the Church to proclaim the gospel to all men everywhere, we are talking about the essential and fundamental service of the servant Church; the Church would no longer be "Church" if she ceased to give men the bread of the Word and of the Eucharist. However, we cannot, in any discussion of the mission of the Church, forget that Christ's manner involved more than a simple and objective presentation of the grace of salvation, though that is his ultimate and central gift. His years of ministry were characterized by a deep and realistic oneness with human needs and the human condition. Jesus, as John McKenzie reminds us,

> . . . is not the conquering kind, not the prophet or sage, not the lawmaker. He is the Son of Man confronted with the realities of the human condition. He does not achieve his deliverance through war and conquest, through preaching and teaching to large numbers or small, through the establishment of great and lasting organized institutions; he achieves his work through sharing deeply in the common experience of men. . . . He achieved unique success not by being different from other men, but by being entirely like them.[35]

His life consisted in going about "doing good" (Acts 10:38), healing the sick, calming the anxious, consoling the afflicted, feeding the hungry. These were his credentials and means: the signs of service to the Father and to all mankind. So the Church — you and I — must communicate God's saving deed and spread the good news by identifying ourselves with Christ the servant . . . in helping men to be more fully human, even if our service does not culminate in the ultimate act of service, the explicit passage into Christ through baptism and the Eucharist. The Pastoral Constitution on the Church and the Modern World of Vatican II expresses an acute awareness of the importance of this dimension of the Church's mission. The Church must always define itself as the servant of the Father's plan, but it must also turn to mankind and tell men of its sympathy and understanding, and make whatever contributions she can to the agonizing problems which men face. Only in this way can the Church be an adequate sign that God has entered decisively into human history in Christ and proclaim to men their vocation to become brothers of Jesus, able to call upon God as their Father.

---

[34] Edward Schillebeeckx, "The Church and Mankind," Concilium, Vol. 1 (Glen Rock, N. J.: Paulist Press, 1964), pp. 98–100.

[35] John McKenzie, The Power and the Wisdom (Milwaukee: The Bruce Publishing Co., 1965), p. 101.

CHAPTER SEVEN

The Historical Foundation of the Church

> To carry out the will of the Father, Christ inaugurated the king-
> dom of heaven on earth and revealed to us the mystery of the
> Father. By his obedience He brought about redemption. The
> Church, or in other words, the kingdom of Christ now present in
> mystery, grows visibly in the world through the power of God.
> — Lumen Gentium, no. 3

1. John the Baptist and the Foundation of the Church

Fulton Oursler has called him "the roughest and toughest of all the
saints." There was also something mysterious about the thirty-year-old
man who has spent much of his early life in the hermetically sealed,
forbidding wasteland called the desert of Judea. He was the last of the
prophets, who had come to announce not the coming but the very
presence of the Messiah.

> In those days John the Baptist arrived to preach in the desert of Judea, and
> his theme was: "You need a change of heart; the kingdom of heaven is

close at hand." This is the man spoken of by Isaiah the prophet, who says: "A herald's voice rings out in the desert: 'Make straight his paths!' " (Mt 3:1–3; cf. Is 40:3).

The change of heart demanded by John in anyone who wished to enter the long-awaited kingdom was a radical change of both outlook and conduct, a whole new set of dispositions. And the rite of lustration or immersion in water was used by John as a symbol of such a change; consequently, the hermit from the Judean desert came to be known as John the Baptist.

In one sense this "conversion" was largely a personal matter; in another sense it meant a conversion from the popular mentality which conceived the kingdom of God as a "nationalistic" kingdom, a liberation of the People of Israel from all foreign domination and occupation. The religious character of God's kingdom was all but lost in this preoccupation; the Jews of these times still longed for their Messiah, but on their own terms, and these were largely temporal. It was a time of deformed expectations, when Jesus was ready to come into the midst of his own. And, because the liberation he offered did not mesh with the contemporary anticipation, his own received him not.

The beginning of the revelation took place on the banks of the Jordan where John was baptizing,[1] when his cousin, Jesus, came unannounced to receive John's baptism — like us in all things, sin alone excepted — and to inaugurate his messianic mission of teaching, healing, suffering, dying, and rising. He was, as the voice rang out, "the beloved Son" of God, but he had been made man in order to redeem man, and so he submitted to this rite of lustration in the name of all whom he would save.

The baptism of Jesus also inaugurated the foundation of the Church. Because the Church is bound up with the total work of man's redemption and salvation, which is its mission, its foundation cannot be considered as set in any one single act of Jesus; the foundation of the Church is rather the overall effect of every act of his life, since all of his life is redemptive in purpose.

2. Two Phases of the Church in the Preaching of Jesus

However, we can distinguish two phases of the Church, as Jesus reveals it: the earthly and the heavenly. The heavenly phase will be inaugurated only with the last judgment, when the Son of Man will "send his angels," and "the saints will shine like the sun in the kingdom of their Father" (Mt 13:40–43; cf. also Mt 26:31–35, 45–46.) The earthly phase of the

---

[1] Cf. Mt 3:13–17; Mk 1:9–11; and Lk 3:21–22.

Church, preceding the heavenly stage, embraces the mortal life of Jesus and the "era of the Church."

Within the mortal life of Jesus, all of which moved consistently toward the formation and foundation of the Church, we see the beginnings of salvation in his preaching, the exercise of divine power over Satan and the breaking of his bonds over men, the formation of the messianic community, the inauguration of the kingdom (cf. Mt 12:28; Lk 17:21).

The "era of the Church," properly speaking, is the direct realization of the promise: "You are Peter, and upon this rock I will build my Church" (Mt 16:18). Note that Jesus says "I will build. . . ." Even though all of his life moved toward the foundation of the Church, certain of his actions may be regarded as directly achieving this foundation; they would be the institution of a new covenant at the last supper, the death and resurrection of Jesus.

In considering the historical foundation of the Church, we are concerned with the earthly phase of the Church: the mortal life of Jesus and the "era of the Church." Obviously, there are certain major events, both in the life of Jesus and the era of the Church, significantly connected with the foundation of the Church. It is these that we will review in the remainder of this chapter.

In order to avoid any possible misunderstandings it seems advisable to preface our study of the major events in the foundation of the Church by a brief comment on the historical character of the Gospels. Every reputable biblical scholar today recognizes that the Gospels were not intended as biographies of Jesus. Moreover, only in a very few instances would contemporary scholars maintain that the sayings and discourses attributed to Jesus represented his *ipsissima verba*. And yet, despite the fact that the Gospels were not intended as biographies or as history in the modern scientific sense, the writers of the New Testament do show an urgent concern to maintain the tradition about Jesus handed down by eyewitnesses. The tradition was the content of the "good news," of redemption in and through Christ, and it was the duty of the leaders of the apostolic community to guard this carefully (cf. Acts 6:3-4; 1 Cor 11:23-26). Yet great freedom was exercised with respect to the details of the life and work of Jesus, as can be seen by a careful comparison of the accounts found in the four Gospels. This does not imply that all the details are not historical; but it does imply that the emphasis was on the meaning or significance of these events as they were understood by the early Christian community. And this understanding, a process guided by the Holy Spirit, of the events in Jesus' life was not always given immediately but was worked out over an extended period of time by the early Christian community. The whole matter is summed

up quite well by John L. McKenzie as follows: "The Primitive Church
. . . was very deeply concerned that its witness should present the reality
of Jesus Messiah and Lord with all possible fidelity. The Church was
satisfied that popular anecdotal memory could present this reality."[2]

3. The First Major Event in the Foundation of the Church: The Choice of the Twelve

The masters of Israel, the Jewish rabbis or teachers, customarily chose a
coterie of disciples, who would not only sit at the feet of the master, but
who would hover about him, striving to imitate everything from his
speech mannerisms to his mental processes. It is clear from the gospels
that John the Baptist had such a group (Lk 7:18). We know that Jesus,
too, formed a large group of disciples, from whom he chose a smaller
"inner circle" who were to be his constant companions,[3] leaving house and
home. In the Gospel of St. Matthew, we read of an unnamed scribe volun-
teering for this inner circle: "Rabbi, I would like to follow you wherever
you go" (Mt 8:18). The number of Jesus' total following seems to have
varied. Luke, in his narration of the Sermon on the Mount, speaks of
"a large number of disciples" (Lk 6:17), which he distinguishes from
"the great many people" who had come to hear Jesus speak and to be
cured. However, after the promise of the Eucharist, which was an explosive utterance because it seemed to suggest cannibalism as the price
of discipleship — "unless a man eats my body and drinks my blood . . ."
— the following of Jesus seems to have dwindled to few more than the
Twelve chosen as disciples of the inner circle. John writes: "Thereupon
many of his disciples went back to their old life and would no longer
associate with him" (Jn 6:66).[4]

From this larger group, we have said, Jesus chose twelve in a special
way and for a special role. The choice of a limited number for a special
function seems to have been unique with Jesus.[5] The question is debated

---

[2] The Power and the Wisdom (Milwaukee: The Bruce Publishing Company, 1965),
p. 44. Here it is crucially important to consult the Pontifical Biblical Commission's
1964 "Instruction on the Historical Truth of the Gospels." The text is given along
with a commentary by Joseph Fitzmyer, S.J., in Historical Truth of the Gospels (Glen
Rock, N. J.: The Paulist Press, 1965).

[3] Cf. Mk 3:13–15; the total discipleship of Jesus is mentioned 170 times in the
Gospels.

[4] In fact Jesus' question (Jn 6:67) seems to imply that only the twelve remained
with him.

[5] Cf. André Feuillet, "Les grandes étapes de la fondation de l'Église d'après les
Évangiles Synoptiques," Sciences Ecclésiastiques 11 (1959), pp. 5–21.

as to whether Jesus gave them the title of "apostles," or whether this was done by the early Christian community, to whom an *apostle* was one entrusted with a special mission and with the power to act in the name of the sender. That there were twelve apostles is definite, and the number is obviously symbolic of the twelve tribes of Israel. Just as the new People of God was to replace Israel, so the twelve are to be the nucleus of this new messianic community, the fulfillment of the original People of God consisting of the twelve tribes of Israel. There is a strong indication here that Jesus wished to show the continuity between Israel and the Church, between the old and the new covenants as stages in salvation history.

These twelve are the "remnant,"[6] spared by God when the divine judgment falls upon the adulterous bride, Israel; chosen to be the nucleus of a new People, they are not the debris of the past but the seed of a new kingdom. Their election and instruction takes place as the Jewish people, under impetus from its priesthood, was turning away from Jesus.

Their names are given in all three Synoptic Gospels and in Acts, and always in a discernible mnemonic scheme, which suggests the oral tradition from which the written Gospels were eventually formed. It is Mark who indicates the method of election and its purpose:

> He then went up the hillside, where he summoned into his presence men of his own choosing. They came forward to join him; and he formed a group of twelve, who were to be his constant companions. His intention was to send them on preaching tours, equipped with the power to heal sicknesses and to drive out demons (Mk 3:13–15).

We know from Luke (6:12) that Jesus spent the whole previous night in prayer, and we are reminded by Mark that these were men "of his own choosing" (Mk 3:13). At the Last Supper, he reminds them: "Not that you chose me; no, I have chosen you" (Jn 15:16).

A cursory reading of the earliest Gospel, that of Mark, indicates that Jesus must have spent the greater part of his public life in the private instruction of these twelve. They were his constant companions, who would someday bear his person and authority in bringing his message of salvation to the world. It is to them that he explains the parables, the mysteries of the kingdom of God (Mk 4:10–11); he calls them his own disciples (Mk 4:34) and gives them careful instructions about their mission (Mk 6:7 ff.). He frequently takes them aside (Mk 6:31) for private instruction, and expresses wonder when they do not understand him (Mk 7:17). He journeys with them outside the boundaries of Pales-

---

[6] The "remnant theme" appears in 1 Kings, Amos, and repeatedly in Isaiah. See also Ezek 16:60, in which "an everlasting covenant" is mentioned in connection with the remnant of the People of Israel.

tine (Mk 7:24 ff.), and during this long interval Jesus does not preach to the people. After his instruction on the "leaven of the Pharisees," he once more voices disappointment in their failure to understand (Mk 8:13–21). Again they journey outside Palestine (Mk 8:27), during which the famous interrogation by Jesus and confession of his divinity by Peter takes place (cf. Mt 16:13–20 along with Mk 8:27–30). He gives them the first hint of his passion and death (Mk 8:31), and gives confidential answers to their questions (Mk 9:28–29).

On a secret journey with them, Jesus "wished to remain incognito, because he was engaged in teaching his disciples" (Mk 9:30). They seek further private interpretations from him when his public preaching eludes their understanding (Mk 10:10). He again takes them aside to forewarn them of his impending passion, but he assures them of his resurrection (Mk 10:32–34). Shortly after this, he tells them in a private audience how they are to exercise the authority to be given to them (Mk 10:42–45). On the day of palms, the grand entrance into Jerusalem and into its temple, he retires late in the day to Bethany, taking only the twelve with him (Mk 11:11). After his prediction to a larger group of disciples, he gives the famous eschatological sermon in answer to the confidential questioning of four of the twelve (Mk 13:3 ff.). Just before the passion begins, he eats the paschal lamb (the Last Supper) with the twelve (Mk 14:17 ff.), which concludes with the long instruction and the special prayer (given more extensively in Lk 22 and Jn 13–17).

In the choice and instruction of the twelve, the whole life of Christ is moving toward the formation and institution of the Church. He is confiding to them his doctrine, which he clearly tells them is the message of his Father (cf. Jn 15:15, 17:7–8). He assures them that he will send them another Advocate, the Holy Spirit, who will "refresh your memory of everything I have told you" (Jn 14:26). Besides his doctrinal teaching, he commits to them the sacraments, by which the divine life will be shared and nourished in men.[7]

Jesus makes it clear that he is choosing them for this instruction that they might in their turn teach it to others (Mk 3:14–15; Mt 4:19–20; Jn 17:20). He sends them out on a preliminary missionary tour (Mt 10:5), and instructs them to proclaim his teachings, given in private, "in broad daylight . . . from the housetops" (Mt 10:27).

During his own public life, Jesus both sends the twelve out on missionary tours and intimates their future mission which they will discharge

---

[7] It should be noted that the actual institution of the sacraments takes place during the resurrected life, though there is considerable instruction given to the apostles during the public life concerning at least three of the sacraments: baptism, the Eucharist, and penance.

after he is gone. In Mt 10 we find the record of one of these preliminary teaching missions (see also Lk 9:1–3). He tells them to announce the kingdom of God and to heal the sick (Lk 9:1–3), which was his own message and mission (see Mt 4:17, 10:8). He tells them that "he who befriends you befriends me, and he who befriends me befriends him whose ambassador I am" (Mt 10:40). Those who refuse to hear the apostles on these preaching tours are faced with severe judgment: "I tell you that on Judgment Day it will go less hard with Sodom and Gomorrha than with that town" (Mt 10:14–15).

In his instructions to the twelve, Jesus is clearly thinking about the continuation of his mission through the apostles after his own death. In what is called "the missionary sermon," recorded in Mt 10, the evangelist collects various instructions of Jesus about the future mission of the apostles.[8]

All of this personal and private instruction to the apostles, as well as the nature of his message, would be enigmatic apart from the intention of Jesus to found his people, the Church. It certainly must be regarded as the first major step or event in the historical foundation of the Church by its Lord.

4. The Second Major Event in the Foundation of the Church: The Promise to Peter

> Then Simon Peter spoke up: "You are the Messiah, the Son of the Living God." Jesus acquiesced and said to him: "Blessed are you Simon, son of Jona. It was my Father in heaven that revealed this to you, and not flesh and blood. And I, in turn, say to you: You are Peter, and upon this rock I will build my Church, and the gates of hell shall not prevail against it. I will give you the keys of the kingdom of heaven, and whatever you bind on earth shall be bound in heaven, and whatever you loose on earth shall be loosed in heaven" (Mt 16:16–19).

The man called Simon Peter, in this momentous passage from Matthew's Gospel, had been a fisherman. His brother, Andrew, and a friend named John had been enthusiastic followers of John the Baptist, and one day, when Jesus was passing by, John had pointed to him and said: "Behold, there is the Lamb of God!" Andrew and his friend John had tagged along after Jesus, and they were startled when he turned and asked them: "What is it you seek?" (Jn 1:38.) They did not know what to say, so they asked like little boys: "Rabbi, where do you live?" Their stumbling question was answered by an invitation that was to change their destinies.

---

[8] Especially Mt 10:17–23; 24–26; 34.

"He said to them: 'Come and see'" (Jn 1:38). John, the friend of Andrew, recalls in his Gospel that it was about four o'clock in the afternoon, and that they stayed with Jesus the rest of the day.

The impression must have been a profound one, for Andrew went running to his brother Simon, and breathlessly announced: "We have found the Messiah!" (Jn 1:41). So Simon went to see, and it was a strangely mysterious meeting. The supposed Messiah simply looked at Simon and told him: "You are Simon, the son of John; but you are going to be called 'Cephas' (which in our language means 'Peter')" (Jn 1:42). Simon must have been quite puzzled at his new name; it was not a man's name at all, but simply meant a craggy mass of rock. Besides, with Semites a name is an almost sacred thing. It was not a mere label, but somehow the name contained the man himself. For example, "hallowed be thy name," which we say in the Lord's Prayer, would mean "may you be glorified." To change a man's name at all was always significant. Among Semitic peoples victors in war did this to their vanquished rivals, to indicate their domination over those rivals. In the sacred history of Israel, God himself had changed the names of persons who were to play important roles in salvation history. Abram had become Abraham, Jacob had become Israel; and now Simon, the son of John, had become Cephas (Aramaic), which is the same as Petros (Greek), the craggy mass of rock, the kind of foundation on which a wise man builds his house to withstand the battering of torrential storms.[9]

It was not until much later that the mystery of this first meeting and the change of name cleared up for Simon. It was evening at a little village near Caesarea Philippi, when Jesus made his momentous announcement: "You are Peter [the rock], and upon this rock I will build my Church" (Mt 16:18). All of the apostles were well aware that Jesus had changed the name of Simon; all the evangelists had recorded it (Mt 10:2; Mk 3:16; Lk 6:14; Jn 1:42), and when the Aramaic Cephas (formed from the Aramaic word kepha, the craggy mass of rock) was taken over into Greek, it was significantly not transliterated according to an almost universal linguistic law, but to emphasize its significance was translated. It was either as Cephas, or its Greek equivalent, Petros, that Simon was known in the primitive Christian community; and the only logical explanation is that this small community knew the significance and importance of that name. Simon, the son of John, was the rock upon which the Lord built his Church.

That this name, Peter, indicated a function and office is reflected most clearly in the pre-eminence of Peter in the whole narrative of the New Testament. He is mentioned in the Gospels 114 times, far more than any

---

[9] See the parable of Christ, recorded in Mt 7:24–25.

of the other apostles. He is the obvious spokesman of the whole group. His name is always listed first in all the catalogues of apostles' names. He is present at the special occasions of Christ's life, e.g., the Transfiguration and the Agony in Gethsemani. Christ lived at his house, cured his mother-in-law, delivered his first sermon from Peter's boat, and gave him the place of prominence in episodes like the tribute of the drachma (Mt 17:24–27). On many occasions Peter speaks for all the apostles (e.g., Mt 15:5),[10] and is the most conspicuous apostle at the Last Supper (Mt 23:33 ff.).

Peter has a special apparition of the risen Christ (Lk 24:34), presides at the election of Matthias (Acts 1:15–26) after the defection of Judas Iscariot necessitates a replacement to fill up the symbolic number of twelve. It is Peter who gives the first Christian sermon (Acts 2:14–20), and who works the first recorded miracle of the apostles (Acts 3:1–11). He condemns Ananias and Sapphira (Acts 5:1–11) and Simon Magus (Acts 8:20–24). After James the Less takes over the government of the Church of Jerusalem, Peter visits many of the newly founded Churches: Samaria (Acts 8:14), Galilee (9:31 ff.), Lydda (9:32 ff.) where he works a miracle, Sharon (9:35), and Joppa (9:36–43). He presides over the council of Jerusalem (Acts 11) where it is his word that settles the great dispute over the manner in which the Gentiles may enter the Church. He seems also to have visited for inspection the Churches of Antioch (Gal 2:11), Corinth (1 Cor 1:12), and Asia Minor (1 Pet 1:1). There is a strong and reliable tradition that he died at Rome, a martyr under Nero, between A.D. 64–67, and very recently the excavations under the present cathedral of St. Peter in Vatican City have substantiated the tradition that he was buried there.

It was to this man that a special role, that of the rock of foundation which would hold the whole building of the Church in place, was promised by Christ. This has to be considered as a major event in the foundation of the Church, toward which the whole of Christ's public life consistently moved. Catholics have come to realize that the function of being the "rock of foundation" of the universal Church is the function of supreme and universal authority, so that all the others, even the apostles, are subordinate to him. It is through cohesion with this supreme authority that all the human tendencies to division, rivalry, and dissolution — the rains and the winds that buffet the Church from within and without — are ultimately checked.

It is incomplete to view this metaphor of the rock without studying its consonance with the two subsequent metaphors used by Christ in the same logion: the promise of the "keys of the kingdom of heaven," and

---

[10] Cf. also Acts 3:12–16; Acts 4:1–22.

the power "to bind and loose." When the three metaphors are taken together, as they should be in any competent exegesis, there is only one logical conclusion: Christ promised supreme and universal authority over his people, to be exercised as his own vicar.

In relation to the power of the keys, we must presume that Christ was trying to communicate a reality to the apostles, and that he was using a metaphor which they would have understood. The meaning of this particular metaphor can be rather clearly traced in its biblical usage, which is supreme vicarious power.[11] Strack-Billerbeck, in the well-known New Testament commentary, propose many examples of this usage from rabbinical writings, and they conclude: "The handing over the keys means the handing over of power to a caretaker, of whom the dictum has it: the commissary is as the one who gave him the commission."[12] The usage, with reference to Christ, in the Apocalypse (3:7; 1:18) is the same in connotation: power over the kingdom.

Christ is, of course, the true ruler of his Church. However, in this world, from which he has ascended, he is not visibly present to rule men. In the context of Mt 16:16, it is clear that Christ is talking about a Church in this world, to be built upon the rock of Simon Peter.[13] The second metaphor illuminates and clarifies the first: since the Church is a social organization, it will require a visible authority, and this is the sense in which Peter will be the rock; he will be the rock of foundation, the source of unity and stability, the vicar with supreme power who holds the keys of the kingdom.

The third metaphor, that of binding and loosing, is a still further clarification. In rabbinical usage it connotes the moral power of prohibiting or permitting. Peter will exercise this precise power, and whatever he does in the discharge of this responsibility on earth will be ratified in heaven. "Whatsoever you bind on earth will be bound in heaven."

The fact that Christ later confers the same binding-loosing power on the other apostles (Mt 18:18) is not really a great difficulty. Supreme and universal authority does not exclude the possibility that others might also have true authority. As is obvious, supreme authority does not necessarily imply exclusive authority.

---

[11] A classic example is found in Is 22:19–22; in connection with this text see also 2 Kings 18:18. Roland de Vaux notes in his commentary on 1 Kings in the Bible de Jerusalem, that the function of the "minister of the royal palace" was the same as that of the oriental vizir, the prime-minister.

[12] See Vol. I, Col. 736 ff.

[13] The metaphor of "building a people" would have also been familiar to the apostles. Scattered throughout the Old Testament are repeated usages of "The House of Israel" to designate the People of God that was Israel. Cf. Amos 5:25, cited by St. Stephen in Acts 7:42. The precise metaphor of "building a people" is found in Jer 1:9–10; 31:4; 31:28; 33:7.

5. *The Third Major Event in the Foundation of the Church:*
The Last Supper

For centuries theologians have been preoccupied in proclaiming the real
and sacrifical character of Christ's words at the Last Supper; only recently
has the relation of the Last Supper to the foundation of the Church come
into clear focus. The main text to be examined is Lk 22:14–20.

It is significant that Christ chose a paschal meal as the scene for the
Last Supper. The feast of the Pasch was the supreme solemnity of the
Mosaic religion; this solemnity not only commemorated the liberation of
Yahweh's people from the iron fists of the Egyptian Pharaoh, as a distant
past fact of history, but it somehow actualized that event in the present,
making it possible for every Jew of every age to participate here and now
in the meaning of that divine favor which led his fathers out of Egyptian
slavery and sent them on their way to the promised land. Christ uses the
occasion of this celebration to replace the imperfect solemnity of the
Passover, by which contemporary Jews participated in the meaning of
their past and the saving mercy of their God, with the Eucharist, destined
to be for all Christians a true actualization of and a participation in the
redemption of Christ. Once more Christ is emphasizing the continuity
of the history of salvation. "This cup is the *new* covenant sealed by my
blood, which is about to be shed for your sake" (Lk 22:20).

We know, too, that new alliances were sealed in two ways: by a
sacrifice of the *blood* of a victim animal and by a *banquet* of celebration.
At the banquet celebrated with his apostles, Christ was holding up the
cup of what had been wine, with the (paraphrased) words: "This is my
blood, sealing the new alliance of covenant, here at this messianic banquet." It was truly the messianic banquet, foretold in the Old Testament,
which assembles the new People of God and celebrates the new alliance
or covenant of God with man.

". . . sealed by my blood, which is about to be shed for your sake."
There is here a clear allusion to Calvary and the agonizing death Christ
would die on the cross. This freely accepted death is the price of man's
redemption. "The Son of Man has come . . . to give his life for the
redemption of many" (Mt 20: 28). His blood is the blood of a sacrificial
victim, but this victim has freely accepted his death, and therefore even
in anticipation he can offer it in oblation to his Father. The means of
man's redemption, by divine appointment, involve the union of men with
this victim. Salvation is to be acquired through incorporation into Christ.
Men are saved not by their individual responses to God's loving initia-
tives of mercy and love, but by joining Christ in his response, the perfect
response of submission and love made to the Father.

We remember that the ancient covenant between God and Israel was sealed by a blood covenant at Mount Sinai.[14] The effect of this covenant was that Israel became the People of God.[15] Now the new covenant, sealed by the blood of Jesus, joins a new people to God. This promised, new covenant is predicted quite a few times in the prophets of the Old Testament.[16] In Ezekiel, the "new covenant" is also intimately connected with the coming of the Messianic King.[17]

At the Last Supper Jesus explicitly applied this prophecy of Isaiah (53:12) to himself: "Yes, I tell you, this Scripture text must be fulfilled in me: 'And he was classified with the lawless.' Indeed, my career is now at an end" (Lk 22:37). The "pouring out of his blood for the remission of sins" is a rather clear allusion to the canticle of the Servant of Yahweh in Isaiah 53:1-12. That his is the blood of "the new covenant" would seem quite clearly to indicate the new messianic covenant promised by God to his Servant:

> I am the Lord, I have called you in righteousness, I have taken you by the hand and kept you; I have given you as a covenant to the people, a light to the nations . . . (Is 42:8).[18]

But there can be no covenant without a People which is allied to God by the covenant, and he who institutes a covenant joins himself to a new people; finally, whoever pours out his blood "for the redemption of many" acquires this new People at the price of his blood. The "many" who receive the fruits of Christ's redemption are by this blood constituted a new People of God, joined to him by a new covenant.

It should be noted, too, that there is an obvious coherence between the proclamation of a new covenant and the institution of a new eucharistic cult of worship to be offered by this newly created People of God. The People of Israel, who were covenanted to Yahweh on Mt. Sinai, received from Yahweh definite prescriptions concerning cult, especially concerning sacrifice and the Paschal Feast.[19] Now, at the Last Supper, in the context of the same Paschal Feast, Jesus is proposing a New Pasch, a new sacrifice, a new feast, to be continued in perennial re-offering by his disciples. "Do this as my memorial" (Lk 22:19).

The Last Supper is not only an historic moment in the foundation of the Church, but it is the very source of stability of the Church until, as St. Paul says, "the Lord comes."

---

[14] Read Ex 24:3-8.
[15] Read Ex 19:5-6; Cf. also Dt 7:6; 26:16-19.
[16] The classic text is Jer 31:31-34.
[17] Read Ezek 34:23-25; 37:24-27.
[18] Is 49:8 repeats the line "I have made you a covenant to the people."
[19] Read Ex 12:1-28; 23:15.

The fact is that I have received as coming from the Lord, and have passed on to you, how the Lord Jesus on the night of his betrayal took bread into his hands and after he had given thanks broke it and said, "This is my body which is given up for you; do this in remembrance of me." In the same way, after he had finished supper, he took the chalice into his hands and said, "This chalice is a new covenant sealed with my blood. Do this, as often as you drink it, in remembrance of me." In reality, every time you eat this bread and drink the chalice of the Lord, you proclaim the Lord's death until he comes (1 Cor 11:23–26).

The memorial that the Lord asks, and which Paul says "proclaims the Lord's death until he comes," is the Christian Eucharistic celebration. It is the anti-type of and the equivalent of the Paschal meal of the Israelites, the means by which the divine favor of redemption is not only remembered gratefully[20] but also the means by which redemption is made contemporaneous to all Christians of every generation and age. The "many" (Mk 14:24; Mt 26:28) of every generation and age will participate in the saving mercy and presence of God's Son through this sacrifice and banquet. This is the memorial celebration of God's new people . . . until he comes, at the end of the world, to gather those who have loved him and to bring them to his Father's home for the heavenly and eternal banquet.

6. The Fourth Major Event in the Foundation: The Death and Resurrection of Jesus

The Feast of the passover was now approaching, and Jesus knew that his time for passing from this world to his Father had arrived. He had always loved his own who were in the world; and now he gave them a last proof of his love (Jn 13:1).

From what has been said, the death of Christ on the cross is obviously the greatest single historic moment in the foundation of the Church. It is the moment of redemption, the moment when the blood which seals the new covenant, establishing a new people, is actually shed. Both Paul and John call Christ on his cross "our paschal lamb."[21] The paschal lamb was the sacrifice that recalled the redemption of the Israelites from the slavery of Egypt. Christ's death on the cross is the sacrifice that redeems all mankind from the slavery of sin. This is the way John the Baptist had announced him: "Behold the Lamb of God . . ." (Jn 1:29). St. Peter

---

[20] The Greek word *eucharistia* means "a thanksgiving." It was used in the primitive Church (*The Didache*, St. Ignatius of Antioch, *et al.*) to refer to the Mass, the Eucharistic celebration, as the grateful remembrance or memorial service in which Christians recall, and enter into, God's mercy to us in Christ.

[21] Cf. also 1 Cor 5:7: "In fact, Christ, our paschal victim, has been sacrificed."

writes of the redemption: "You were not redeemed with corruptible things, as gold or silver . . . but with the precious blood of Christ, as of a lamb unspotted and undefiled" (1 Pet 1:18–19).

The Fathers of the Church frequently refer to the Church as the New Eve, born from the side of Christ, during the sleep of death. With Christ's release from this life and his going to the Father, he becomes a "life-giving spirit" (1 Cor 15:45). Out of his death rises a new creation: the Church, the People of God, sealed to God forever by his death. Paul tells the Ephesians that "through the blood of Christ" all hostility between Jew and Gentile has been broken down, because Christ has abolished the Law so that "of the two races he might create in himself one new being . . . reconciling both in one body to God by the cross (Eph 2:13–16).

Pope Pius XII wrote in his encyclical on the Mystical Body that Christ, the divine Redeemer, began the building of the mystical temple of the Church when by his preaching he announced his precepts; he completed it when he hung glorified on the cross; and he manifested and proclaimed it when he sent the Holy Spirit as Paraclete in visible form on his disciples.[22] Although the whole public life of our Lord was moving toward the establishment of the Church, which is his Body, it was only when these activities were signed by the sign of the cross that the torrents of grace were released from head to members. Pope Pius wrote:

> It was by his blood shed on the cross that God's anger was removed, and as a result all the heavenly gifts, especially the spiritual graces of the New and Eternal Testament, could then flow from the fountains of our Savior for the salvation of men. . . . It was on the tree of the cross, finally, that He entered into possession of the Church, that is, all the members of his Mystical Body; for they would not have been united to this Mystical Body through the waters of baptism except by the saving power of the cross. . . .[23]

Christ had become the head of the Mystical Body in the womb of the Blessed Virgin Mary, the Pope declared, but "by the power of the cross our Savior exercises *fully* the office itself of Head of the Church . . . our Savior, by his death, became, in the full and complete sense of the word, the Head of the Church. . . .[24]

Somehow, then, the death of Christ releases the torrents of grace to the whole human race and brings Christ into the full exercise of his headship of the Church, which was born from his side, opened by the soldier's lance, during the sleep of his death.

---

[22] *Mystici Corporis*, America Press Edition, par. 33.
[23] *Ibid.*, par. 37.
[24] *Ibid.*, par. 38 (italics mine).

To understand the meaning of Christ's death in relation to redemption and the foundation of the Church, one must understand the meaning of death. It is only in the act of dying that one can release the fullest volitional force of love and dedication. Greater love than this no man has. During life, we can give God only our transitory acts, the consecration of individual moments, actions and powers, to his love and service. But, while these actions direct my life and soul to God, it is only in one act that I can give God everything, not only my transitory acts but the faculties that produce those acts; only in one act, my act of dying, can I transfer *everything* to God in an act of loving abandonment and submission. It was this way with Christ, too. His humanity had not yet acted according to its full power, neither as united to God nor united to humanity. Only in his death as the definitive action, irrevocable, ineradicable, and final, could he deliver himself up entirely for us. Only in his act of dying could he be wholly obedient to the laws of our universe and unreservedly given to the work of our redemption. All other actions, with us as with Christ, prepare the way for the final act of dying; all other actions culminate in this. In the act of dying the will of man sums up the totality of its being; it is the act of the total man, body and soul, the climax and culmination of all human life and moral action.

Christ's death is the recapitulation of all the other redemptive actions of his life, and represents the full acceptance of his mission. It is the moment of unreserved consent. In his death he cast himself wholly into his Father's will.[25] It is this significance of the act of dying that gives meaning to the words of Christ, addressed to the downcast disciples on the road to Emmaus: "Was it not necessary that the Messiah should undergo these sufferings and thus enter into his glory?" (Lk 24:26.)

Christ had a command from his Father, the mission of redemption. He called it the "baptism wherewith I am to be baptized" and said that he was "straitened until it be accomplished" (Lk 12:50). He avowed that his one purpose was to do the will of his Father. "My meat is to do the will of him that sent me, so that I might bring his work to completion" (Jn 4:34). And, in the course of this obedience, he became "obedient unto death, even to the death of the cross" (Phil 2:8). His death was, as it is with all men, the final and utter commitment to the will of God, the utter surrender of obedience. Consequently, when he was about to die on the cross, he could say with his final breath, "It is completed!" (Jn 19:30.)

Clearly it is impossible for the blood of bulls and goats to take away sins. For this reason at his entrance into the world Christ says: "Sacrifice and oblation you did not wish, but you have fitted together a body for me.

[25] Cf. Jn 3:16.

You took no pleasure in burnt offerings and sin offerings. Then I said: 'Here I am; I have come to do your will, O God,' as it is written in the roll of the book."

After he had said "Sacrifices and oblations and burnt offerings and sin offerings you did not wish, and took no pleasure in them" — offerings prescribed by the Law — he then said: "Here I am; I have come to do your will." He thus abolishes the former [the Law] to establish the latter [the submission of obedience]. It is in virtue of this "will" [of the Father] that we have been sanctified through the offering once and for all of the body of Jesus Christ (Heb 10:4–10).

With this final act of obedience and the irrevocable act of surrender, the way is opened for the total effusion of grace, which is the life of the Church. He himself had made this clear, that his death was a condition for this total effusion:

"But I tell you the truth; it is to your advantage that I depart. Unless I depart, the Advocate will not come to you; whereas, if I depart, I will send him to you" (Jn 16:7).

The relation between Christ's resurrection and the foundation of the Church, which is quite clear in St. Paul, and which was realized by the early Church, was somehow overlooked and finally forgotten in the history of theology. Father Bruce Vawter points out, in his article on "Resurrection and Redemption,"[26] that Paul clearly teaches the resurrection as a cause of man's spiritual regeneration.

For if the dead rise not again, neither is Christ risen again. And if Christ be not risen again, your faith is without foundation, for you are yet in your sins (1 Cor 15:16–17).

Jesus Christ . . . who was delivered up for our sins, and rose again for our justification (Rom 4:23–25).

The Greek Fathers of the Church took Paul literally, that Christ rose for the purpose of our justification, though their exegesis is admittedly vague. The Latin Fathers, in attempting to integrate the effect of Christ's death and his resurrection, unfortunately tended to minimize the causality of the resurrection. They seemed to interpret this causality as a merely moral causality, i.e., the resurrection is a motive for faith (which, of course, it is), a complement to the passion and death of Christ. Gradually, in the Latin Fathers, the resurrection became an accessory after the fact, and the causality of the resurrection lost all its meaning. After Trent, which was concerned chiefly with meritorious causality, the realization of the causality of the resurrection, which is admittedly not meritorious, was lost completely.

---

[26] Bruce Vawter, "Resurrection and Redemption," *The Catholic Biblical Quarterly* 15 (Jan. 1953), pp. 11–23.

Only recently, as theological emphasis has fallen upon the doctrine of the Church, the Mystical Body and our incorporation into Christ, has the doctrine, which St. Thomas spelled out rather clearly, of the redemptive value of the resurrection been brought back into focus.[27] The resurrection of Christ, according to St. Thomas, is the efficient and exemplary cause of our resurrection, in fact, of all salutary effects. It is the model, too, of what it produces; but its causality is based on man's incorporation into Christ's body.

The causality of the resurrection is plainly not meritorious causality. In fact, the resurrection is not really an action of Christ, but of the Father who raises his Son from the dead into glory. Death is the final term of merit, and Christ's act of dying was his final meritorious act. But God uses the resurrection, not as a meritorious cause, nor simply as an exemplary cause, but as in instrumental, efficient and exemplary cause of the spiritual regeneration of men and the formation of the Church. God, of course, in the principal cause of our redemption and the Church. The humanity of Christ, to which we are engrafted in the Mystical Body, is in the resurrection the instrument of divine power and goodness.

St. Thomas says that what causes Christ's resurrection likewise causes ours. This is no doubt what St. Paul means when he writes to the Romans: "He who raised Jesus Christ from the dead, will give life to our mortal bodies" (Rom 8:11). Of this St. Thomas says, "It is the very resurrection of Christ, by the power of the divinity united to Him, which is the quasi-instrumental cause of our resurrection, for the divine operations are effected through the medium of the Body of Christ. . . ." It is God, then, who uses the humanity of Christ as an instrument to produce our resurrection. Our resurrection, in this context, refers to our being raised from the death of sin to the life of grace.[28] The resurrection of Christ is the efficient cause of our resurrection by the divine power which "by its presence touches all places and times."[29]

All understanding of the connection between Christ's resurrection and our redemption or resurrection is conditioned by our understanding of the union with Christ that we enjoy in the Mystical Body. When God the Father raised his Son from the dead he was simultaneously raising all of us who would be joined to Christ in the Mystical Body. From Christ's fullness we have all received. The Christ to whom we are engrafted, whose members we are, is the risen Christ. The fullness of life,

---

[27] Cf. Ferdinand Holtz, S.C.J., "La valeur soteriologique de la Résurrection du Christ selon S. Thomas," *Ephemerides Theologicae Lovanienses* 29 (1953; 1954), pp. 609–645.

[28] The text being treated is Rom 8:11; cf. also Rom 6:4 and Eph 2:6–7.

[29] The quotations from St. Thomas are found in his *Summa Theologiae*, III, q. 56, a. 1, ad 3.

which was in Christ, and in which we participate, is the fullness of the risen life. In raising his Son from the dead, God is raising us to incorporation with his risen Son. We have said that this causality is based on the fact of our incorporation into Christ. We receive of his fullness, and therefore each mystery of the life of Christ produces in his humanity an effect which corresponds to that which must be and is produced in us. The whole supernatural life of the Church is entirely in Christ. Paul writes to the Corinthians, "from him [God] comes your union in Christ Jesus, who has become for us God-given wisdom and holiness and sanctification and redemption . . ." (1 Cor 1:30), and to the Romans "Yes, we were buried in death with Him by means of baptism, in order that, just as Christ was raised from the dead by the glorious power of the Father, so we also may conduct ourselves by a new principle of life" (Rom 6:4).

Notice that Paul is saying that the Father has raised Christ so that we may live the life of grace. Christ recapitulates all human history in his own history, and contains all the effects of grace in his own fully-graced humanity. Therefore, we who receive of his fullness, because we are his members, can live the life of glory through grace, even in this present life, because Christ of whom we are members has been glorified in the resurrection. We are indeed the risen, triumphant, glorified Mystical Body of Christ. It is in this precise way that the humanity of Christ is the efficient-instrumental cause of all the graces that come to his members.

Because faith and hope are divine gifts, coming through Christ, the author of Hebrews always unites the exaltation of Christ by his passion and resurrection to our supernatural powers of faith and hope:

> We can enter the sanctuary with confidence through the blood of Christ. He has opened up for us a new, living approach . . . Let us come forward with sincere hearts in full assurance of the faith . . . and let us not waver in the hope we cherish (Heb 10:19–23).

In the early Christian community it was the resurrection that occupied the central position of the kerygma or proclamation of the good news. The presentation of the resurrection in this early preaching was not only the resurrection as a factual, historical event, but as a salvation-event. In our use of the resurrection as an apologetic argument, we can easily forget that the resurrection was not simply a return of Jesus to his former earthly life but to a new and glorified state of life. Peter makes this point in his sermon recorded in Acts 2:22–36. Jesus' resurrection makes him the "source of life" (Acts 3:15) and the "firstborn from among the dead" (Col 1:18). The fact of Christianity and the Church is the result of this resurrection. The effusion of grace on the Christian community effected by the Holy Spirit, is the result of this salvation-event, the resurrection. Peter preached:

> God has raised him up, having put an end to the pangs of death, because it was not possible that death should hold Him. . . . Therefore, exalted by the power of God, and receiving from the Father the promised Holy Spirit, he has poured forth that which you see and hear (Acts 2:24–33).

We remember that Jesus tried to tell his disciples that the passion and resurrection were a necessary part of his messianic accomplishments:

> From that time on Jesus began to make plain to his disciples that it was necessary for him to go to Jerusalem, to suffer much at the hands of the elders, high priests, and scribes, to be put to death, and on the third day to rise again (Mt 16:21).

Obviously the apostles did not understand this necessity of Christ's dying and rising. "May God spare you, Lord," Peter was quick to add, "this must never happen to you" (Mt 16:22). After the resurrection, the promised Holy Spirit is poured upon them, and the whole perspective is different. This same Peter acknowledges the pouring out of the spirit as an effect of the passion and resurrection (Acts 2:17–20). Christ has been glorified for the salvation of the People of God (Acts 3:26).

The essence of Christian existence is the incorporation into the Body of Christ, membership in Christ. The Christ in whom all Christians are united, and from whose fullness all Christians receive, is the living, glorified Christ. And because the risen Christ is the glorified Head of his Body, then truly the Church is the Body of Christ. As "firstborn from among the dead" and "the source of life," the risen Christ is the new Adam, the head and cause of a new creation, a new humanity. If we are one with this risen, glorified Christ, then we are also risen and glorified already. We already share the fruits of the resurrection because we are one in the risen Christ.

> As for us, our home is in heaven, and it is from there that we eagerly await our Savior, the Lord Jesus Christ. It is he who by an exercise of the power which enables him even to subject the universe to himself will refashion our lowly bodies, forming them to his glorious body (Phil 3:20–21).

> By grace you have been saved. Together with Christ Jesus and in him, he raised us up and enthroned us in the heavenly realm, that in Christ Jesus he might show throughout the ages to come the overflowing riches of his grace springing from his goodness to us (Eph 2:6–7).

In a sense the reality of the existence of the Body of Christ, the Church, has its beginning in the "now" of the resurrection, for the resurrection is not merely an historical event bound to space and time, but it is truly the source of grace and salvation in all times and in every place.

The resurrection is the unending salvation-reality which makes the historical event of the resurrection an ever-present reality. Salvation, in its fullest meaning, implies glory and union. These are ours because glory and union belong to Christ and we belong to, and are engrafted to, him. It is true both for him and for us, that without Calvary there could be no resurrection, but without the resurrection Calvary would have been an empty tragedy. The Church is the Body of the Risen Christ, "firstborn from among the dead" and "the source of life."

We have said that the Church is a resurrected Church because its Lord is risen. Appropriately, St. Paul quotes an early Christian hymn in his letter to the Ephesians: "Awake, sleeper, and arise from the dead; and Christ will give you light" (Eph 5:14). Over his Church the risen Christ "exalted by the power of God, and receiving from the Father the promised Holy Spirit, . . . has poured forth what you see and hear" (Acts 2:33). This effusion of grace began when Christ, after his resurrection, breathes upon the apostles; "Receive the Holy Spirit" (Jn 20:22). On the day of Pentecost, which is taken from the Greek pentekoste, meaning "the fiftieth," presumably the Christian name for the feast that was celebrated on the fiftieth day after the Passover, the great charismatic effusion took place (Acts 2:4). It was the Church's public manifestation, her official debut. It was the day of the anointing of the Church at the dawn of her messianic mission, just as the Lord of the Church, who was conceived by the Holy Spirit (Lk 1:35) had been anointed by the Holy Spirit at the beginning of his messianic mission (Acts 10:38; Mt 3:16). It was the seal of the Holy Spirit, placed upon the Church, just as the same Spirit places the seal (of confirmation) on the Christian who is already consecrated by baptism (Acts 8:17; cf. also 2:38).

7. Conclusion

There are those who see the destruction of Jerusalem as the final sign or manifestation of the Church. The destruction of Jerusalem represents, in this exegesis, the final revelation that the Church has replaced Israel as the new People of God. Jesus had himself predicted the future destruction of the holy city and its temple as a divine judgment upon the people who would reject him (cf. Mt 23:37–38; 24; 1–3; 24; 15–22).

Christ had also predicted that such a judgment was to come upon the Jews of his own generation (cf. Mt 23:36; 24:34; Mk 13:30; Lk 21:32). He had foretold that his own generation would witness the institution and the spread of the Church (cf. Mk 9:1), and he had connected these two events in the parable of the evil vine-dressers (cf. Mt 21:33-41).

The coming of the lord of the vineyard for the punishment of the evil vine-dressers who have killed his son, it would seem, is a clear allusion to the destruction of Jerusalem. At the same time the kingdom is turned over to others who would cultivate it with zeal and fidelity. We recall that, during his own lifetime, Jesus limited his preaching and that of his apostles to the Jews alone (cf. Mt 15:24), and that, even after the ascension of Jesus, the apostles preached for several years only to the Jews (cf. Acts 11:19-20).

With the destruction of Jerusalem the final manifestation of God is apparent. There remains only the second phase of the Church, the heavenly phase, when "the saints will shine like the sun in the kingdom of their Father" (Mt 13:43).

From the moment of the incarnation, then, the movement of the entire life of Christ was directed to the foundation of the Church as the sacrament of human salvation. All the actions and intentions of Christ were a part of this great salvation-event. In the call and instruction of the apostles, in the institution of the Last Supper, in the death by crucifixion, and in the glory of the resurrection, in the manifestation of Pentecost and the destruction of Jerusalem — in all these major events the Church has been fully revealed and realized. Now she is the pilgrim Church on the road to her destiny, to the day and hour which no man knows (Mk 13:32), when the saints will shine like the sun in the kingdom of their Father. It is the Church of anticipation and vigilance.

> And I saw the holy city, the New Jerusalem,
>   coming down out of heaven from God,
>   made ready as a bride adorned for her husband.
>
> And I heard a loud voice from the throne saying:
>   "Behold the dwelling of God with men,
>   and He will dwell with them.
>
> And they will be His people,
>   and God Himself will be with them as their God.
> And God will wipe away every tear from their eyes,
> And death shall be no more:
>   neither shall there be mourning,
>   nor crying,
>   nor pain any more,
>   for the former things have passed away" (Apoc 21:2-5).

CHAPTER EIGHT

Authority in the Church

Such, then is the basic reality of the Church as the People of God
and the community of salvation. Within this community, however, are persons with special functions and powers. These are
the ordained ministers. They receive their functions and their
powers in a consecration given by the action of Christ in a sacrament, though this consecration does not alter their essential
equality with other members as regards their personal relation to
Christ. Although the powers and functions are given from above
by the action of Christ, they are given to be exercised as a service
within the community and in union with it, not independently
of it. . . . They must act then in union with the community. They
are there to represent its faith and see that it is handed on by
sound teaching; they are there to preside over the liturgical celebration of the assembly, not to celebrate instead of the community; they are there to watch for the signs of the Spirit's action
within the community and discern true from false; they are there
to guide and to rule, so that the freedom proper to all Christians
will be exercised with order. . . . The basic reality remains the
community. Ministers are not outside of it ruling it as from a
great height.[1]

---

[1] From an editorial, The Clergy Review, July, 1963.

1. The Danger of Scandal

Moral theologians treat the difficult subject of scandal. We may not, prescinding from the specifics, be the occasion of the spiritual disedification or ruin of others. We must make every reasonable attempt to avoid this even when our subjective consciences are undisturbed. Perhaps this general principle is applicable to the Catholic stance before the world, and especially in its exercise and public image of authority. Oftentimes the hierarchical authority, exercised and defended within Catholicism, has meant to many both inside and outside the Church absolute control, monarchial power, suppressed human rights and dignity, disregard for the individual, and the relegation of the faithful to the status of sheep.

The Catholic vocabulary has also seemed to many to be scandalous. There are words and concepts, like excommunication, interdict, and anathema, as well as numerous taboos, which are unintelligible to the average sincere Protestant. Our traditional "marriage laws," our laws forbidding communication with non-Catholics in the worship of God, as prescribed in the code of canon law, and our "infallible definitions" all may well seem to those not in communion with Rome very much as though man is playing at being God.

2. Authority in the Church as a Role of Service

The first thing that must be said about all authority in the Church is that there is only one authority, that of Christ, the Lord of the Church. All who exercise authority, at any level, in the Church, do so because they participate in the authority of Christ. We trace this authority back to the Gospels, to a Christ of infinite patience and humility, who tolerated a class of twelve reluctant learners with great affection and endurance. In the Gospels we view this Christ washing the feet of his apostles, and we hear him greet them after their classic defection during his passion and death with the reassurance of "Shalom!" This was the Lord, who being God did not think that the majesty of his divinity was a thing to be clung to.[2]

We find this Lord of the Church telling his apostles that the man who strives to be a little lord in his kingdom will find himself in the lowest place. He was instructing men to whom he wished to commit at least a limited charge over his flock; and he was greatly concerned that these men would be gentle and understanding in their exercise of his authority which would be vested in them. He is in this matter very explicit:

[2] Cf. Phil 2:5–7.

Jesus called them into his presence and said to them: "You know that the distinguished rulers of the Gentiles lorded over their subjects, and that their princes tyrannize them. That is not to be your way! On the contrary, he who would be a prince among you must be your *servant*, and he who would be a leader among you must be the *slave* of everyone. Why, even the Son of Man did not come into the world to be served but to serve and to give his life as a ransom for many" (Mk 10:42-45).

It is important to realize that our Lord is not saying that there will be no authority in his Church; in the fullness of his message he unmistakably confers his authority on the apostles. He is saying that those in authority are to act as *servants* and *slaves*, words which would have had sharp edges and jarring meanings in the ears of the apostles.

Just as everything within Christianity is to be characterized by love, so in the exercise of authority in the Church, the only worthy motive and manner is that of love.

By *this* shall men know that you are my disciples, that you have an enduring love for one another. . . . This is my commandment: Love one another as I have loved you. . . . This is all I command you: Love one another (Jn 13:35; 15:12, 17).

Our Lord rarely used the word "obey," and seems to put very little stress on the virtue of obedience as such.[3] To obey was for him a definite thing to do, something concrete and material, a matter-of-fact action to be performed, doing the will of another.[4] Although he did not talk much about obedience as such, it is evident that his whole life was a submission to many authorities. He was obedient, first of all, to the authority of his Father's will, obedient "even to the death of the cross" (Phil 2:8). He also submitted to human authority, both domestic and political. He obeyed his parents, when he "went down to Nazareth and was subject to them" for thirty years of his short life (cf. Lk 2:51). Similarly, he obeyed civil and religious authorities (cf. Mk 12:17). And finally he said: "Whoever breaks one of these least laws and teaches others to do likewise shall be counted least in the kingdom of heaven" (Mt 5:19).

Yet obedience was never a fetish with Christ, never the letter of the law devoid of spirit. With seemingly great liberty of spirit, he bypassed ancient Jewish laws and customs, excepted himself from the Sabbath regulations, ate with unwashed hands — all in favor of a higher law.

If submission to authority in the Church means in its most general connotation compliance to law and commands, it can be distinguished from other types of obedience. It is not a domestic obedience, that of

---

[3] Cf. Jacques Guillet, *Jesus Christ, Yesterday and Today* (Chicago, Franciscan Herald Press, 1965).

[4] Cf. Karl Rahner, "Reflections on Obedience," *Cross Currents* 10 (1960), p. 370.

children to their parents, for such obedience always works toward the eventual transcendance of itself. Nor is the obedience of a Catholic a civil obedience which concerns itself with the temporal common good of a group, although there is room for this type of obedience in the Church because of the many unavoidable exigencies that arise from the nature of the Church as a community. Nor is the obedience of a Catholic that pseudo-obedience which avoids responsibility and initiative under the pretext of deferring to the decision of others.[5] The obedience within the Church is meant to be a fulfilling type of obedience, humanly fulfilling as well as divinely maturing. The exercise of authority in the Church is, as the Vatican Council repeatedly points out,[6] a role of service designed to give a fullness of life to its subjects. Human maturity, obviously, is gained when we become responsible for our own lives, down to their last details.[7] No one of us can turn his will over to another. Finally, obedience in the Church precludes that servility which proceeds from fear of authority, and which is opposed to intelligent obedience. Father Adrian Van Kaam notes that "Obedience comes from the Latin *ob-audire* which means 'to listen to. . . .'" It is "essentially an attitude of attentiveness to God's will, followed by a prompt and joyful response."[8] The obedience of a Catholic is meant, of course, to be an intelligent obedience, a reflective obedience. Father Häring writes:

> Even a servant is expected to reflect on his master's command if he desires to carry out the commission in conformity with his master's intention. How much more should the children of God try to enter into the genuine beauty and deep significance of God's design by a ready response of obedience.[9]

In the New Testament the words "authority" and "power" are rarely used; and positions of power are referred to primarily as functions of service within the community. Father McKenzie distinguishes authority within the Church from authority in general, remarking that "it is natural to consider authority in the Church as a species of authority in general . . . but such a conception . . . is false to the New Testament idea of Church authority."[10]

Father McKenzie also distinguishes between the two types of natural

---

[5] Richard Vaughan, "Obedience and Psychological Maturity," *Review for Religious*, 21 (1962), p. 428.

[6] See especially the *Constitution on the Church*, chap. 3, and the *Decree on the Bishops' Pastoral Office*.

[7] Rahner, *op. cit.*, p. 371.

[8] Adrian Van Kaam, "Together in Obedience," *Envoy* 1 (1965), p. 1.

[9] Bernard Häring, *Christian Renewal in a Changing World* (New York: Desclee, 1964), p. 75.

[10] From *Authority in the Church* by John L. McKenzie, S.J. (New York: Sheed and Ward, Inc., 1966), p. 5. Copyright © 1966 by Sheed and Ward, Inc.

societies: domestic and political. All others are conventional, created by men for a particular end which is not specified by human nature and the conditions of human existence. He writes:

> In conventional societies the basis of authority is contract; the authority is established by the mutual consent of those who form the society, and these are free also to determine the constitution of the society.[11]

The authority of natural societies rests on a moral basis and the authority of conventional societies rests on a contractual foundation. Only a moral basis makes obedience a morally good act.[12] The Church, according to Father McKenzie, forms a third type of society because its constitution and its final end differ from each of these other societies. The end in the family is the maturity of its subjects; the end of the state lies in the temporal common good of society; the end of conventional societies is determined by contract; but the end of the Church is the common good, not of a natural society nor of a contractual association, but of a community in charity living the life of the Spirit.[13]

Father McKenzie further maintains that in the apostolic Church authority was exercised ordinarily by persuasion and exhortation, rather than by direct command. Both Christ and his apostles considered a position of authority one of leadership in the service of love to the community.[14] Though this idea was foreign to the civil authority of the time, it was precisely what Christ had in mind for his Church when he said:

> In the world, kings lord it over their subjects; and those in authority are called their country's "benefactors." Not so with you: on the contrary, the highest among you must bear himself as though he were the youngest, and the chief among you must act like a servant. For who is greater — the one who sits at table or the servants who wait on him? Surely the one who sits at table. Yet here am I among you like a servant (Lk 22:25–27).

The terms used by Paul and the apostles to indicate positions of leadership or authority refer to a task or activity of service performed in the community. There were various offices such as those of apostles, doctors, prophets, evangelists, teachers, pastors, bishops, presbyters, ministers, leaders or superintendents, presidents, stewards, or administrators. But, as Yves Congar points out, "All of these offices are included in the diakonia (service), even that of the apostle. . . . All of the apostles identify superiority of rank with the maximum degree of humble and loving service."[15] Within the Church, Father McKenzie writes:

---

[11] *Ibid.*, p. 8.
[12] *Ibid.*, p. 11.
[13] *Ibid.*, p. 12.
[14] Cf. Mk 10:42–45; 1 Pet 4:10; 1 Cor 9:19.
[15] Yves Congar, "Historical Development of Authority," in *Problems of Authority*, John M. Todd, ed. (Baltimore: Helicon Press, 1962), pp. 120–121.

Authority is only one of the operations of the Spirit, one of the organs of the body. The full life of the body, moved by the Spirit, demands the healthy function of all the members; no one member, even authority, may assume functions which are not its own.

Love is the supreme motivation both of the officers and of the other members of the Church; with this motivation anything like a power structure is forever excluded from the Church. Love is the only power which the New Testament knows.[16]

Archbishop Roberts concurs with Father McKenzie, when he writes:

When the Church becomes a power structure, unless that power be the power of love, it takes on a secular character. When coercion replaces inspiration and love, the Church takes on a secular character; it can even take on the unpleasant aspects of the police state.[17]

Authority is a role of service, and the power of those who exercise this authority is the power of love, which asks the question: What can I do for those I love? What can I confer upon their lives? How can I help them to be fulfilled, to grow, to achieve, to be truly happy? To possess authority in the Church always connotes responsibility, the responsibility indicated in these questions. Archbishop Roberts writes: "No one can climb to the summit of authority using the one leg of power. The other leg — responsibility — must go with him every inch of the way."

Authority must seek growth, creativity, and new life. There may well be times when it has to be exercised in a negative way, by denying dangerous liberty. Those in authority in the Church may have to order us down from dangerously thin branches of the tree in which we may be climbing, but for the most part authority should seek to make the life of the ordinary Christian a more fruitful and a fuller life. Vatican II reinforces this concept:

And that duty which the Lord committed to the shepherds of His people, is a true service, which in sacred literature is significantly called "diakonia," or ministry.[18]

Priests, prudent cooperators with the episcopal order, its aid and instrument, called to serve the People of God, constitute one priesthood with their bishops, although bound by a diversity of duties.[19]

For the nurturing and constant growth of the People of God, Christ the Lord instituted in His Church a variety of ministries, which work for the good of the whole body. For those ministers, who are endowed with sacred powers, serve their brethren, so that all who are of the People of

---

[16] McKenzie, op. cit., pp. 82, 85.
[17] Archbishop Thomas Roberts, Black Popes (New York: Sheed and Ward, 1954), p. 11.
[18] Lumen Gentium, no. 24; cf. also Acts 1:17 and 25; Rom 11:13; 1 Tm 1:12.
[19] Ibid., no. 28.

God, and therefore enjoy a true Christian dignity, working toward a common goal freely and in an orderly way, may arrive at salvation.[20]

This power they use only for the edification of their flock in truth and holiness, remembering that he who is greater should become as the lesser and he who is the more distinguished should become as the servant (cf. Lk 22:26–27).[21]

The whole notion of authority in the Church is primarily that it is a function of service, and the manner in which it is to be exercised is the manner of a servant and a slave. The motive of those who exercise this authority in the Church as well as the motive of those who accept authority in the Church is the common motive of love. It is the only power which the New Testament and Christianity recognizes.

All of the members of Christ's Body, which is animated by the Holy Spirit, are open to the inspiration of the Holy Spirit; and it is the *community as such* which must act, not simply those who are in authority. There is no doubt that in the final moment the decision rests with those who possess authority in the Church. However, mere human competence is not the sole criterion. Responsible examination and consultation must always precede such a final moment if there is to be a well-founded hope that the community that is the Church will actually be doing the will of God and possessing the truth of God.

A true understanding of what we have been saying here implies the necessity of dialogue in the Church, which we will take up later at length, as well as a theological listening for the will of God, which must occur at the highest levels of authority within the People of God. The Holy Father, in order that he might find the will of God and the truth of the Holy Spirit, consults the bishops and asks the faithful for suggestions. He listens to the Spirit acting within the whole People of God. And while this procedure is true at the highest levels of authority, it is also the way authority must proceed all the way up and down the fabric of authority within the Church. This view implies that every member of the Church must really strive to live by the Spirit and let the Spirit act in and through him. Otherwise, those who are in authority will find the will of God in the community of the Church only by coincidence.

A final but fundamental requirement, if authority is to be exercised as a role of service within the Church, is the willingness to delegate responsibility and power, and to let the *principle of subsidiarity* function on all levels of authority. Delegation of responsibility and power and the principle of subsidiarity are not precisely the same, but they are closely related. Delegation is a substitution of authority in which the authority

---

[20] *Ibid.*, no. 18.
[21] *Ibid.*, no. 27.

of the superior is given to a subject. Subsidiarity rather implies the sharing of authority, from the highest to the lowest authority in the community of the Church, giving some responsibility to all. The principle of subsidiarity has been effectively proposed by Pope Pius XI in *Quadragesimo Anno,* and repeated by both Pius XII and John XXIII. Pius XI writes in his encyclical:

> It is a grave injustice . . . and disturbance of right order for larger and higher organizations to arrogate to themselves functions which can be performed efficiently by smaller and lower bodies.[22]

The serious application of the principles of delegation and subsidiarity within the Church not only would lighten the burdens of those in authority, who cannot be well-versed in all the knowledge needed today to govern efficiently and to mediate God's will, but it would also benefit the individual works of the Church and would be psychologically beneficial to the members of the Church who would then be able to practice initiative and critical judgment in a personal, rewarding, and responsible way. A psychologist has written recently:

> If you are a person with authority . . . you may realize that if those who work under you want to sabotage your efforts, one good way is to withhold the information you need to make intelligent decisions. To act intelligently you must be as well informed as possible about the consequences of various alternative courses of action available to you. You have to depend on your subordinates for both adequate information and adequate implementation of your program. This is where good interpersonal relationships are important.

> The superior who takes over subordinate functions fosters apathy and hostility in subjects. . . . If the person in authority is formal, rigid and fearful, subordinates will tend to act toward him in the same way. If he is free and really human, his subordinates will tend also to feel free and reasonable with him and thus to become mature and responsible.[23]

In summary, we must return to the importance of charity. If the response in love that is made by Christians to a God of love is to be defined largely in terms of the love and service of our neighbor, then authority and obedience are essential, just as they are essential in any community. But the nature of authority and obedience depend on the nature of the end of that community, and not *vice versa.* The religious community of the Church does not have merely a natural end. The end toward which the religious community of the Church is directed is that perfection of charity in the life of the Spirit, which is the life of the Church. Therefore, as Father McKenzie indicates, we must look to the Church to find that basis for authority and obedience which is peculiar to this com-

---

[22] Pope Pius XI, *Quadragesimo Anno,* May 15, 1931, DS 3738 (DB 2266).
[23] John Meany, "The Use of Authority," *America* (March 26, 1966), pp. 409, 411.

munity. The basis is not power but love. *Love is, and must always be, the supreme motivation both of those who govern and of those who obey.*[24]

3. The Authority of Christ and the Hierarchy of the Church

The Vatican Council, in its *Constitution on the Church*, Chapter 3 (Nos. 19–21), summarizes the doctrine of authority in the Church as follows:

> The Lord Jesus, after praying to the Father and calling to Himself those whom He desired, appointed twelve men who would stay in His company, and whom He would send to preach the kingdom of God. These apostles He formed after the manner of a college or a fixed group, over which He placed Peter, chosen from among them. He sent them first to the children of Israel and then to all nations, so that as sharers in His power they might make all people His disciples, sanctifying and governing them. Thus they would spread His Church, and by ministering to it under the guidance of the Lord, would shepherd it all days even to the consummation of the world.

> They were fully confirmed in this mission on the day of Pentecost in accordance with the Lord's promise: "You shall receive power when the Holy Spirit comes upon you and you shall be witnesses for Me in Jerusalem and in all Judea and in Samaria and even to the very ends of the earth" (Acts 1:8). By everywhere preaching the gospel, which was accepted by their heirs under the influence of the Holy Spirit, the apostles gathered together the universal Church, which the Lord established on the apostles and built upon blessed Peter, their chief, Christ Jesus Himself remaining the supreme cornerstone.

> That divine mission, entrusted by Christ to the apostles, will last until the end of the world, since the gospel they are to teach is for all time the source of all life for the Church. And for this reason the apostles, appointed as the ruling authority in this society, took care to appoint successors . . . in order that the mission assigned to them might continue after their death, they passed on to their immediate cooperators . . . the duty of confirming and finishing the work begun by themselves. . . . Thus, as St. Irenaeus testified, through those who were appointed bishops by the apostles, and through their successors (the bishops) down to our own time, the apostolic tradition is manifested and preserved.[25]

> Therefore the Sacred Council teaches that the bishops by divine institution have succeeded to the place of the apostles, as shepherds of the Church and he who hears them, hears Christ, and he who rejects them, rejects Christ and Him Who sent Christ.

> For the discharge of such great duties, the apostles were enriched by Christ with a special outpouring of the Holy Spirit coming down upon them, and

---

[24] McKenzie, op. cit., p. 85.
[25] Cf. St. Irenaeus, Adv. Haer., III, 3, 1; PG 7, 848; III 2, 2; PG 7, 847.

they passed on this spiritual gift to their helpers by the imposition of hands; and it has been transmitted down to us in episcopal consecration. . . . But episcopal consecration, together with the office of sanctifying, also confers the office of teaching and of governing, which . . . is so conferred and the sacred character so impressed, that bishops in an eminent and visible way sustain the roles of Christ Himself as teacher, shepherd and high priest, and that they act in His person.[26]

It might be well to summarize here the facts of theological data concerning the Christian and his obedience to Christ in the Church:

I. Christian obedience is fundamentally commitment to the Lord Jesus Christ. He is the one mediator through whom the truth and the will of God comes to us; and therefore the one and only authority in the community of the Church is its Lord.

II. However, the structure of the organic unity that is the Body of Christ is a hierarchical structure. There is a distribution of gifts by the Holy Spirit according to the office or function of each member within this body.[27] Still the Father "has subjected every single thing to his [Christ's] authority and has appointed him as the universal head of the Church" (Cf. Eph 1:22–33).

III. The charismatic gifts, through which the Holy Spirit works in the Church, correspond to the offices or functions within the Mystical Body, but all of these gifts and offices tend to the unity and the building up of the Body of Christ.[28] Consequently, the distinctions of hierarchy do not beget exclusiveness or division but unity through cooperation. The head and the feet are not the same, but they must work together.

IV. The supreme authority in the Church is possessed by the apostles and their successors, the bishops of the Church. However, this does not in any way diminish the reality of the "variety of ministries" to which Vatican II refers.[29] Furthermore, even though Paul, in his listings of the gifts of the Holy Spirit, always mentions the apostles in first place, he always lists the gift of prophecy as a charismatic gift, and usually in the second place (cf. 1 Cor 12:28).

V. Authority in the Church is a role of service. Just as all the ministries of the Church must work toward the building up of the Body of Christ, proceeding toward this "common goal freely and in an orderly way,"[30] so authority in the Church must serve the whole Church by seeking its growth, creativity, and the deepening of its life.[31]

---

[26] Cf. St. Cyprian, *Epist* 63, no. 14; PL 4, 386.
[27] Cf. 1 Cor 12:4–31.
[28] Cf. 1 Cor 12:12–13; chap. 13; Rom 12:4–13; Col 3:12–17; Eph 4:1–16.
[29] Cf. *Lumen Gentium*, no. 18.
[30] *Ibid.*, no. 18.
[31] *Ibid.*, no. 18, 24, 27, 28.

VI. The authority implied in the hierarchical offices of the Church is mediatorial in its purpose and function. The *raison d'être* of authority is to bring the Church into encounter with God. It is meant to produce within Christians an ever-deepening commitment to the Lord of all by causing the community to confront, and helping it to submit to, the absolute divine authority of Christ. The *Constitution on the Church* says:

> Therefore, the Sacred Council teaches that bishops by divine institution have succeeded to the place of the apostles, as shepherds of the Church, and he who hears them, hears Christ, and he who rejects them, rejects Christ and Him Who sent Christ.[32]

VII. Alienation, therefore, from the service of the hierarchy is alienation from Christ. Although the hierarchy is seriously obliged to exercise its authority in the manner of a servant and a slave, Christ has made it clear that, if one refuses this service, he can have no part with Christ. This was the lesson to the reluctant Peter, as recorded in St. John's Gospel: "If I do not wash you, I have nothing more to do with you." The hierarchy must offer its service as a physician would who offers health and life as a service, not as a command which he is prepared to sanction by coercion. One need not accept this service, but if he does not he is refusing his own health. So the servant-hierarchy offers the community a diagnosis of Christian existence and the medicine of revealed truth. Nevertheless, the encounter is really with the absolute divine authority of Christ, and the choice is between the health of obedience and the sickness of disobedience, and even possibly between the life of obedience and the death of disobedience.

VIII. If the hierarchy is to mediate the divine will and the divine truth in this way, it does not create the divine will or truth. The will of the hierarchy is not automatically the divine will that must be mediated to the Church. The hierarchy must seek to find the will of God, not to become it. Therefore, it is imperative that the servant-hierarchy listen to the entire Church, in which the Spirit of God is working. It is the whole Body in which the Spirit works, and evidence of the will of God is to be found in all the parts. The whole Body is structured with joints and ligaments, and bound by these to the head, and thus life and growth is to be found in all the parts.[33]

In conclusion, there is an enormous responsibility of the hierarchy to mediate, whether in doctrine or discipline, the will of God, given to us through his Son who is the only Lord of the Church and its only authority. At the same time there is an equally enormous responsibility for all the faithful to be obedient to the service rendered by the hierarchy.

[32] *Ibid.*, no. 20; cf. Lk 10:16.
[33] Cf. Col 2:19.

Apart from this service, there is only separation from Christ, whose person is borne by the hierarchy. The Church is neither a kingdom of little lords and tyrants, nor is it a democracy. It is a hierarchically structured community of love. When the hierarchy consults the entire Church in an effort to find the indications of the working of the Spirit and finally exercises its own ultimate power of discrimination and discernment of spirits, it must be done out of and in the spirit of love, of loving service. When the entire Church speaks out in its contribution to the Church's total understanding of God's truth and will, and in the end submits in the spirit of obedience to its Lord, both the exercise of freedom and the submission of obedience must be acts of love. "By this shall men know that you are my disciples, that you have an enduring love for one another" (Jn 13:35). If the hierarchy fails to exercise its authority in the spirit of service and fails to consult the action of the Holy Spirit in the entire Church, it will fall into the malpractice of excessive maternal care, of legislating with too great haste and in too minute detail, of ruling too much. If the faithful fail to love the Church, and to speak out forthrightly in areas open to discussion, they will fail the Church and its Lord.

4. Teaching Authority in the Church

There are various aspects of the redemption effected by Christ. He redeems us as *priest* in his act of sacrifice and atonement, as *prophet* in his role as teacher, bringing God's self-revelation to men, and as *king* in his office of governing his people. All three of these messianic, redemptive offices he committed to the apostles and, as the Church has always believed, to their successors.

> Go into the whole world and preach the good news to all creation. He that believes and is baptized will be saved: He that does not believe will be condemned (Mk 16:16). . . . Whoever receives you, receives me (Mt 10:40). . . . Whoever hears you, hears me, and whoever spurns you spurns me (Lk 10:16). . . . But should the people not make you welcome and not listen to your preaching, leave that house or town, and shake the dust off your feet. I tell you the plain truth: On Judgment Day it will go less hard with Sodom and Gomorrha than with that town (Mt 10:14–15). . . . I have made known to you all that I have heard from my Father (Jn 15:15). . . . Go therefore and teach all nations . . . teach them to observe all the commandments I have given you (Mt 28:19–20). . . . Just as the Father has sent me, so I send you (Jn 20:21). . . . You will receive power when the Holy Spirit comes upon you, and you will be my witnesses in Jerusalem, and in all Judea, and Samaria, and even to the very ends of the earth (Acts 1:8). . . . There is still much that I might say to you;

but you are not ready for this at present. But when he, the Spirit of truth, has come, he will conduct you through the whole range of truth" (Jn 16:12–13).

With this commission and the help of the Holy Spirit, the apostles begin their labors of preaching and teaching "filled with the Holy Spirit" (Acts 4:8–31). They have a very clear realization, after Pentecost, that God is teaching through them.[34] Their word is the word of God.[35] They are so sure of this that Paul instructs the Galatians:

> Let me tell you that, if even we ourselves or an angel from heaven should proclaim to you a gospel other than that which we have preached, let him be accursed. I repeat what I have said: If anyone proclaims to you a gospel other than that which you have received, let him be accursed (Gal 1:8–9).

The suspicion that authority necessarily encroaches upon freedom can result from a poor orientation. Man's ultimate freedom is conditioned upon his possession of the truth, which Paul says "is in Jesus" (Eph 4:21). Paul teaches us, in his letter to the Galatians, that "Christ has set us free to enjoy freedom. Stand fast then and do not be caught again under the yoke of slavery. . . . You were running the race splendidly. Who prevented you from continuing to submit to the truth?" (Gal 5:1–7.) The whole Pauline emphasis is precisely this: We must submit to the truth that is in Jesus in order to be free. Christ himself told us this same thing:

> Jesus then said to the Jews that had just begun to believe in Him: "If you make my teaching your rule of life, you are truly my disciples; then you will know the truth, and the truth will make you free" (Jn 8:31–32).

We must submit to the truth of Christ in order to be truly free. It is, ironically, in this submission that man finds liberation. The teaching and the person of Christ are, for the Christian, the truth. The real issue is not whether authority in the Church restricts my freedom; the real issue is rather this: Do those who bear authority in the Church bear the Person of Christ, and do the teachings of this authority represent the teachings of Christ? If the answer to these questions is yes, then my freedom is endangered only in my rejection of this authority.

In his lifetime, Jesus insisted that his message was not his own but that of his Father. "For the message you have delivered to me, I have delivered to them" (Jn 17:8). The meaning is that the words spoken through the mouth of his sacred humanity did not originate in that humanity; the message is from God who speaks to us through his Son. And, just as the Father has sent Christ, so Christ sends his apostles.

---

[34] Cf. Acts 5:32; 15:28.
[35] Cf. Acts 6:2.

"My teaching is not my own invention, it is his teaching whose ambassador I am" (Jn 7:16). "So I am making them my ambassadors to the world" (Jn 17:18).

It is clear that the teachings of the magisterium do not all have the same doctrinal value or command the same fullness of assent on the part of the faithful. We might outline the teaching authority of the Church and the expected response of the faithful as follows:

I. THE ROMAN PONTIFF

A. *His extraordinary or solemn Magisterium:* This embraces only the absolute, irreversible peremptory judgments which are called *definitions.* These definitions, or *ex cathedra* pronouncements, may be made about any matter which is included in the deposit of divine revelation, and, if such a matter is defined the response is an internal, religious, and absolute act of faith. Definitions may also be made about truths which are not themselves revealed but are so closely connected with revealed truths that errors in these matters would easily lead to errors of faith.[36] If a truth is defined from this secondary area of infallibility, the response is *not* an act of faith, since faith is the response to God revealing. Nonetheless a definition of this kind does demand an assent which is absolute, internal, and religious. The definition of a *revealed truth* raises it to the status of a dogma. The definition of a truth from the secondary area does not result in a dogma, but the truth becomes a matter of irrevocable assent because it is defined. The Roman Pontiff can define in any type of document, and there is no special formula, but it must be clear that the Pope is intending to define. The law of the Church says that nothing is to be regarded as a definition unless the intention to define is manifest.[37] The Pope is always infallible, by the assistance of the Holy Spirit who will not permit the universal Church to be involved in an error of faith, when he is defining. It is a dogma, i.e., revealed by God and proposed infallibly by the Church, that the Roman Pontiff is infallible when he is defining revealed truths.[38] It is theologically certain that he is infallible when defining truths from the secondary area, e.g., pronouncing a Council to be Ecumenical, theological conclusions, the preambles of faith, dogmatic facts such as the condemnation of certain doctrines or writings, laws passed for the universal Church as in harmony with the divine law and apt for the promotion of holiness, the solemn

---

[36] Cf. the Acts of Vatican I, *Col. Lac.*, no. 414 d, 415, 416.
[37] Cf. Canon 1323, 3.
[38] Cf. *DS* 3074 (*DB* 1839).

approbation of religious orders, and the solemn canonization of saints.[39]

B. *His ordinary Magisterium:* This embraces any teaching in the general area of faith and morals intended for the universal Church, but not intended to be a definition. These teachings are called authoritative, but are not regarded as infallible. They can be proposed in any type of document or address, e.g., encyclicals, allocutions, radio addresses, etc. The decrees of the Biblical Commission and the Congregation of the Faith, as organs of the Holy Father, are included under this magisterium. The assent to be given to teachings of the ordinary, papal magisterium is internal, religious, but *conditional.* The condition of this assent could be worded this way: I give my assent to this teaching *unless* (1) the Church shall some day teach me otherwise, or (2) the opposite shall become obvious to me as a competent judge of the matter which the teaching concerns.

II. THE COLLEGE OF BISHOPS (INCLUDING THE BISHOP OF ROME)

A. *Their extraordinary or solemn Magisterium:* This embraces all truths taught by the bishops of the world in an Ecumenical Council. Not everything taught by a Council, however, is to be regarded as defined doctrine; but the same principle applies to the extraordinary Magisterium of the Council which applies to that of the Pope: there must be an intention to define and this must somehow be made clear. Usually the *Acta Concilii,* which includes the secretary's narration of discussions, etc. preceding actual balloting, clarify the intentions of the Council fathers. Again, the Council may define revealed matters, thus requiring the assent of faith on the part of the universal Church. The revealed truth which is defined in this way itself becomes a defined dogma. Or the Council, as the Roman Pontiff, may define a truth not revealed in itself but closely connected to the deposit of revelation; the truth, in this case, is taught infallibly, but the assent, although it is absolute and irrevocable, is not the assent of faith. The matter proposed is that found in the decrees of the Council, which have been promulgated with papal approbation.[40]

B. *Their ordinary and universal Magisterium:* This embraces all the truths taught by all the bishops dispersed throughout the world, i.e., not in Council. If the bishops are teaching a given truth as revealed by God,

---

[39] Cf. *Col. Lac.,* no. 416–417; also see DS 2880 (DB 1684); DS 3017–19 (DB 1797–19); DS 3886 (DB 2314); esp. DS 3892 (DB 2320); DS 2001–07 (DB 1092–96); DS 2678 (DB 1578); DS 1728 (DB 931); DS 1731–32 (DB 934–35); DS 1613 (DB 856); DS 1645 (DB 879); *Lumen Gentium,* no. 43–45.

[40] Cf. DS 3011 (DB 792); also see *Lumen Gentium,* no. 25.

it becomes a matter of faith and a dogma, and the assent to be given is the absolute assent of faith. It may be difficult to know if there is such a consensus of the dispersed bishops, but it is possible to verify this perhaps by research into catechisms, the statements of groups of bishops, local episcopal synods, etc. Although a given teaching, when taught as revealed, is a matter of faith and infallibly true, it is not a definition.[41]

5. Authority and Private Judgment as Complementary Forces in the Church

There is no doubt that, in any community like the Church, there is need for external authority. The problem is to reconcile authority with the human rights to think for oneself and to make truly human choices. While one may be able to achieve this reconciliation in theory, the practice will be inevitably hard. Furthermore, the practice may well be complicated by a real resentment for authority, which may well be caused by the manner in which authority is exercised. We know that authority in general does not necessarily dehumanize people, yet there are many examples available to us in which this has been a real danger.

In general, when we address ourselves to authority, the first question of interest is the competence of that authority to direct us. And when we address ourselves to the authority of the Church, that competence is based not only on human resources, but on the activity of the Spirit who gives each grace according to the office or role he plays in the life of the Church.[42] The Church claims to speak in the name of Christ. But this claim is not subject to the scrutiny of merely natural reason. If I accept this vicarious role of the Church, in its exercise of doctrinal and moral authority, it will be simply because God has given me the grace to believe this. We cannot hope to persuade or convince others, on merely natural grounds, that the Church does in fact bear the authority of Christ. Only God can make a man a believer. It is very necessary to accept the authority of the Church for what it is, and to know that only faith can illuminate the true nature of this authority. Flesh and blood have no power to reveal it, but only our Father who is in heaven. The jury of one's own mind is not competent to pass verdict on this claim. Faith is a supernatural gift and will always be such.

To assent to the Church's authority, even though this assent is made

---

[41] A definition is always a formal and explicit statement of the truth in question; this statement is made either by the Pope in his solemn magisterial office or by an ecumenical council. Cf. *Constitution on the Church*, no. 25.

[42] Cf. 1 Cor 12:4-11.

possible only by God's grace, remains, nevertheless, a *personal, intelligent,* and *free* act. For those who have accepted the faith in adulthood, this is a patent reality. For born-Catholics it is a question of gradual adjustment to adult faith, and may well imply many crises of faith.

But private judgment remains active and vital to the life of the Church, even after the initial private judgment that is the act of faith. When the Church teaches, we must ask if the speaker is truly qualified to speak for the Church, and if what he is saying is in accord with the traditional faith of the Church preserved in the Scriptures and in Sacred Tradition. Private judgment must also ask about one's own competence and understanding. Is my understanding of the traditional faith of the Church and the meaning of this speaker here and now a complete or competent understanding?

Granted that private judgment will ask these questions, it remains also a check on the orthodoxy and the competence of judgments passed by the Church, in its magisterial statements short of defined truths. Theologians have always recognized the reality of the *sensus fidelium*. There is, as we have said earlier, a connatural instinct in the faithful of Christ for the truths and will of God. It is based upon the activity of the Holy Spirit, who is the soul of the Church, in all of the Body of Christ. We have discussed in the previous part the *doctrinal* Magisterium of the Church. Perhaps it is even more to the point to discuss the power of the Church to direct the *moral* lives of the faithful.

When a representative of the Magisterium seeks to direct the conscience of a man, to form that conscience, the same questions essentially must be asked. Is he qualified to speak for the Church, and is what he is saying in accord with the traditional moral teachings of the Church? Also we must ask if he is within the scope of his authority, which is primarily the deposit of faith and connected matters. Members of the hierarchy are qualified to speak authoritatively only in the areas of religious and moral issues.

Even after these questions are asked, personal judgment must remain vital and operative. None of us can shift the responsibility to face the question of whether it is right or not to obey in any given instance, where we might suspect that the direction being given to us is not truly in accord with the will of God. St. Thomas Aquinas summarizes this responsibility as follows:

> Every man is bound to examine his own actions according to the knowledge that God has given him, whether natural, or acquired, or infused from above: For every human being is bound to act according to reason.
>
> Although the prelate is superior to his subjects, nevertheless God, from whose precept the individual conscience derives its binding force, is superior

to the prelate. . . . Hence, although it is not fitting that the subject pass judgment on the content of the prelate's command considered in itself, it is proper for him to pass judgment on whether or not he should obey this command. For it is this which is his personal concern.[43]

The important thing is that we act out of love and be seriously intent upon the will of God. There can be no real obedience in the Church, which has any merit before God, unless there are free, responsible judgments made by those who are obeying. This, of course, involves risk. There will always be a vital tension, which is a healthy thing, between authority and these responsible judgments of the faithful. There are no easy answers. The important thing is to realize that private judgment acts as a check upon authority in the Church, but is not of itself opposed to authority. They must be seen as complementary forces. Furthermore, the one who is obeying in the Church must accept the utterances of authority in the way that they are intended. Very often authority may distinguish between what is true and false, or between what is right and wrong, as opposed to that which it considers safe or not safe.

And finally there is need for an articulate dialogue in the Church from which alone the truth of the Holy Spirit can emerge. There is need for free speech and public opinion, which we shall take up in a subsequent chapter, not only to check the use and direction of authority, but also to direct the attention of authority to the true needs of the Body of Christ, and to apply the truth of Christ to our contemporary world and life. For this, of course, there is needed in the Church a mature, dedicated, and articulate laity.

6. The Special Problem of Non-Defined Teachings of Authority in the Church

One of the growing realizations of our present generation is that, while we know some things about absolute truth, we do not possess absolute truth. Many of our conclusions and much of our knowledge, therefore, are of a tentative nature. We must understand that authority in the Church is a site of encounter with Christ, who has committed his own prophetic mission to the Church. In all duly-constituted authority in the Church, it is Christ who is teaching, teaching us the truth that alone can make us free. We have said that, in those cases where the Church is defining revealed doctrine, the encounter with Christ is clear and unquestionable. It is the call to an absolute assent of faith. The problem

---

[43] De Veritate, q. 17, a. 5, ad 3 and 4.

is rather with teachings that are short of this definition-status. I am still in encounter with Christ — "He who hears you, hears me!" — yet I know that, in such teachings, God may not override human haste or human ignorance.

The word *assent*, which is the word used by Vatican II,[44] is a strong word, with serious connotations. It seems to be descriptive of that state of mind when the giver of assent has consciously reached an ultimate possession of truth. All assent would seem to be by its very definition absolute assent. Yet in the case of the non-definitive judgments or teachings of the Magisterium there is no guarantee of this ultimate possession, no guarantee of infallibility or irreversibility. It would seem, therefore, that the response to these teachings be a *conditional* assent: I assent unless or until the Church teaches me otherwise, or my professional competence in the matter absolves me, for the sake of intellectual honesty, from assent. And yet there is something uncomfortable and unmanageable in this solution. It seems, in its wording, to create a state of schizophrenia, if assent connotes a certain finality in the process of knowing. It seems to ask the mind to say an absolute *yes* and *maybe* in the same moment and matter, to *close* and *remain open* at the same time. The problem can be especially difficult for a scholar, since it seems to ask him to make a final judgment, in the sense that all judgments are final, and to keep investigating the very matter he has already judged.

Perhaps a more manageable solution can be proposed if we make a slight epistemological re-orientation and adopt a new set of terms. The new epistemological orientation would presuppose that there are other pre-judgmental or pre-assential states of mind besides simple apprehension and mere opinion. In his *Grammar of Assent*, Cardinal Newman suggests the word *inference* to indicate a tentative but probable certitude. It is a type of notional, as opposed to real, assent; for the sake of clarity we can call it *the act of inference*. Whereas assent is an act of judgment, precluding all reasonable fear of error and an act which of itself excludes the possibility of error, the act of inference is a pre-judgmental act and state of mind, which does not of itself exclude the possibility of error. It is, of its nature, not final and absolute. Of its nature it points toward finality, toward judgment, toward the absolute, but remains of itself tentative and hypothetical.

Assuming such a pre-judgmental state and act of the mind it would seem that the response to teachings of the Church, which are non-definitive, involves *both* an act of assent and an act of inference. I *assent* to the larger, contextual truth that Christ is acting, teaching, and directing my life in the authority of the Church. To a specific teaching, how-

---

[44] Cf. *Lumen Gentium*, Chap. 3, esp. no. 25.

ever, which is forwarded to me through a non-definitive statement of the Magisterium, I offer the adherence of *inference*, which is of its nature tentative.

The merit of this approach seems to be that the conditions proposed, if we use the terms "conditional assent," are compatible with my act and state of mind. They do not appear to be compatible with the finality and ultimate possession, which of itself guarantees immunity from error, and which is connoted in the word assent or judgment. It is important to note that, at the same time, I do *assent* to the presence of Christ in the Magisterium. The reverence begotten in this assent for specific teachings would seem to guarantee respect for teaching authority in the Church, to preclude frivolous rebellion and denial. It will also beget a deeper sense of prudence and tact in forwarding the data of my own enlightenment, which would take all the necessary precautions to avoid undermining general respect in the Church for the authority of Christ which obviously resides in the Magisterium. This reverence is very clearly a part of the *sentire ecclesiam* (thinking with the Church) and the habit of theology which characterizes the fully-formed Catholic theologian.

More will be said about the nature of and the response to authority in the Church in the subsequent chapter, which will deal specifically and at length with the need for free speech and public opinion in the Church.

CHAPTER NINE

Free Speech and Public Opinion in the Church

Let him [the bishop] not refuse to listen to his subjects, whom he cherishes as his true sons and whom he exhorts to cooperate readily with himself.

They [the bishops] also know that they were not ordained by Christ to take upon themselves alone the entire salvific mission of the Church towards the world. On the contrary, they understand that it is their noble duty to shepherd the faithful and to recognize their ministries and charisms. . . . For we must all "practice the truth in love and so grow up in all things in Him who is the Head, Christ . . ." (Eph 4:15).

These faithful are by Baptism made one body with Christ and are constituted among the People of God. They are in their own way made sharers in the priestly, prophetical and kingly functions of Christ, and they carry out for their own part the mission of the whole Christian people in the Church and in the world.

He does this [Christ continues His office of teaching] not only through the hierarchy, who teach in His name and with His authority, but also through the laity whom He made His witnesses and to whom He gave an understanding of the faith [sensu fidei] and an attractiveness in speech so that the power of the Gospel might sound forth in their daily social and family lives.

— Lumen Gentium, nos. 26, 30, 31, 35

1. The History of Repression and Recent Enlightenment

The great gasp of surprise, the shock of most non-Catholics during the sessions of the recently terminated Vatican II resulted from the apparently new knowledge that Catholics are allowed to debate. And it was not, surprisingly enough, just a private game in which laymen and assistant priests indulged surreptitiously; even the members of the hierarchy could argue, and right under the nose of the Pope in Vatican City. The impression of many centuries was, and not without basis, that the Church is monolithic, authoritarian, and an inflexibly structured society, in which all communication is a one way street: from the top down. It goes without saying that Vatican II has only dented this impression; it has not destroyed it. To put the status of free speech and public opinion in proper perspective, we must ask ourselves how this image of the Church was created.

For several hundred years the Church has been on the cultural and intellectual defensive. In the fourteenth and fifteenth centuries, theology was a game of abstract speculation, conducted among an elite scholarship which spoke only to itself. The discussions of these theologians were highly impersonal and seriously irrelevant. In reaction to this, there arose the exaggerated humanism of the Renaissance. However, before Catholic scholars could integrate this new learning and speculation into the existing culture, the Church found itself reeling under the trauma of the Reformation. The theologians of the Church came out of their towers of irrelevant speculation, and hammered out a theology of the Church on the anvil of controversy. It was, unfortunately, a purely juridical concept of the Church which they proposed.

Through the ages of Enlightenment, Deism, and Darwin, theories which were characterized by the rising smokestacks of new industries and the triumph of the test tubes of the physical sciences, the Church once more took on a familiar defensive posture. Instead of incorporating these advances of learning for what they were worth, she insisted on telling her children not to play with the "bad boys" of philosophical speculation and scientific laboratories. This protective outlook tended to isolate Catholic philosophy and theology from the mainstream of cultural thought and social change. Seminaries turned out a clergy trained largely on biblical fundamentalism and ecclesiastical juridicism.

The Church in America was born as the child of the Church in Europe. Church leaders in this country were immigrants, of limited education, and in need of the qualities and confidence of true leaders. Worst of all, they were isolated from the American community, and so they quickly fell into the same mold, the posture of defense, in which the hands are held over the eyes and ears. It has been called the ostrich-complex. The Church in America chose to develop along her own prim-rose path instead of developing along with and integrating with the changing American secular society. These years of isolation and separation make the task today look herculean.

In defense of the early American Catholics, it must be said that they for a long time experienced an unfriendly and even hostile atmosphere, and, being immigrants, were subject to the blind fury of prejudice and even violence by reason of their faith. This very often discouraged these Catholics from taking part in the secular society which was evolving around them. They made no contribution to public opinion within the life of a new democracy because they very often found public opinion set against them in advance. This forced upon them the defensive posture of isolation. While this ghetto mentality is still evident in some places and at some times, it is largely a relic now of the early days of American Catholicism.

Catholics have also withdrawn from the mainstream of public opinion within the Church because they felt that their beliefs were unique and had to be defended by the only competent defenders, the clergy. It is recalled that Cardinal Gibbons rejected the proposal that Catholics form separate labor unions, like those found in Europe, lest the faithful be contaminated by mixing with anarchists and socialists. He pointed out that this was "one of the trials of faith which our brew of American Catholics are accustomed to meet almost daily and which they know how to disregard with good sense and firmness."

In 1889 free speech and public opinion within the Church attempted to rise above the repression of the past, and at the Catholic Congress called in Baltimore, Maryland, a congress which had been organized by laymen in cooperation with the hierarchy, the then current practices within the Church were freely criticized and a wide range of opinions were expressed concerning the Church and the world with which it is in dialogue. The attempt became known in Europe as the heresy of "Americanism," and Roman reaction to it tended to discourage all free expression of opinion in the American Church. A papal encyclical on the supposed heresy tended strongly to support this discouragement. Lay leaders in the Church, feeling chastised for their efforts, withdrew into oblivion; and their voice was not heard again until the last thirty years, when the emphasis on the doctrine of the Mystical Body, the renewal of the liturgical movement, and the emphasis on the role of the laity in the social apostolate which was strongly supported by new developments of a theology of the laity, encouraged the renewal of personal engagement in the life of the Church.

The necessity of freedom of speech and public opinion within the
Church is obviously related to the theology of the Mystical Body and
the corporate effort of that Body to build itself up. The theology of
the New Testament, dictating personal responsibility for the Church's
life and activity on the part of all, is strongly supported in the writings
of the Fathers of the Church. These Fathers demonstrate a considerable
variety of opinion on matters which are today considered settled. Saints
and others who were less than saints have spoken up to bishops and
even to popes. Even ladies, like Catherine of Siena, have participated
vigorously in this dialogue. The debates of Vatican II were hardly an
innovation in the life of the Church. Even though the recent history
of the Church is largely a history of repression, free speech and public
opinion have always been very important in the development of the
Church. The defensive postures of the Church, as evidenced in over-
governing and legislations dictated by fright, are, in a sense, atypical.

The Church, like everything that lives, must be growing, renewing
itself. Composed of living members, the Church is the strongest when
the members which compose it are most mature, and maturity for
thinking men involves a constant effort to rethink what is already known,
and a never-ending struggle to assimilate what is yet to be acquired, and
to relate and apply all of this knowledge in Christian living. As human
generations continue to replace their predecessors, human thought patterns and the vehicles of expression undergo a radical change. And even
within one generation the diversity of simultaneously existing cultures,
or the object of the Church's mission to which no people or culture
is alien, calls for the rethinking, reformulation, and reapplication of the
revelation of Christ. The Church must be a light to the whole world,
and preach the Gospel to every creature. She is a part of human civilization, and clearly one of the most important parts. The Holy Spirit, who
guards and influences the Church, works in these men as they are, in
their own cultural and historical perspectives, in their thinking habits and
in their language of communication. Pope Pius XII once wrote:

> The Church is unchanging, indelible in her document of foundation, given
> to her by Christ and sealed with the blood of the Son of God: however,
> the Church spreads out, assumes new forms with the ages into which
> it penetrates, making progress, but not indeed by any change in its nature,
> as St. Vincent of Lerins said so well: The religion of the soul has to imitate
> the process of bodies, which although they increase the number of their
> years in development and growth, nevertheless remain the same bodies
> that they always were.[1]

---

[1] Pope Pius XII, *Radio Message* on the 25th anniversary of his own episcopal consecration, May 13, 1942.

This is vital to understanding the place of freedom of speech and public opinion in the Church: we must remember that the Church is a growing and self-renewing organism, and that each generation has a contribution to make in the form of a deeper penetration of the truth entrusted to the Church and a new application of this truth to the daily lives and situation of men. We must also remember that the Holy Spirit works in the Church of each generation, assisting it to make this contribution and these applications.

If one understands the true nature of the Church and its mission, it will be obvious to him that the Church badly needs an intelligent, responsible, and articulate membership. He will also understand that it is not only the right but in fact the duty of all to contribute to public opinion within the Church. Pope Pius XII described this need of the Church as follows:

> Public opinion is the natural portion of every normal society composed of human beings. . . . Whenever there is no manifest expression of public opinion at all, and above all whenever one must admit that public opinion does not exist at all, this lack must be regarded as a fault, a weakness and a disease in the life of that society. . . . In conclusion, we wish to add a few words about public opinion within the pale of the Church. Only those will be surprised at this who do not know the Catholic Church, or at least know her only badly. For after all she, too, is a living body, and there would be something lacking in her life if there were no public opinion in the Church — a lack for which the pastors as well as the faithful would be to blame.[2]

Every part of the mission of the Church has been given to it by Christ. Just as Christ received his pastoral charge from his heavenly Father, he in turn bestows it upon the Church. He commits to the Church his role of prophet or teacher, of priest or sanctifier, and of king or ruler. He empowered his apostles and their successors, the bishops, to teach, sanctify, and to govern in his name. However, traditionally in the Church the bishops have shared their pastoral charge both with the priests and the faithful of their dioceses, however differently in each case. The bishop was never intended to discharge his pastoral obligations by himself, and so he ordains men to the priesthood and gives them a specific sharing in his apostolic mission, which is a continuation of the mission of Christ himself. Priests are cooperators in the bishop's holy orders. They participate in his priesthood, and they share in the ministry of the Word and assist him in the government of the diocese. But the bishop also shares his pastoral charge with *all of the faithful of his diocese.* Through the sacrament of baptism, all Christians begin to share in the life of Christ, and this life is necessarily redemptive and involves the salvation of all

---

[2] Pope Pius XII, Address published in *L'Osservatore Romano,* February 18, 1950.

men; it is a life that is inseparable from mission. Consequently, through baptism, and in a special way through the sacrament of confirmation, all Christians take on the life and mission of the Church, as the Church extends in time and space the pastoral mission of Christ himself. The fact that the Church is hierarchical does not mean that it is divided into two separate groups, an active hierarchy and a passive faithful.[3] In a recent pastoral letter, Cardinal Cushing defines the nature and necessity of public opinion as follows:

> For us, public opinion may be described as the beliefs, attitudes and judgments held by members within the Church, and especially those views which are expressive of the usual working of the Spirit, making ever more manifest the divine truth within it. This will include an expression of views concerning those contemporary areas of life and action where the Church's teaching needs to be applied more fully or with greater precision. A further element will also show itself in public opinion as a reaction to abuses which, through human frailty, may at any time be developing within the Church as an institution. Public opinion then is an existent and visible force within the Church which consists in the confluence of many individual opinions on those matters which touch upon the Christian life. The more mature the society and the more committed its members become to the implications of their faith, the more sure are we to have a living ferment of Christian thought among them.

> The necessity of such a body of opinion within the Church is evident on many counts. Basic to them all, as we have said, is the consideration that the adult Christian is a member of the Church by Baptism and through the act of Faith — and this last is itself a free and responsible answer to the call of God within him. Through the sacrament of Confirmation also the Christian is brought through grace to a new maturity and this demands of him an adult responsibility within the Church. While all members have the teachings of the Church and its means of sanctification open to them as guides and aids in their individual growth into the full stature of a Christian, this growth should also be, under God, a process of responsible self-creation and self-achievement.[4]

It has been suggested that our country has not produced a proportionate number of outstanding theologians because of the suppression of dialogue within the Church as well as with members of other faiths. The idea, hopefully in descendancy, that freedom of speech and the expression of opinions in the Church will lead to the risk of error and mistakes, is both naturally and supernaturally difficult to accept. The activity of exploration of ideas and discussions, intended to find the truth by confrontation with the thoughts of capable peers, can hardly

---

[3] Cf. Richard Cardinal Cushing, *The Church and Public Opinion*, Pastoral Letter published on Good Shepherd Sunday, 1963, copies available from the Daughters of St. Paul, Jamaica Plain, Boston, Mass. See esp. pp. 8 and 9.

[4] *Ibid.*, pp. 11–12.

lead us astray. No Catholic need enter such a venture with the idea that the contents of his faith might be compromised; but he could well enter the venture with the hope that his faith and the understanding of Christian mysteries will be deepened. Only in this way will the truth become vital and significant to him.

The age is hopefully past when discussion, challenge, and the expression of opinions could provoke questions of loyalty and allegiance. Hopefully, too, the age is past when terminology is to be identified with truth. The emphasis of the past on a scholastic approach to philosophy, the consideration of moral and liturgical problems from a monocultural viewpoint has been so uniform that ideas formulated in any but the traditional way have fallen under the cloud of a certain suspicion. There was no effort to find and assess the idea itself; it just did not sound right.

We are the Church. We are in a sense, also, the future of the Church. The present and the future direction of the Church, the success or failure of carrying out our Christian mission is contingent upon the full exercise of our responsibility. Likewise, we must witness to the freedom which public opinion connotes. It is a necessary part of human development and fulfillment. Men today judge a society in terms of its potential to fulfill them. Men of today are engaged in extensive corporate and social activities. They will reject a Church of conformism, of authoritarianism, of prohibition and police-state censorship. They will reject a Church which seems to ask an abdication of the finest human faculties, intelligence and free will. The Church was never intended to be restrictive of human development, and we must not let it create this image before men.

2. The Origin and Clarification of Ideas: Judgments and
   Assent Within the Church

Ideas originate with people. They can, of course, have their genesis anywhere or in anyone, but more than likely ideas are born in the educated or in those who are becoming educated. Today we expect ideas to be the product of university or professional circles, and the result of a corporate intuition, research, and discussion. It is the mark of an educated person, as well as his function, to employ himself in the discovery of new insights and the exploration of difficult problems. A member of the Body of Christ should sense a personal urgency to do this, since his intelligence and education are vital if the Church is to understand and to influence the modern world. The work of restoring all things in

Christ is needed today more than it ever has been, with all the new forces which man has created. There can be no place in the Church for the "ghetto mentality" or the "siege mentality." Theologians of the Church will have to ally themselves with psychiatrists, sociologists, scientists, demographers, and communication artists. The Church can no longer rely on the knowledge that comes from the top down. All the understanding and intellectual initiative in the Church must be pooled to preach the gospel to every creature in today's world.

Ideas not only can but must rise out of such intellectual ferment, of the inquisitive and open minds of every member of the Church. Ideas do not and cannot originate only with authority; in fact, the only real hope for intelligent and constructive use of authority in the Church is the honest and open exchange of insights, ideas, perspectives, and knowledge. The complexity of modern civilization, which requires many diverse intellectual competencies in order to consider and work toward the solution of today's problems, leaves the Church no real choice.

This has been reflected in the statement that theology today has become a theology of question rather than a theology of statement, and only a pooling of expertise in the Church can adequately expose the questions. Only after this, an adequate exposé of the questions, is there any hope to propose approaches that might eventually lead to solution. This attitude is the supposition of all modern learning and pedagogy. As each discipline matures, the statements of its leading scholars become more and more tentative. In the initial stages of every intellectual pursuit there are always pioneers who act as pontiffs. However, as the relationships and problems of the pursuit begin to float to the surface, the prevailing attitude of the involved is to wonder at how much is yet to be learned rather than to rest on the oars of accomplishment. This trend is now being felt in the world of theology. Authority is growing more cautious about final and definitive pronouncements, realizing that valid judgments usually require vast amounts of information; and realizing, too, that while we know some things about absolute truth, we do not possess it.

There is no call to have the Church in her magisterial function abdicate her claim or role to be teacher and guide, but she must show herself less unwilling to admit her ignorance about the revelation in her possession. She might well make a point of demonstrating her eagerness to learn about the world in which and for which she exists. She must be willing to sit as a disciple at the feet of those members who have devoted considerable talent and energy to the study of this world.

From the origin of ideas the intellectual progress moves toward the clarification of those ideas. These concepts, of course, are not what we call final conclusions. Ideas, in this present usage, indicate the absence of final conclusions. Ideas are those notions which are proposed to stimulate thought, to advance research, and to indicate the need for deeper insights and clearer formulation. A conclusion says that something is or something is not. These conclusions or judgments have their origin in ideas, in hypotheses that have been proposed, but progress is achieved only by the presentation of many ideas. After their presentation they must be tested, altered, clarified, and related in dialogue before any judgment of a definitive nature can be made. One finds evidence in the specialized journals of today that this is the way scholars in a given field pool their resources and intelligence. The authors of such articles do not consider their contributions definitive but rather tentative and part of a corporate effort.

In the area of theology there is a great need for caution. Prefabricated or false conclusions can only deter the progress of theology and draw suspicion to themselves. Theologians, just as other scholars, must be given the range of expression that they need, including journals, conventions, lectures, etc. for an adequate presentation of ideas. But they must also be aware and visibly aware that their opinions are not definitive. They must stand in the position of debt to other scholars, and be willing to draw from the total intelligence of the Church. It is vital that the whole Church participate in this clarification of ideas through dialogue because all knowledge has the nature of a continuum; all the parts of reality are related, and so the Church must manifest a vital interest in and extend a sincere encouragement to the clarification of ideas in all areas of human life.

There are without doubt occasions on which it is necessary to pass judgment. The Church is entrusted with the conservation and integrity of the deposit of revelation and faith. And it may well happen that an idea, hostile at least in appearance to this deposit, will be growing in importance and posing a real obstacle to the faith of Christians. If the Church in her total membership has been involved in the clarification of this idea, as it grew, she is in a much better position to judge its merits and dangers, and to the extent that the idea has developed within the body of the faithful, there is proportionately less danger that the idea would develop along lines inimical to the Church and to society.

There have been instances in the past when the Church has found herself in the unfortunate and embarrassing position of having to pass judgment on ideas the implications of which and the meaning of which she did not fully understand, but whose effects were being felt in areas for which she has direct responsibility. The members of the society that is the Church are citizens in two worlds; they are members also of a civil society, and are contributing members of their own cultural milieu. Catholics are engaged in the groundswell movements of science, philosophy, sociology, psychology, economics, and the physical sciences. Oftentimes theories or applications of theories, such as evolution, arise from these movements which have moral or doctrinal implications. The Church realizes that she needs more than the contents of revelation to assess the danger or lack of it in such theories. She needs more than divine revelation to make judicious application of Christian principles to an ever-changing and ever-growing world. She also needs a penetrating knowledge of that world, for which she is dependent on her total membership.

Perhaps in certain instances of the past the authority of the Church has been too quick to intervene. However, the Church seems to be coming to an increasing awareness of the tentative and almost groping nature of speculation and the complex nature of man and the world he lives in. On the other hand, the Church has also, in the past, been urged to precipitous action by the manner in which certain ideas have been presented. This seems to be a critical point. Many of the decisions of the past, perhaps precipitated by fear, have been provoked by individuals and ideas challenging traditional understanding, and made in glowering, hostile, and blatantly critical terms. The compatibility of a given idea with the truth which the Church concurs may all too often be judged in the manner in which the evidence is presented. A prudent, calm, and charitable presentation of evidence, as opposed to a shrill declamation of supposed facts, is less likely to occasion precipitous judgments by the Church.

If the hierarchy is the appointed final power of discrimination in this dialogue of origin and clarification of ideas, it is obvious that recognition and respect for this fact does not preclude public opinion and freedom of speech in the Church. Even in cases where the teaching authority of the Church has passed judgments, there is still a necessary reliance on the continued work of all the faithful to clarify further and to apply what has been taught.

We have previously said that the assent to teachings of the Magisterium short of definitive status is a conditional and not absolute assent. It may well be that the Church herself will issue a subsequent declaration, reversing its original decision. It may also be true, in the case of such declarations, that the opposite will be manifest to a competent scholar. Since this type of teaching is by presumption a case in which the guarantee of God's infallibility cannot be invoked, if a competent scholar sees clear evidence which obviously controverts a given, non-definitive teaching, the demand of obedience falls away. Ordinarily, such a departure would involve a high degree of professional competence in the area of consideration. But the question of free speech and public opinion becomes a thorny problem in such a case and should be considered. It is not a purely hypothetical case. It is important that the competent scholars continue their research, and continue to advance reasons and insights through legitimate channels with prudence, respect, and tact until the matter is clarified. This may well be a long and painful process, made more difficult by the complexities of modern civilization. It is again a question of the vital tension and adjustment to be made between thinking with the Church and love of the truth. Only love of the truth and love of the Church should motivate the scholar in this predicament.

Prudence is the virtue in demand. Prudence must first inspect the competence one possesses and the facts of which he is sure. Premature judgment in the case of either, and imprudent expression can easily tend to undermine the respect that should exist in the Church for legitimate authority. Prudence must also inspect the teaching of the Church in the matter. It may well be that the judgment of the Church has not been expressed in terms of *right* and *wrong* but in terms of *safe* and *not safe*. No specific rules of thumb can be given for behavior in such a case. Both facts must be faced honestly and honestly respected: the authority of the Church and the possibility that the tentative conclusion or decision of the Church will have to be altered. Obviously, the intellectual honesty and personal integrity of a scholar may be involved by the teachings of the Magisterium. Still no expression of disagreement should take the form of disrespect or attack. In the context of free speech and public opinion, it might be well to reflect that such disagreement would have a lower incidence if free speech and public opinion were exercised adequately in the Church, and were to go into the discussion of the issue and the subsequent decision. To the extent that this exchange is open, honest, and respectful, the ultimate decision will be more solidly founded, more accurately applied, and more willingly accepted. We must recall that authority in the Church, by the definition of Christ, is a function of service. It is not to be tyrannical, self-complacent, or inconsiderate. As we have said in the previous chapter, authority and public opinion are meant to be complementary forces.

Etymologically, criticism is not an offensive word. The Greek word *krinein* means to separate or discern. All that has been said in this chapter about the origin, clarification, and formation of judgments is involved in the work of criticism. In popular usage, however, it often connotes something quite different, something destructive, contagiously dangerous, and inspired by the spirit of aggression. In this sense, criticism undermines all the structured benefits of free speech and the circulation of opinion in the Church because it closes off communication, stifles initiative, and very often forces those in authority into a posture of defense and reaction.

Christian criticism should be:

1. competent: The critic should know whereof he speaks.
2. constructive: The criticism should be of itself designed to effect a good.
3. constrained: The critic must not lash out, but take into consideration the possibility of his own error and exaggeration, and be moderated by a sensitivity for the human feelings of others.
4. considered: The critic should regard the total picture, assess the good in balance with the bad, and consider the good or evil that will result from his criticism.
5. committed: The critic must be a committed person, committed to the total good of the Church. There is less danger that he will be unkind and narrow if his criticism results from his love for the Church and not his own personal indignation.
6. compassionate: The critic should presume good will in others and display a certain humility, sensitivity, and tact in forwarding his opinions.
7. charitable: The only effective and Christian criticism must be this in both motive and manner.

3. The Current Status of Public Opinion and Vatican II

Today there is considerable discussion about public opinion and freedom of expression or its absence in the Church. A decade ago it was hardly an issue. However, since 1961 the question has become one of the major debates in the Church. The contention of many is that authoritarian pressure has, intentionally or unintentionally, intimidated priests and the laity alike in this matter of communication within the Church. John Cogley expresses the frustrations felt by the laity as follows:

> The layman seems intimidated by the difference between the daily reality of marital love, which he knows, and the images presented by priests: He then hesitates to speak for fear of violating orthodoxy.

> I was thinking . . . of the creation of an atmosphere, within the Catholic community, where there would be more confrontation between theologian and untutored laymen — untutored in the science of theology that is; less fear of incorrect or imprecise expressions of theological concerns, on the part of the laity; more patience on the part of theologians and willingness to understand what the laity are saying, in their own uncultivated language;

and with less concern for the niceties of theological terminology, a stronger emphasis on genuine communication.[5]

Father William Doty points out that:

> . . . the common interests of the Church and the whole community should be consulted before controversial positions are presented in the public forum. This does not involve the elimination of freedom of discussion but rather preserves it and enhances the dignity of this freedom and assures its proper effectiveness.[6]

To this the well-known Hans Küng adds however:

> The virtue of prudence has often been falsified in the Church in a very time-serving way: Made to mean being careful only to say what is opportune, i.e., what is pleasing to those in charge.[7]

The supposed cases of repression have not been limited only to the suppression of the voice of the laity. Daniel Callahan has this to say of the problems clerics have encountered:

> There is little, of course, that the laity can do to encourage clerical freedom of speech. Yet since the priest is so rarely free to raise a public voice in his own behalf in this respect, it may fall to the layman to raise some questions for him. These will do for a start: Granting the necessity for clerical obedience, is it either necessary or good for clerical freedom of expression to be hindered? Should not the priest have as much right as any other Catholic to say publicly what he will on controversial questions? If, as most now grant, a layman has the right to disagree with a bishop on non-doctrinal matters, should not the clergy have the same right? We do not pretend to be fully clear on the answer to these questions, but we think it is time to ask them — if we read the recent cases of censorship and suppression of clerical opinion correctly, they can be hidden questions no longer.[8]

In spite of these de facto problems discussed in the public debate on freedom within the Church, Vatican II is quite definite in proclaiming that freedom forms the hard core of Christianity:

> . . . let it be recognized that all the faithful, clerical and lay, possess a lawful freedom of inquiry and of thought and the freedom to express their minds humbly and courageously about those matters in which they enjoy competence.[9]

---

[5] John Cogley, "In Search of Honesty," Commonweal, 79 (1963), p. 706.

[6] William Doty, "Controversy Within the Church," America, 114 (April 9, 1966), p. 482.

[7] Hans Küng, "The Church and Freedom," Commonweal, 78 (June 21, 1963), p. 348.

[8] D. Callahan, "Clerical Freedom: Recent Cases of Suppression of Clerical Opinion," Commonweal, 78 (April 19, 1963), pp. 86–87.

[9] Pastoral Constitution on the Church in the Modern World, no. 62.

Therefore this Vatican Synod urges everyone, especially those who are charged with the task of educating others, to do their utmost to form men who will respect the moral order and be obedient to lawful authority. Let them form men too who will be lovers of true freedom — men, in other words, who will come to decisions on their own judgment and in the light of truth, govern their activities with a sense of responsibility, and strive after what is true and right, willing always to join with others in cooperative effort.[10]

All these considerations demand too, that, within the limits of morality and the general welfare, a man be free to search for the truth, voice his mind, and publicize it; that he be free to practice any art he chooses; and finally that he have appropriate access to information about public affairs.[11]

In fidelity of conscience, Christians are joined with the rest of men in the search for truth, and for the genuine solution to the numerous problems which arise in the life of individuals and from social relationships.[12]

Today public opinion exerts massive force and authority over the private and public life of every class of citizen. Hence the necessity arises for every member of society to do what justice and charity require in this matter. With the aid of these instruments, then, each man should strive to form and to voice worthy views on public affairs.[13]

By unremitting study they [priests] should fit themselves to do their part in establishing dialogue with the world and with men of all shades of opinion. . . . In the present age . . . it does not escape the Church how great a distance lies between the message she offers and the human failings of those to whom the Gospel is entrusted.[14]

One might wonder, in his effort to voice opinions and exercise his right of free speech, about the possibility of scandal. Certainly, opinions must be forwarded with tact and a certain sensitivity to the feelings and peace of others, but as has been pointed out, there is the possibility of the "scandal of silence":

I believe we must risk the scandal of controversy — precisely to avoid the "scandal of silence," the scandal of the pathetic gesture, the scandal of hypocrisy. Above all, we should avoid the scandal of the phony dialogue — confined to a policed press or to polite meetings in the chancery. We need the world's public opinion in the act, and the world needs to know our agony.[15]

Hans Küng has pointed out in a recent article that:

---

[10] *Declaration on Religious Freedom*, no. 8.
[11] *Pastoral Constitution on the Church in the Modern World*, no. 59.
[12] *Ibid.*, no. 16.
[13] *Decree on the Instruments of Social Communication*, no. 8.
[14] *Pastoral Constitution on the Church in the Modern World*, no. 43.
[15] John O'Connor, "Controversy within the Church: A Rebuttal," *America*, 114 (April 9, 1966), p. 484.

It was Gregory the Great who said, "But if scandal is taken as the truth, it is better to allow scandal to arise than to neglect the truth."[16] And Thomas Aquinas stressed the necessity for free criticism, *correctio fraterna*, even to ecclesiastical superiors.[17]

Vatican II gives general descriptive lines along which the dialogue of free expression and public opinion within the Church might follow:

> Practical recognition has to be given to the human dignity of the laity and their own proper role in the mission of the Church. They should open their minds, express their needs and desires freely and confidently and the priest is to be a good listener, recognizing their experience, competence, and the special gifts given them by God. Freedom and room for movement should be left them when they are given a task, and they should be encouraged to act on their own initiative.[18]

> Since it is the mission of the Church to converse with the human society in which she lives, bishops especially are called upon to approach men, seeking and fostering dialogue with them. These conversations on salvation ought to be distinguished for clarity of speech as well as for humility and gentleness so that truth might always be joined with charity and understanding with love. Likewise they should be characterized by due prudence, allied, however, with that trustfulness which fosters friendship and thus is naturally disposed to bring about a union of minds.

> Laymen should also know that it is generally the function of their well-formed, Christian conscience to see that divine law is inscribed in the life of the earthly city. From priests they may look for spiritual light and nourishment. Let the layman not imagine that his pastors are always such experts, that to every problem which arises, however complicated, they can readily give him a concrete solution, or even that such is their mission. Rather, enlightened by Christian wisdom and giving close attention to the teaching authority of the Church, let the layman take on his own distinctive role. Often enough the Christian view of things will itself suggest some specific solution in certain circumstances. Yet it happens rather frequently, and legitimately so, that with equal sincerity some of the faithful will disagree with others on a given matter. Even against the intentions of their proponents, however, solutions proposed on one side or another may be easily confused by many people with the Gospel message. Hence, it is necessary for people to remember that no one is allowed in the aforementioned situations to appropriate the Church's authority for his opinion. They should always try to enlighten one another through honest discussion, preserving mutual charity and caring above all for the common good.[19]

> Every layman should openly reveal to [his pastors] his needs and desires with that freedom and confidence which befits a son of God and a brother

---

[16] *In Ezek. Hom.* 7; *PL* 77, 324.

[17] Hans Küng, "The Church and Freedom," *Commonweal*, 78 (June 21, 1963), p. 348; cf. St. Thomas, *Summa Theologiae*, II–II, q. 33, a. 1–4.

[18] Note to no. 9 in "Decree on the Ministry of Priests," from *Documents of Vatican II*, Guild Press Edition, Walter Abbott (ed.), p. 553.

[19] *Pastoral Constitution on the Church in the Modern World*, no. 43.

in Christ. An individual layman, by reason of the knowledge, competence, or outstanding ability which he may enjoy, is permitted and sometimes even obliged to express his opinion on things which concern the good of the Church. When occasions arise, let this be done through the agencies set up by the Church for this purpose. Let it always be done in truth, in courage, and in prudence, with reverence and charity toward those who by reason of their sacred office represent the person of Christ. . . . Let sacred pastors recognize and promote the dignity as well as the responsibility of the layman in the Church. Let them willingly make use of his prudent advice. Let them confidently assign duties to him in the service of the Church, allowing him freedom and room for action. Further, let them encourage the layman so that he may undertake tasks on his own initiative. Attentively in Christ, let them consider with fatherly love the projects, suggestions, and desires proposed by the laity. Furthermore let pastors respectfully acknowledge that just freedom which belongs to everyone in this earthly city. A great many benefits are to be hoped for from this familiar dialogue between the laity and their pastors: In the laity, a strengthened sense of personal responsibility, and renewed enthusiasm, a more ready application of their talents to the projects of their pastors. The latter, for their part, aided by the experience of the laity can more clearly and more suitably come to decisions regarding spiritual and temporal matters. In this way, the whole Church, strengthened by each one of its members can more effectively fulfill its mission for the life of the world.[20]

From all the texts of Vatican II and the other quoted material, one might conclude that the most necessary requirement for a successful dialogue within the Church and on the part of the Church with the society in which it lives is charity. However, there is an obvious call for open minds, much listening, and the encouragement of initiative and honesty. Recognizing that the ultimate powers of discretion lie with the hierarchy in matters of faith and morals, it is necessary that such a dialogue precede the final decisions of that hierarchy, a dialogue in which opinions circulated with openness and honesty will be purified. In the last analysis it is only such a dialogue, incorporating free expression and the existence of a vigorous public opinion within the Church, that will keep that Church alive and spiritually healthy.

---

[20] Lumen Gentium, no. 37.

CHAPTER TEN

The Liturgy and the Church

The Liturgy . . . is the outstanding means whereby the faithful may express in their lives and manifest to others the mystery of Christ and the real nature of the true Church.
— Vatican II, Constitution on the Sacred Liturgy, no. 2

1. The History of Liturgical Malaise

Only in this present generation has the liturgical movement finally "arrived." Until this recent arrival, a liturgical malaise has afflicted the Western Church, and this malaise had its roots in the Middle Ages. It was in the Middle Ages that the language of the liturgy, clerical Latin, because it was no longer the language of the people, caused the faithful to withdraw more and more from active participation. At the same time another divorce was in process: between the monks and the faithful. The actual connotation of this division was between fervent Christians and those second-raters, who did not care enough about the things of God to enter monasteries. As a result, the faithful peacefully accepted their status as outsiders and as the non-initiate who drew little value from liturgical celebrations because they were given little understanding of the meaning of these celebrations. Finally, the Church and its hierarchy became progressively allied to the wealthy classes, with the general result that the faithful became more and more anti-hierarchical and consequently anti-sacramental.

To the extent that the liturgy did reach the People of God in the Middle Ages, it was devotional in nature. Long prayers were inserted by the priest before the Canon of the Mass, preparation for communion was prolonged, and communions became increasingly more rare because of indifference in some and because of the stimulated fear of unworthy reception in others. The Fourth Council of the Lateran (A.D. 1215) felt compelled to legislate in the matter, because communions had become so infrequent, and prescribed the paschal communion or, as we call it, the Easter Duty. This devotional posture of the Church introduced a growing interest in guardian angels and saints whose biographies contained far more fiction than fact. The veneration of relics very often became practices of pure superstition.

During the twelfth century, with its many social upheavals and agitations, the Church seemed to split two ways: many left the Church as the alliance of ecclesiastical and political power was tightened; they rejected the hierarchy and with it the sacramental, liturgical life. Others became hermits and recluses, but they did not enter monasteries as the monasteries of the time were in possession of the same soiled linens as the pompous hierarchy. These self-proclaimed hermits specialized rather in a misanthropic Christianity, gilded by private devotions and prayers in honor of obscure saints.

In the thirteenth century, the great mendicant orders of St. Francis of Assisi and St. Dominic Guzman came into existence. Although the liturgical life of both orders was substantial, it was seemingly only a complement to religious life, especially among the Franciscans, where the accent fell on poverty. Meanwhile the theological doctors of both orders were hard at the work of developing a systematized theology, a hard and fast science of God. Ultimately, this theology became a sort of metaphysics, a deductive science, crowding out the patristic presentation of salvation history. Theology and preaching, consequently, separated at the fork of this road and each went its own way: theology to the ivory towers of speculation and preaching to the smoking pulpits of fear and maudlin devotions. Neither had the true spirit of the liturgy, which is fundamentally biblical, a continual renewal of the historical events of salvation. It is the proclamation of the Christ-event in such a way that Christ is given contemporaneity with every generation of men.

The result of all this was that the Church lost its sense of Christian unity and community, as asceticism became a personal effort and encounter instead of a corporate worship of God. The Church also lost its sense of history, and the historical dimensions of salvation. The fervent wanted to become saints on an individual basis instead of dynamic members of the People of God; and they sought to achieve this sanctity through interior renunciations and dramatic, external penances rather than by the fullest use of God's appointed means: the Mass and the Sacraments. At the end of the Middle Ages, the spirituality of the Church was largely superstitious, and was built on practices of personal devotion, indulgenced and extra-liturgical prayers. Salvation was viewed as an individual affair with God. "Jesus and I and let the rest of the world go by." The whole spirit of the liturgy was lost.

In 1545, the Council of Trent passed decrees and the Holy See assumed total jurisdiction in all liturgical matters; the Sacred Congregation of Rites was created in 1588, chiefly as a means of safeguarding uniformity in liturgical celebrations. The new emphasis, after Trent, fell upon rubrics, directions for external actions, to be cherished as a kind of court etiquette. The Fathers of Trent discussed the possibility of a liturgy in the vernacular, but compromised by prescribing that the faithful should be instructed in the vernacular on the meaning of the Sacrifice of the Mass. The Reformers were using the vernacular in their liturgies — Luther since 1525 — and perhaps the Fathers of Trent feared that following the Reformers into the vernacular might be a path to further theological errors. And so, the Council of Trent unified the rites and reformed the liturgical books, but it also tended to prolong the medieval spirit of separation of clergy and laity, by laying an undeserved halo on the head of Latin as the liturgical language, and opened the door to a multiplicity of devotions and accretions outside of the true liturgy.

2. The Concept of the Church and Its Effect on the Liturgy

The presentation of the Church that grew out of the Reformation anger is hardly one that prepares men for an understanding of the liturgy. Instead of accenting Christian unity in Christ and through him, it was a polemical presentation, apologetic and defensive rather than explanatory. It emphasized one reality — unquestionably a valid and necessary truth — but one which does not very clearly promote liturgical spirit: *Ubi Petrus Ibi Ecclesia* (Where Peter is, there is the Church). Our submission to the Pope as Christ's Vicar is a submission to Christ whose person the Pope bears in teaching, ruling, and sanctifying the Church. But Christ is present to his Church in another, sacramental way: *Ubi Eucharistia, Ibi Ecclesia* (Where the Eucharist is, there is the Church). The Church is the People of God, adoring, thanking, petitioning him while on journey to its ultimate fulfillment and destiny. The imbalance of the post-Reformation ecclesiology is that it stressed a juridical Church at the expense of the vision that it is also a sacramental Church. The external lines of the institutional Church were drawn indelibly; the interior lines of the divine life pulsing within the Church and the unity of its members in Christ became almost invisible. Such a concept of the Church does not foster the true liturgical spirit. The concept of the Church which underlies the true liturgical spirit is that of the People of God, prolonging the mystery of Christ in human history; it is the Church as the Body of Christ, prolonging his saving presence in time and extending that presence in space. It is a community fused by love to Christ, through whom it is united to God himself, who is a community of love: Father, Son, and Holy Spirit.

It is in its act of public worship, in the Eucharistic Assembly, that this community is most perfectly itself. The important thing to be realized about the liturgy is that it is an act of a People, a Community of Love. There are no isolated individuals, even though some members of the community have special powers and functions. The Body of Christ is a living organism. Every offering of the whole Christ to the Father is an act of the whole community as a community. The Eucharistic Assembly is the calling together of this People of God, this assembly of the redeemed. Together we are offering the whole Mystical Body, Christ the Head and we his members to the Father. This is the sacrificial aspect of the Mass which is also a communal banquet, a love-feast or agapē. It is in this moment of Christ's coming, the moment of communion, that the bonds of unity of this whole community are proclaimed, strengthened, and renewed. In the Mass we are the People of God worshiping together; and our assembly is a sign of our unity in Christ. It is an act of embrace, in which we are joined not only to Christ but to all those who are in Christ's community. It is only in the light of this understanding that we can understand why the *Constitution on the Sacred Liturgy* of Vatican II calls the Liturgy:

> . . . the summit towards which the activity of the Church is directed, the font from which all her powers flow. . . . The Liturgy . . . is the outstanding means whereby the faithful may express in their lives and manifest to others the mystery of Christ and the real nature of the true Church.[1]

If we think of the Church, then, as the People of God, formed by God's love, we can see the sacred liturgy as that people celebrating the mystery of God's love. It is the privileged site of proclamation of the great manifestation of God's love, the Christ-event, the most wondrous

---

[1] *Constitution on the Sacred Liturgy*, no. 2, 10.

of God's works. It is quite clear that the unity in love and life for which God has formed this people in Christ is most perfectly realized in the Eucharistic celebration. This is the moment when Christians most perfectly experience the Christian mystery of their union in Christ. This is the experience that alone can make truth, the truth of God's love and the truth of Christ and his Church, a meaningful and relevant truth. There is, obviously, a part of truth that can never be communicated from person to person, but can only be experienced. One can hear the awesome facts of salvation repeated eloquently and indefinitely but these truths can never be truly learned until they are experienced, and the liturgy is the opportunity par excellence for this experience.

The moment of the liturgy is the moment when the Christian can experience the we of Christian vision, but he must be prepared for this moment by instruction. He must reflect on this moment afterward in order to achieve a fuller understanding. But both the preparatory instruction and the subsequent reflection can never be anything but irrelevant without the experience itself. Like an Indian summer, a haunting melody, or moonlight on water: to know it really, I must experience the fact of the Church, the vital unity of men in Christ. This experience will make baptism, by which the Christian is incorporated into Christ, not a past event but a continuing, daily, and progressive thing. For we are baptized into unity, into the death and resurrection of Christ, and our lives in Christ are a part of this community gathered together in liturgical celebration.

Since all sacramental rites or actions are intended to signify, to tell us what Christ is doing in these sacraments, we need to know the significance of these rites or actions so that we can respond properly. Consequently, the rites of the liturgy are in need of constant reform and renewal, for each generation must encounter Christ and experience its Christian identity in a meaningful way. To keep this encounter and experience of Christian community vital, the liturgical rites must clearly signify what they produce. The fathers of Vatican II were profoundly aware that the Mass and the sacraments belong to the category of signs, which must kept vital and meaningful. The Constitution on the Liturgy says:

> In this restoration [of the liturgy] both texts and rites should be drawn up so that they express more clearly the holy things which they signify. . . . The Christian people so far as possible, should be enabled to understand them with ease and to take part in them fully, actively and as befits a community.[2]

---

[2] Ibid., no. 21.

The restoration of the vernacular is a part of the restoration of the sincerity or genuineness of these signs; for language is the basic element of the sacramental sign. It is the supposed privilege of a people to speak its own language, and it would seem to be the right of God's People when they speak to him. Until recently the missal in English has dubbed in our own language for us; attending Mass was like going to a foreign movie with subtitles in English. The restoration of the vernacular will perhaps do away with the need for private reading, which is as distracting from the Mass as it would be at a movie: we miss the action going on. The implementation of the *Constitution on the Sacred Liturgy* will take time, and is in the hands of the Post-Conciliary Commission. The worshiping habits of God's People cannot be changed overnight; the whole notion of sign depends upon gradual introduction and familiarity. Signs have to be tested and above all explained. The Council Fathers have given the Church a remarkable impetus; the whole Church, however, must respond. The *Constitution* unmistakably implies this:

> Zeal for the promotion and restoration of the Liturgy is rightly held to be a sign of the providential disposition of God in our time, as movements of the Holy Spirit in His Church.[3]

3. *The Liturgy and Encounter With the Contemporaneous Christ*

We have spoken earlier of the necessity of an encounter with Christ that is both vital and perceptible to the senses. We have described faith in the terms of this encounter, as a vital experience of God present to us in the saving presence of Christ. This is the whole notion that underlies the People of God, joined to God through his Son. We have said that the liturgy is the privileged site and best living expression of this encounter. Through the principal liturgical celebration, the Mass, which is a re-presentation of Christ's saving act, we must somehow realize that that saving act is here and now and visibly present to us. We must make his saving act save us. Through the Mass and the sacraments Jesus acts here and now, giving us the gift of divine life, nourishing that life in us, and restoring us to that life when we have undergone spiritual death because of our sins. The Mass and the sacraments are not merely ceremonies or services, but rather occasions of personal encounter between Christ and his People. Such is the function of the liturgy: to make such an encounter and experience possible to the People of God in every generation and in every place throughout the world. It offers us a personal and

---

[3] *Ibid.*, no. 43.

intimate exchange of divine-giving and human response, such as that which the first Apostles of Christ experienced.

We recall the encounter between God and Abram, and the promise of God to this man. We recall that the destiny of Abram was changed by this encounter; he was to be the father of a new people whom God would adopt as his own. This was the whole significance of changing his name from Abram to Abraham, since among Semitic peoples the change of a name indicates the change of destiny. In the Old Testament we find this People of God in the bondage of Egypt, and the saving act of Yahweh through which his people was released to seek the land he had promised them. We recall that the blood of a lamb was spread over the doorposts of the Jewish families, and they were consequently spared the ravages of the Angel of Death. Likewise, we remember how the Jews celebrated this saving act of God in their Passover feast, of which the main course was the lamb, the figure or sign of liberation. In the book of Exodus we followed the People of God in their journey to the foot of Mt. Sinai, where Moses, as the prophet of God, sealed the covenant between God and his people by the sacrificial offering and the sprinkling of blood over the heads of the people together with the banquet which was not so much a celebration of, but, together with the sacrifice, a means of sealing their alliance with God.

For the thirteen hundred years between Moses and the coming of Christ, the Passover meal was a "memorial service," unlike anything that we know in our present culture. It made the saving act of God, liberating his people from the slavery of Egypt, present to every Jew in every generation of those thirteen hundred years. When a Jew celebrated the Passover meal, he was somehow entering into an event made contemporaneous by this celebration, and consequently called a memorial service.

We recall that Christ, in his very first encounter with Simon the son of John, changed his name to Peter, the Rock. Subsequently, the same Christ promised Peter that upon this rock he would build or call together a new People, and that Peter would be the rock upon which this new house of God would be constructed. Later in the manifestation of his miraculous powers, when he multiplied the loaves and the fish, the Jewish people clamored to make him their king. He declined this invitation, making clear to them that his kingdom was a kingdom of faith. They rejoined that they were men of faith, and that they even believed that Yahweh had given their fathers manna in the desert when they were starving. To this, Christ remarks that they ate the manna and died but:

"I am the bread of life," replied Jesus; "He who comes to me will never hunger, and he who believes in me will never thirst. . . . The bread which I speak of, which comes down from heaven, is such that no one who eats of it will ever die. I am the living bread that has come down from heaven. If one eats of this bread, he will live forever; and, furthermore, the bread which I shall give is my flesh given for the life of the world. . . . What I tell you is the plain truth: Unless you eat the flesh of the Son of Man and drink his blood, you have no life in you. He who eats my flesh and drinks my blood is in possession of eternal life; and I will raise him from the dead on the last day; for my flesh is real food and My blood is real drink. He who eats my flesh and drinks my blood is united to me, and I am united with him" (Jn 6:35–57).

The apostles were as puzzled as everyone else standing there that day, but there was one difference: they believed in the person of Jesus and had faith that someday he would clarify these strange words. The enigma that cost Jesus almost all of his following on that day, because they thought he was suggesting some form of cannibalism, was unraveled only at the Last Supper. He had told them that he would celebrate his last Passover meal with them, and asked them to make the necessary preparations. The necessary preparations involved bread and wine and the lamb. However, instead of dipping the bread into the dark red sauce, as was customary and passing it around to the others joining in the memorial service, St. Luke tells us:

Then he took some bread, and when he had given thanks broke it and gave it to them, saying "This is my Body which will be given for you; do this as a memorial service of me." He did the same with the cup after supper, and said "This cup is the new covenant in my blood which will be poured out for you" (Lk 22:19–20).

The memorial service, requested by Christ, and which is our Eucharistic celebration, is the same to the Christian as the Passover celebration was to the Jew. It makes the event of salvation present to all Christians of all generations. When a Christian goes to this celebration or memorial service, the saving act of Christ dying and rising for us, is present to him, not as a simple recollection of a past event but is actually present in that Christ is offering himself truly and really to his Father at this moment and giving himself to us as the bread of life. It is in this surrender of Christ to the Father that we as his members are joined. In the Mass, Christ, the high priest and principal celebrant of every Mass, makes himself present under the sacramental veils of bread and wine, now joined by all the members of his Mystical Body, and presents himself to the Father for the whole world. It is a renewal and ratification of the covenant or alliance, sealed by Christ's blood on Good Friday. It is a re-enactment of Christ's total surrender to his Father in which we participate for our salvation.

Such is the function of the liturgy for public worship of the People of God: to make such an encounter and experience possible to every member of the People of God. It is quite obviously just as real for us in our Eucharistic celebration as it was for the apostles in the very first Eucharistic celebration. The essential elements of the Last Supper — the instruction, the offering, the consecration, and communion — are the essential elements of our Eucharistic celebration. The difficulty is that, as the apostles and their successors continued to fulfill the precept of Christ to "Do this as my memorial service" (Lk 22:19), an elaborate ritual or rite developed in place of the original setting of the meal taken together. Because of the historical difficulties mentioned at the beginning of this chapter, we have somewhere along the way lost the idea that we are the People of God. Especially at this moment, which is in fact a renewal of the covenant or pact, we stand before God not as individuals but as his People, gathered to him in his Son. The Last Supper and our Eucharistic celebration are both an offering to God and a family meal. The People of God is gathered together around its Lord who is truly present. If the inner reality of the Church is that it is a community of love, joined to God by a participation of and in his life through Christ the Lord from whose fullness all receive, then this is *the* moment of the Church, the moment when she is most clearly herself; the moment when she expresses most clearly in her actions what she truly is. It is through the liturgy, then, that the Church says what she is and becomes what she was intended to be: a community of love, united in Christ, and through him to the community of love in heaven, the Trinity. In the liturgy, especially in the Eucharistic celebration, the Church re-presents the very act by which it came into existence as the People of God, covenanted to God by the blood of his Son. The *Constitution on the Liturgy* tells us:

> In the liturgy the whole public worship is performed by the Mystical Body of Christ Jesus, that is, by the Head and His members. From this it follows that every liturgical celebration, because it is an action of Christ the priest and of His Body which is the Church, is a sacred action surpassing all others; no other action of the Church can equal its efficacy by the same title and to the same degree.[4]

Although the Eucharist stands by itself as an unique encounter with Christ, the other sacraments are also liturgical events that we must learn to regard as true encounters with Christ. In the Eucharist the liturgical symbols of bread and wine are simply veils under which Christ is truly and really present just as he was present in his visible humanity two thousand years ago. In the other sacraments Christ is not present in this same sense. In these other sacraments, the signs of the liturgy are rather *gestures* or *actions* of Christ. The baptismal water and the chrism of confirmation do not become Christ himself, but rather they become his

---

[4] *Constitution on the Sacred Liturgy*, no. 7.

actions. They are the visible signs of Christ in the act of healing and giving growth. When we receive these other sacraments, Christ is communicating his life to us through these signs.

As we read the Gospels, we see Christ in the lifegiving ministry of resuscitating the apparently dead daughter of Jairus (Mk 5:41-42), and we see him as he touches the eyes of the blind man and restores his sight (Mk 8:22-26), and as his touch on the ears and the tongue of the deaf-mute open a whole new world of speaking and hearing to the man (Mk 7:32-35). We see Christ speaking to the lepers and cleansing them of their hideous disease (Lk 17:12-14).

These healing actions of Christ are contemporaneous to us in his sacraments. He reaches out to cleanse us and give us growth in baptism; he strengthens our weaknesses in confirmation, and touches us in the healing words of absolution in the confessional. His hand is felt upon us in the anointing of the sick, and the sores of our sins are closed and the life of Christ flows through us once more. Appearing to his apostles after the resurrection, ". . . He breathed upon them and said to them 'Receive the Holy Spirit; whose sins you shall forgive, they are forgiven them; whose sins you shall retain, they are retained'" (Jn 20:22-23). Today, Christ in his Church still breathes upon certain ones and conveys special powers to them in the sacraments of confirmation and holy orders.

In the Gospels Christ's deliberate gestures were designed to accomplish a definite purpose, to give life and power and strength. The sacraments are the same kind of powerful and purposeful gestures. Through them Christ conveys his life to us; and his life flows directly from the gesture itself, for the sacraments produce that which they signify. If it is the Eucharist that brings us Christ in his person, then the other sacraments, which are part of our liturgical life, bring him to us in his actions.

The liturgical life of the Church also embraces what are called sacramentals. They involve the other liturgical events not directly connected with the Eucharist or the other sacraments but bring us in contact with our salvation by bringing us into the presence of the saving life of Christ. We recall, again from the Gospels, an incident that occurred on the road of Palestine when a woman suffering from a hemorrhage struggled through the crowd and touched the hem of his garment and was immediately cured (Mk 5:25-29). In this case the power of Christ was operative even though our Lord did not actually do anything himself. In fact, the Gospels tell us that he had not even noticed her until he felt ". . . that power had gone forth from him," and he turned to the crowd and asked, "Who touched my cloak?" In this case there was no gesture of Christ, as in the case of the daughter of Jairus. It was simply the presence of Christ and the woman's great faith in him that effected the cure. "If

I touch only his cloak, I will be saved," the suffering woman said, and she was right about this. Christ himself confirmed her in her faith: "Daughter, your faith has saved you" (Mk 5:34).

The sacramentals are something like the cloak of Christ, those things whose use because of their connection with Christ can bring him and his life to us. The liturgical symbol in the case of the sacramentals is neither the presence of Christ nor his saving action but it is Christ present to us so that we may reach out in faith to touch him. We are lost in the great crowd struggling for contact with his saving power, and if we use the signs the way the woman touched the hem of his garment, we, too, will experience the same power that always goes out from him. The present Canon Law of the Church defines these sacramentals as ". . . certain rites, actions, or particular things which the Church customarily uses, in imitation of the sacraments, in order to obtain through her intercession, certain effects especially of spiritual character."[5]

Thus when I bless myself with holy water or kneel for one of the blessings of the Church or take part in the blessing of food at the time of eating, I am like the woman grasping at Christ's garment, and the action becomes for me a contact with Christ. The gesture of such a sacramental makes Christ's saving presence present to me. But the sacramentals depend for their efficacy on my firm belief that, before Christ, I am in the presence of my salvation. My faith is essential if the power of Christ is to go out from him to me. In the use of the sacramentals, it is not so much that Christ is approaching me to fill me with his life but that I am approaching Christ in faith and hope. These sacramentals are not simply memory devices, but actually as institutions of the Church itself bring me into the presence of Christ and afford the possibility of personal encounter with him.

Some of the sacramentals are bound up with the sacraments and as such are in a special category. Such things as the anointings in baptism and the ceremonies of ordination to holy orders are, like the sacraments themselves, more properly the actions of Christ, for they belong to the sacrament. In the case of these sacramentals, rather than giving his grace of healing or the granting of life in one word or gesture, Christ our Lord uses a more deliberate procedure. We can recall the occasion on which he spat on the ground and made a clay of the spittle to place on a blind man's eyes commanding him to go wash in the pool of Siloe.[6]

Sometimes Christ heals by one word of command, as in the words of absolution of the sacrament of penance. In other sacraments, his procedure is more elaborate and surrounded by other rites which belong to

---

[5] Code of Canon Law, Canon 1144.
[6] Cf. Jn 9:6–7.

the decisive action of Christ and are also for our benefit. These other sacramental actions, part of a rite used in the conferring of a sacrament, are meant to impress upon us something of the significance and importance of what Christ is doing for us. He comes to us to give us his life and he is beginning to act even as he approaches us.

However, in all of the liturgical life of the Church it is always the same Christ Who is, one way or another, bringing salvation to us. It is the whole saving life of Christ that confronts us in every liturgical action. Just as the presence and the actions of Christ took different forms and had different effects, during his life on this earth, so the liturgical signs which bring us into contact with Christ tell us what is the nature of that contact and what effect it will have, but this is always in common: it brings us into encounter with Christ himself.

The obvious stress, however, of the liturgical life of the Church is its emphasis on community, on corporate worship. This is not meant to de-emphasize the need for a deeply personal response to God, for it is only through the deepening of my personal response to God through Christ that I will deepen the bonds of community and the life of the community of Christ. It was the personal responses of Abraham, Moses, and the mother of Christ which brought the People of God into existence; and it will be through the deeply personal responses of Christ's members today that the People of God will be brought to its fulfillment and destiny. "For them I sanctify myself in truth, that they also may be sanctified in truth" (Jn 17:19). Still the thrust of the liturgy is to bring the Christian to a sense of identity as a member of Christ's community, all bearing the same life and destiny. The mystery of this unity is the mystery of Christ living and acting in us.

4. The Liturgy and Christian Identity

The task of the Christian is to put on Christ, and the liturgy helps us not only to join Christ in his act of love for his Father, but also in his act of love for mankind. Salvation is never put on as a private ornament but as a corporate gift. The Christ whom we put on in the liturgy is the total Christ, Head and members. We are saved and we worship with Christ and with all the members of Christ who are incorporated into him. This liturgy is not only an expression of our community in salvation and worship but it effects this unity. God's saving gestures in his Son still act to form a community, the new People of God which is the Church. Like the people of Israel we become a people through the saving events of our history. And the saving events of these, our times, are the Mass, the sacraments, and the whole saving action of Christ in his Church, which is the liturgy. It is the liturgy, principally, which makes us here and now the People of God. In the Mass we meet in order to ratify solemnly the covenant which God has made with us in his Son, and when we eat the sacrificial meal together we are drawn deeper into Christ and into one another. Through the liturgy God tightens the bonds of love and life that bind us to him and to one another in his Son. The Christian accepts his identity as a Christian in belonging to a new community, a new family, and a new fellowship. St. Paul expresses the unity in the Church this way:

> But God Who is rich in mercy by reason of his very great love wherewith he has loved us even when we were dead by reason of our sins, brought us to life together with Christ . . . and raised us up together and seated us together in heaven in Christ Jesus, that he might show in the ages to come the overflowing riches of his grace and kindness toward us in Christ Jesus. . . . For his workmanship we are. . . . Therefore you are no longer strangers and foreigners, but you are citizens with the saints and members of God's household: You are built upon the foundation of the Apostles and the prophets with Christ Jesus himself as the chief cornerstone. In him the whole structure is closely fitted together and grows into a temple holy in the Lord: In him you too are being built together into a dwelling place for God in the Spirit (Eph 2:4–6; 10:19–22).

Our Lord himself prayed:

> Yet not for these only do I pray, but for those also who through their word are to believe in me, that all may be one, even as you Father in me and I in you; that they also may be one in us, that the world may believe that you have sent me. And the glory that you have given me, I have given to them, that they may be one, even as We are one: I in them and you in me; that they may be perfected in unity . . . and that the world may know that you have sent me, and that you have loved them even as you have loved me (Jn 17:22–23).

It is this unity that the liturgy of the Church expresses and in which Christians experience their unity in Christ and through him with the Father. As the *Constitution on the Sacred Liturgy* tells us, the liturgy is not co-extensive with the total activity of the Church: "The Sacred Liturgy does not exhaust the entire activity of the Church."[7] The Church is also an extension and prolongation of Christ as prophet and as king; through the Church Christ continues to teach and to rule. The *Constitution on the Sacred Liturgy* reminds us that the liturgy is not co-extensive with the spiritual life of the Church:

---

[7] *Constitution on the Sacred Liturgy*, no. 9.

The spiritual life, however, is not limited solely to participation in the Liturgy. The Christian is indeed called to pray with his brethren, but he must also enter into his chamber to pray to the Father in secret; yet more, according to the teaching of the Apostle, he should pray without ceasing. We learn from the same Apostle that we must always bear about in our body the dying of Jesus (the victimhood of Jesus), so that the life also of Jesus may be manifest in our bodily frame.[8]

If it is true that we find our Christian identity in the community of Christ, it is also true that we remain individuals. However, there is no opposition between our Christian communal identity and our Christian individuality. True Christian individuality will show itself in the Christian community and flow into Christian community. All deepening of our personal union with Christ will reflect itself in the public acts of worship in which we proclaim Christ's saving presence and our corporate unity in him as ". . . a chosen race, a royal priesthood, a holy nation, a purchased people . . ." (1 Pet 2:9).

---

[8] *Ibid.*, no. 12.

CHAPTER ELEVEN

Church and State

. . . In their proper spheres, the political community and the Church are mutually independent and self-governing. Yet, by a different title, each serves the personal and social vocation of the same human beings. This service can be more effectively rendered for the good of all, if each works better for wholesome mutual co-operation depending on the circumstances of time and place.

— Vatican II, *Pastoral Constitution on the Church in the Modern World*, no. 76

1. Definition of Terms and of the Problem

One of the most distressing and divisive issues concerning the Church, and perhaps the most topical at this particular moment, is the relationship of the Church with the state. The incarnation of the Church, its very presence in the world, necessarily asks its own recognition; yet the Church must in its turn acknowledge the recognition of another society, civil society. The tensions and adjustments resulting from the co-existence of two autonomous societies have never been completely resolved, either in theory or in practice. The theoretical questions of this co-existence can be summarized as follows: (1) Is the Church a part of civil society or is civil society a part of the Church? (2) Does each society have its own autonomy? (3) Is the autonomy of the state limited or modified by the constitution of the Church?

In general, we see the answers to these questions as follows: (1) The Church is a society distinct from civil society and superior to it. (2) The superiority of the Church does not deprive the state of its own autonomy in matters which pertain to the natural finality or goals of civil society. (3) Matters which concern civil society recede from the dominion of the state when they fall under the authority of the Church. But, before we take up these questions in a more specific treatment of each, it would be wise to define a few terms and the problem itself more precisely.

The Church, in the context of this discussion, is a religious community, universal, supranational, and visible, which is meant to perdure till the end of the world; in this Church there are constituted offices of juridical authority to teach, rule, and sanctify. Like all societies, the Church is a moral union of men engaged in the prosecution of a recognized end or finality through mutual cooperation. The unique feature of the Church as a society is that it is a supernatural society because its end or finality is supernatural, i.e., above and beyond merely human resources and the boundaries of this world. Obviously, a society can be elevated to such a status only by God.

Civil Society is that natural and perfect society toward which all men are impelled by human nature and human instinct. It too involves the prosecution of an end or goal through mutual cooperation of its members. More specifically, the end or finality of civil society is "the common good," the peace and prosperity of its members. These notions are borrowed from philosophy, in particular, ethics; we cannot stop to prove them here. The autonomy of civil society, which we wish to vindicate, means this: there is a self-sufficiency in governing, so that the state need not consult the Church in those things which, according to the law of nature, fall under the end or finality of the natural, civil society.

The State, as we understand it here, is not identified with civil society; it is rather this civil society with relation to actual government. Civil society is a larger notion and reality than the state. Many things pertain to civil society which do not pertain at all to the State, e.g., art, culture in general, the practical vision of human life, the sciences. These are clearly a part of the responsibility of civil society but do not fall within the scope of actual government. The state is practically identified with the activity of governing.

We are dealing here with the fundamental problem of Church and state. The existence and function of a state are fundamental data, and true to the philosophy of society as proposed by St. Thomas. Its existence and function are grounded in the natural law, so that the state must exist. Likewise, the institution of the Church by God is regarded as something given. Some Christian theologians have proposed theories of the Church which would truly resolve all the tensions of the two co-existing, autonomous societies. They have described an *eschatological* Church that will begin its proper existence only at the end of the world. Others have insisted that Christ did not found the Church at all, intent as he was on the apocalyptic event that would mark the end of this world, once and for all. These theologians do not seem to be very deeply impressed with the fact that the New Testament, in all its length and breadth and depth, is saturated with a notion of a very concrete institution, very definitely distinct from the hectically excited eschatological literature produced by the oppressed contemporaries of the New Testament, who no doubt hoped for an end to all this, and put their wishful thinking in writing.

Others who have accused the Church of a kind of heavenly-mindedness to the point of disdain for humanity, have pronounced the Church to be a "defective development," the fate suffered by so many pure-ideas in this evil, deforming world. In fact, the history of this co-existence has been marked with many unsuccessful attempts to reconcile by discreditation.

The problem is not that the Church would deny or devaluate this order and the realities of this world, but that it seeks to redeem them. If the meaning of this redemption is understood, it will be clear that the Church does not plan a direct invasion of the temporal order or an absorption by baptism of its possessions, but is simply seeking to preserve that order and those possessions in a state of integrity. When the Christian says with Paul that "all things belong to us, and we to Christ, and Christ to God," he is not denying or appropriating, but affirming and respecting the earthly realities which belong to the temporal order. Creation is not a pretext to love God; it is lovable in itself because it is good in itself.[1] Christopher Dawson has said that the Church has undeviatingly maintained the dignity of human nature in itself and of the material element in man's nature.[2]

In other words, the accusation often made against the Church is precisely the area of her great contribution to both societies: the affirmation of the temporal and the natural values of that order. Judaism could not think of a state, except as subordinate to religion. Historically, it

---

[1] Cf. H. Bouesse, in review of Yves Congar's *Jalons pour une théologie du läicat*, *Lumière et Vie* (1954), p. 144.

[2] Christopher Dawson, *Progress and Religion* (London: Sheed and Ward, 1937), p. 173. Cf. also Gerard Philips, *Le rôle du läicat dans l'Église* (Paris, 1954), p. 70.

acknowledged only "sacral" values. Pagan Rome could not conceive of religion except as a department of state. Manichaeanism, Gnosticism, Docetism, Monophysitism, each in its own way, represented an implicit denial of the temporal, and the Church rejected all of these heresies. Renaissance humanism verged in the other direction, and the Church sought to draw it back to a recognition of the spiritual. Atheistic humanism was outright in its denial of God, and the Church rejected it.

No adequate sense of human history can accept these accusations against the Church, which imply a denial of human values in the teaching of the Church, without rebuttal. In the ruins of a dying civilization, and in the confusion that preceded the rise of another, at the end of the Middle Ages, the Church took over "all education and literary culture, all art, all matters of social welfare such as relief of the poor and care of the sick."[3] Roman Pontiffs founded the universities of Paris, Oxford, Rome, Bologna, and Padua. It was, of course, only a provisory role of the Church.[4] If certain churchmen have, at times, unwisely sought to protect the sovereignty of the Church by the possession of an earthly kingdom — and there is incontrovertible evidence of such — it is nevertheless certain that the doctrine of the Church is not one of aggrandizement, and that the general history of the Church supports her professed intentions to honor the autonomy of civil society and to respect the temporal order and natural values.

The problem of Church and state obviously calls for a solution which will allow a distinction of final goals, and for the delimitation of respective rights and duties. Each is a supreme institution in its own order, and as supreme institutions Church and state are a most remarkable couple. They are inevitably chained to each other and in a sense they will decide their fate mutually, since absolute separation is out of the question. There have been periods in human history when they have smiled at each other and other periods when they have glared at each other. Their interests are often diverse, and yet it is often difficult to recognize their agreements and disagreements. Each is mutually independent of the other and self-governing. Yet, as Vatican II maintains, "by a different title, each serves the personal and social vocation of the same human beings. This service can be more effectively rendered for the good of all, if each works better for wholesome mutual cooperation. . . ."[5] Somehow the problem of

---

[3] *Ibid.*, p. 169. Both Dawson and Philips maintain that the Church has always respected the legitimacy of temporal societies and their power to regulate temporal human activity.

[4] Charles Journet, *The Church of the Word Incarnate* (New York: Sheed and Ward, 1955), Vol. I, p. 202.

[5] *Pastoral Constitution on the Church in the Modern World*, no. 76.

Church and state can be resolved only in a kind of "mutual cooperation," for harmonious collaboration of Church and state has no other alternative than conflict.

2. A Brief Historical Resumé of the Question

Hardly had the Church been born, when the strange drama of Church and state began. For three centuries of violent persecution the state tried to choke the Church to death. The fact that the Church could count only a handful of members at this time makes such savage zeal to destroy her quite difficult to understand. Whatever his motives, the emperor Constantine brought peace, but he took the Church uncomfortably close to his bosom. This was the beginning of what has been called the "Oriental Era," in which emperors began playing popes with all the awkwardness of rank amateurs. This is what is meant by "Caesaropapism" — Caesar making himself pope. Constantine did not distinguish himself for this kind of meddling as much as his successors, notably Constantius. During the fourth century one of these successors, Theodosius, proclaimed Christianity the state religion, a very doubtful favor, especially in the light of the fact that his motivation was undoubtedly political. It has always been a big temptation to wear the Church's halo for one's own purposes.

Constantine's image eventually grew into the person of Charlemagne, the first "Brother Sacristan" who kept both the coffers and the sacristy of the Holy Roman Empire. Two hundred years later, in the tenth century, the Ottos handled the Church with the same kind of dominating paternalism. Then came what has been called the "investiture struggle," in which the principal question was: Who is subject to whom? It was in this struggle that the papacy came of age, and sought not only its own autonomy but began taking its turn at playing the bully. The popes now began to depose emperors in a switch of roles. But this era of arrogance came to a shattering end in the thirteenth century, and the pope of the following century became a court chaplain of the French ruler. In France from Philip the Fair until Napoleon, the accepted doctrine was that which is called "Gallicanism," which put the Church on her obedient knees before the French State.

The Carolingian age had made an incalculable contribution to the problem of amalgamating the spiritual and the temporal: the creation of a pontifical state. The author of this magnificent blunder was Pepin the Short in A.D. 756. In A.D. 774, Charlemagne solemnly renewed the donation, which bequeathed to the Church not only the whole middle strip of Italy but with it a thousand years of suffering. These Papal States did furnish a protection for the pope, but no doubt dimmed the vision of his universal and spiritual mission, of which his predecessors had been so conscious. The resultant ecclesiastical fiscal system and the scars of nepotism, entrusting important posts and Church benefits to one's friends or preferably family, are certain indications that the papacy was fast becoming a temporal power. The death knell of Christendom was beginning to toll in the distance.

With the coming of the violent Boniface VIII in 1294, a man determined to crystallize the policy of ecclesiastical pre-eminence, the downfall looked even more imminent, especially after his conflict with the king of France, Philip IV or Philip the Fair. Pope Boniface died in 1303, and the popes resided in Avignon, France, from 1309 till 1367. The Great Schism, when three separate men laid claim to the papal throne, lasted from 1378 to 1417 and greatly contributed to and publicized the disrepute of the papacy. This would have been the moment for a clear-headed leader who could have formed a stable platform of relations with the State, but none appeared.

During this period of independence from and hostility toward the papacy, national governments grew stronger within themselves. The faithful in general were less and less influenced by the Church. As early as the fourteenth century Pierre D'Ailly and his disciple, Jean Gerson, men of great virtue and deep piety and scholars at the University of Paris, recommended the constitution of a "federal church," within which each national church would enjoy its own autonomy. Their system also sought to restrict Roman primacy by the "conciliar theory" which subjected the pope to ecumenical councils. In 1438 "The Pragmatic Sanction of Bourges," a French law sanctioning the condemned Council of Basel, sided with the conciliar theory and gave legal sanction to the schismatic Council of Basel. This Pragmatic Sanction continued in effect until the Concordat of 1516, and was the most indicative sign and conclusive proof of what had happened to the Church. The pope finally settled the desperate situation, but his prestige was a thing of the past. The prestige of both pope and Church had been dying inch by inch since the time of Pope Boniface VIII in 1294.

After the period of decline, marked by the exile of Avignon and the Great Schism of the popes, came the ultimate stages of decline in the persons of the Borgias. In the history of the Church no name is more suggestive of deceit, scandal, and vice. During the reigns of Innocent VIII and Alexander VI — and we might add Julius II and Leo X — the depravity of the Roman Court was equal to that of any other European Court because these popes guided the destinies of the Church as though it were a completely temporal society. At the death of Leo X, all hope for the grandiose dreams of Innocent III were shattered. There was an immense disgust for the Church in Christians of the time, and this disgust eventually broke its barriers in the Protestant Reformation. The Council of Trent ambitioned Church reform and the restoration of the Church's honor and dignity, but from this point on, Church-state relations could never be the same.

After the Protestant Reformation, religious wars tore all of Europe apart, with the exceptions of Italy and Spain. Catholicism was driven out of England, the Scandinavian countries, a great part of Germany, and a number of Swiss cantons. Due in large part to the papal habit of dealing with other states as a sovereign political power, pontifical debasement had struck the nadir, and only several centuries later would it reacquire some independence and respect.

Within the areas salvaged for the Church, Gallicanism now had its hour. The civil powers, while granting the Catholic Church the privilege of being the state religion, demanded in return strict control over religion. Temporal rulers refused the Church any right of interference in state affairs, and subordinated pontifical jurisdiction to their own discretion. In the end, Gallicanism became an export item and sowed the seed of discord between Church and state everywhere.

The Renaissance and the Reformation developed nationalisms, and brought about the division of western Europe religiously and culturally. The Protestant lands developed the theory of the "Divine Right of Kings," against which Francis Suarez and Cardinal Bellarmine, of the Society of Jesus, forged the Catholic doctrine of Church and state. Although they seemed to be unconscious of it, their theory was a rationalization of a past condition that had not completely disappeared but which was vanishing rapidly. Martin Luther had eliminated the pope as a religious center of gravity and the developing nationalism welcomed his doctrine. Each prince was now the center of religious unity in his own territory, and from this fact the adage was formulated: *Cujus Regio Ejus Religio* (Whose region, his religion). Cross and crown, altar and throne, were now occupied by one man without subjection to outside authority. Religion and politics were hopelessly intermingled, and no one felt quite sure where one ended and the other began. This was the confusion of the "Confessional State."

The eighteenth-century rationalists wanted to construct a naturalistic culture, and, even in the Confessional States, religion was a strong part of the contemporary culture; the whole postulate of supernaturalism was distasteful to them and the whole religious structure odious. Their anger was not so much directed at the general tyranny of these local kings, but against their assumed right to impose ideas, especially religious ideas. These rationalists were not out-and-out atheists, but they were doggedly intent on killing *supernatural* religion and replacing it with a *rationalistic* religion. This inevitably meant: the *separation* of Church and state.

In the United States, Thomas Jefferson was clearly influenced by the Enlightenment. He had cut out with a razor all the passages of his personal Bible which dealt with the supernatural. The American Constitution, drafted eleven years after Jefferson's Declaration of Independence, was the first attempt in history to solve this age-old problem by a separation of Church and state. This was not the separation of the French Rationalists, for the Fathers of the Constitution were not at all opposed to religion; in fact, according to their lights, they were religious men. Even if they had not been such, the people clearly were religious. The Confessional State would never have worked in America; too many religions had already planted their roots in American soil. The French idea of separation was therefore adopted, but with the clear hope that the people would be free to be religious, and not that religion would be interred by their decision.

In the nineteenth century, the French ideal of separation, bolstered by the success of the American experiment, became the battle cry all over Europe. The demand of "tolerance" was not really the *issue*, though it was the *word* of the hour. The Popes favored separation in non-Catholic lands and pluralistic societies, because it gave the Catholics of those lands an opportunity to live and grow, but they resented the cry for separation in Catholic Confessional States. In his *Syllabus of Errors* (1864), Pope Pius IX condemned the proposition: "The Church must be separated from the State and the State from the Church."[6] However, the idea spread and became the universally accepted solution everywhere, including the new, unified Italy that supplanted the era of the Papal States. Against a totally new background Pope Leo XIII tried to explain the position of the Church in three documents: the encyclical letters *Immortale Dei* (1885), *Libertas Praestantissimum* (1888), and *Sapientiae Christianae* (1890).

Catholic thinkers did not look benignly upon this new state of things. The Catholics in France were monarchists and bore an acute hostility toward a new Italian government with all its works and pomps; Spanish Catholics were used to "the cross and crown" merger, and repeated the warning that all republican movements are the children of anti-Catholics. In Latin America, the liberals who spoke hopefully of separation of Church and state were the avowed enemies of Catholicism. In general

[6] *DS* 2975 (DB 1775).

the posture of the Church leaned against the new order of things, although the popes did sign many concordats with various states, in which there was recognition of the separation of Church and state.

The twentieth century brought its own problems and changes. Parliamentary procedures ceded to a new force: totalitarian dictatorships, fascist and communist. These were energized by a new spirit of nationalism, and refused any rights to anyone unless approved by the state. In Italy, Fascism made an uneasy peace with the Church; in Germany the dictator attacked Catholicism and seemed to have absolute subjection in mind. In Communist countries, there was a general hostility and suppression of religion. It was in this historical setting that the voice of Pope Pius XII pleaded for liberty as a requisite for a well-regulated society.[7]

In the wake of the terrible World War II, the question of Church and state came under general scrutiny again. The suppression of Protestant efforts to proselytize in Spain, the Italian divorce laws, the Catholic school system in the United States, the whole question of religious freedom — all emerged as urgent questions in the forums of public discussion.

3. Church and State in the New Testament

It is an interesting phenomenon that only with the advent of Christianity have Church and state found it impossible to live apart and yet difficult to live together. We might say that the first fork in the road of separation occurred at the trial of Jesus[8] when Christ was questioned by the Roman governor Pontius Pilate. Christ tried to explain to Pilate that his kingdom is not really of this world, but that its whole thrust is rather to bear witness to the truth. Pilate immediately lost interest. "What is truth?" he asked. The two spheres and institutions are, in this moment portrayed as distinct entities. Jesus respects the official representative of the state, and the official representative of the state seems to acknowledge his incompetence to settle questions of religious truth. Until that time the ancient state had regarded itself as the subsistent truth, the object of worship. Now, before this power, Jesus proclaims himself to be witnessing to the truth. In a sense, the public sphere of the state loses its "sacral" character in this moment, and Christ's claim to be a witness to the truth is proposed for public validation.

We have already remarked that Judaism could admit only sacral values, and in Paul's letter to the Romans[9] this sacred character of all authority

---

[7] Pope Pius XII, Christmas Radio Address, December 24, 1944.
[8] Cf. Jn 18:33–38.
[9] Cf. Rom 13:1–7.

is obviously in Paul's mind. It is interesting to note that, at the time Paul wrote to the Romans from Corinth, he had just been protected by the moral power of the state when the Roman proconsul, Gallio, saved him from the homicidal tendencies of a mob. But this hardly explains Paul's admiration and respect for civil authority as God's will. The thesis of St. Paul seems to be this: that the state is empowered by God, just as the Church, and he uses the names commonly applied to offices in the Church[10] to describe the public officials to whom obedience is owing. Furthermore, Paul urges this obedience on the grounds that God's power is delegated to these public servants, and so it is not a matter of fear, but a matter of conscience. It is a question of conscience and ultimately, therefore, a question of truth to recognize the state.

The total biblical understanding of civil authority is complex. State power seems to be subject to serious qualifications, and should not be allowed to infringe on the divine sovereignty,[11] and it is regarded as a threat to the bond of love.[12] The kingdom of Christ seems to be portrayed as very far removed from the kingdoms of this earth;[13] the state (politeuma) of Christians is in heaven[14] for "this world in its present form is passing away" (1 Cor 7:31), and "here we have no lasting city, but we are looking for the one which is to come" (Heb 13:14). This thought seemed to dominate much early Christian thinking. Jesus himself preached the complete renunciation of worldly goods[15] and family ties.[16] He saw violent defense — "with the sword" — of his kingdom as futile.[17]

Still, the New Testament leaves little doubt that the Christian is to obey the state, as is clear from the passage of Paul to the Romans as also from the First Letter of St. Peter.[18] It seems to be part of the Christian's acceptance of God's will, as forwarded through the state. Even Christ acknowledged this in his remark: "You would not have the least authority over me had it not been given to you from above" (Jn 19:11). Still the commands of the state never supersede the demands of a Christian's conscience, as is clear from the absolute refusal of obedience on the part of the apostles to the religious authority of the Sanhedrin; they were commanded "to make no utterance and to teach nothing at all in the name of Jesus." To this the Apostles replied simply: "we cannot refrain . . ."

[10] Diakonos, leitourgoi = minister, public servants.
[11] Cf. 1 Kgs 8:7.
[12] Cf. Gal 5:14; Rom 13:10.
[13] Cf. Jn 17:36.
[14] Cf. Phil 3:20.
[15] Cf. Mt 6:19–34; 19:21.
[16] Cf. Mt 19:29.
[17] Cf. Mt 26:52.
[18] Cf. 1 Pet 2:13–17.

and after praying for courage to stand their ground in the face of this threat, "they continued to speak the message of God with firm assurance" (Acts 4:19-31).

Finally, there is the well-known "Render unto Caesar the things that are Caesar's and to God the things that are God's" (Mk 12:13-17). The context for this remark was the question of the poll tax, established in A.D. 6 and payable to the imperial treasury. The Zealots had refused to pay it, but the Herodians and Pharisees had submitted, and now these latter two groups had sent representatives to Jesus with the familiar loaded question. If he told them not to pay the tax, they could deliver him up to Roman authority, as they desired to do. But Christ saw through their deceit, and delivered the verdict that obedience to temporal power does not withdraw one from his obedience to God. They are compatible.

That civil authority is divinely established[19] is clear. It is also clear in the New Testament that the state is established to promote the common good. Society is a work of God, and it is achieved or realized by the cooperation of men. Certainly one functional part of this cooperation is the exercise and acceptance of authority. This function is a continuation of God's role in instituting society. In a recent article by a moral theologian, it is urged that Christians be induced to understand that civil authority contains the divine no less than does religious authority for the difference does not touch the notion of authority as such.[20] The author sees this as the scriptural presentation of civil authority and the state.

4. The Problem of Harmonization in "Mixed Matters"

In his encyclical letter, Immortale Dei,[21] Pope Leo XIII speaks of res mixtae, mixed matters, by which he means those things which pertain to the mission of the Church and at the same time to the responsibility of the state. For example, education, matrimonial laws, clerical privileges, etc. We have already said that, in such matters, the state cannot countermand or contradict the legislation of the Church legitimately because the Church alone possesses the competence to pass laws in these areas. Of course, the state does have jurisdiction over the purely civil effects of such matters, but its legislation cannot be dissonant from the legislation of the Church.

---

[19] Cf. Rom 13:1-5; Tit 3:1; 1 Pet 2:13.

[20] Josef Fuchs, "Auctoritas Dei in Auctoritate Civili," Periodica, 52 (1963) pp. 3-18.

[21] Promulgated under date of November 1, 1885; cf. DS 3172 (DB 1870).

It is the problem of harmonization in such matters that is the most delicate and neuralgic part of the whole Church-state discussion. No one, even the Communists, will challenge the Church's right to deal with and direct the spiritual life of her subjects. In general, Protestantism considers religion as something so utterly spiritual, inward, and private that it can have only spiritual and private manifestations. In general, too, Protestants feel that the outward, social, and public manifestation of religion tends to be "political," and consequently Protestants generally regard all attempts of the Church to apply religious or moral principles to social, political, and economic problems as an impertinence.

The Catholic stance that the state cannot countermand the legislation of the Church becomes a crucial issue in a pluralistic society like our own. The right to follow one's conscience is always and everywhere a sacred right. "Whether it is right to listen to you, in the sight of God, or rather to God, decide for yourselves" (Acts 4:19). Were the majority in a state convinced of the natural obligation for legislation contrary to that of the Church, e.g., abortion, what would the Catholic counsel of action be? It is supposed that it would be one of reasonable resistance. Stronger action would seemingly not safeguard the sacredness of conscience for religious liberty. One is also reminded of the more recent interpretation of "error has no rights," namely that persons do, and the right to follow one's conscience is certainly an inalienable right. In such a pluralistic society, the Church must function in her defense of the truth by an articulate and persuasive promulgation rather than by a suppression of the opposite errors and the human liberty of dissidents.

However, even in such a pluralistic society the thesis of union of Church and state is logical and inevitable. However, in this phrase, the word union must not have the connotation of an amalgam of Church and state. What is meant rather would be a harmonious cooperation and mutual respect. In this sense, the word used by Leo XIII, in his encyclical letter, Immortale Dei, would probably be a better choice. He uses the word concordia, which denotes a harmonious collaboration, in which there would be a mutual consultation, deference to, and recognition of the respective rights of both Church and state. Only in this way would a true and stable peace be possible in the community, especially if the community were to be predominantly Catholic.

When the Rationalists of the eighteenth century called for "separation of Church and state," the call was not simply for the distinction between two distinct entities but for the disdain and contempt of the Church by the state. Others have used the phrase in various ways and with diverse connotations. Each must be studied in its own historical context. However, when we speak of the union or harmonious collaboration of Church and state, as a theological doctrine, we suppose that there is a distinction between the two and yet insist that there must be, in the ideal order, a harmony of relations, a concord between the two institutions. This position would seem to be the most irenic and positive one. Rather than insisting on areas of conflict in negative terms, it rather expresses the meaning of union as a harmonious collaboration, a peaceful relationship of mutual aid, supposing that the Church herself must make a contribution to civil society and to the state by forming in her own ways loyal citizens who respect the law of the land. The Church would do this by inculcating religious motivation for altruistic contributions to and dedication to the common good of human society.

5. The Contribution of the Church to the Temporal Order

We have said that the Church must make a contribution to civil society and to the temporal order, and it will do this when Catholics are truly catholic in the way they think of and use the things of this world. The doctrines of the Church will become normative in a society only when Catholics are prepared to exhibit that inner dynamism and the resultant benefits of these doctrines in practice. However, even in the act of making such a contribution, the Church will always recognize that the state cannot be baptized and elevated by grace; it is not an apt subject for this. The state can be elevated to the Christian vision only indirectly when it is the state formed by a truly Christian people. The state does not make a Christian people, but Christian people can make a Christian state. It is not the structure of the state that can realize the dreams and hopes of the Church, but only the living and universal faith of a whole nation. The state is helpless either to create such a condition or to annihilate it.

The Christianization of public life is a spontaneous by-product of Christian living among the people. The natural state is not Christian in structure or dynamism, but it is capable of becoming Christian just as marriage can become christianized when the partners of the marriage are Christians. The state by its nature, just as marriage by its nature, is never specifically Christian; both the state and marriage can become Christian only by the grace given and received by the individual persons involved.

The work of penetrating the whole of the temporal order and diffusing Christian principles of law, love, and life, is not the work of the state. The state has no vocation to restore all things in Christ. This is the mission of the instrument that God has chosen, his Church. When the people of a state are truly Christian, that state will be Christian; but it is clear that half-hearted Christians cannot sit back and tell the state about its vocation to be Christian. The state as such has no such calling.

This contribution of the Church to the temporal order must be made in the clear recognition that the Church does not have covetous eyes on the prestige of temporal power. She bears enough historical scars to remind her that, when she ventures into worldliness and entanglements, men will easily forget that she is the complement of her Lord and Master, who came into this world not to be served but to serve, and whose mission was not to judge but to save. In 1956, Pope Pius XII spoke to the International Congress of Historical Sciences, meeting in Rome. The whole of his speech was dedicated to an explanation of how the Church contributes to the temporal order and to the natural sciences without absorbing these into her own supernatural order. He tried to clarify the role of the Church within the temporal order, stressing that its influence will not be achieved by absorbing the temporal order or the state, but rather through the presence of fully formed Christians who will furnish the Christian insights and orientation which alone can keep the natural order itself and the state itself from a spiritual vacuum into which violence is prepared to rush. The following are excerpts from Pope Pius' address:

> The Church gladly recognizes the good and great realities of the natural order, even if they existed before her own existence began, and even if they are outside her dominion. The Church's very purpose is *the man*, naturally good, penetrated, ennobled and fortified by the truth and grace of Christ. The Church has made every effort to contribute to the solution of these problems (of the family, society, the State, the social order), and, we believe, with some success. The Church is persuaded, nevertheless, that she is not able to work more efficaciously than in continuing to form these men of the type we have described.

The Second Vatican Council, in its *Constitution on the Church*, describes this contribution of the Church to human society as follows:

> The faithful, therefore, must learn the deepest meaning and the value of all creation, and how to relate it to the praise of God. . . . In this way the world is permeated by the spirit of Christ and more effectively achieves its purpose in justice, charity, and peace. . . . Therefore by their competence in secular fields and by their personal activity, elevated from within by the grace of Christ, let them labor vigorously so that by human labor, technical skill, and civic culture created goods may be perfected for the benefit of every last man, according to the design of the Creator and the light of His Word. Let them work to see that created goods are more fittingly distributed among men, and that such goods in their own way lead to general progress in human and Christian liberty. In this manner, through the members of the Church, Christ will progressively illumine the whole of human society with His saving light.

Because the very plan of salvation requires it, the faithful should learn how to distinguish carefully between those rights and duties which are theirs as members of the Church, and those which they have as members of human society. Let them strive to harmonize the two, remembering that in every temporal affair they must be guided by a Christian conscience. For even in secular affairs there is no human activity which can be withdrawn from God's dominion. In our own time, however, it is most urgent that this distinction and also this harmony should shine forth as radiantly as possible in the practice of the faithful, so that the mission of the Church may correspond more adequately to the special conditions of the world today. For while it must be recognized that the temporal sphere is governed by its own principles, since it is properly concerned with the interests of this world, that ominous doctrine must rightly be regarded which attempts to build a society with no regard whatever for religion and which attacks and destroys the religious liberty of its citizens.[22]

6. Vatican II and the Question of Church and State

John Courtney Murray, the architect of the *Declaration on Religious Freedom* of Vatican II, has written of the deeper significance of this document:

A work of differentiation between the sacral and the secular has been effected in history. But differentiation is not the highest stage in human growth. The movement toward it, now that it has come to term, must be followed by a further movement toward a new synthesis, within which the differentiation will at once subsist, integral and unconfused and also be transcended in a higher unity. . . . There is a new problematic: the unity of these two orders of human life, achieved under full respect for the integrity of each.[23]

The "work of differentiation" of which Father Murray speaks is that which exists between the sphere of the Church in the pursuit of its supernatural mission and the sphere of the state in the pursuit of its natural mission, the prosperity of man. The "synthesis" of which he speaks is the harmonization between Church and state of which we have spoken. Vatican II, in its document on *The Church in the Modern World*, says of this differentiation and synthesis:

If by the autonomy of earthly affairs we mean that created things and societies themselves enjoy their own laws and values which must be gradually deciphered, put to use, and regulated by men, then it is entirely right to demand that autonomy. Such is not merely required by modern man, but harmonizes also with the will of the Creator. For by the very circumstance of their having been created, all things are endowed with

22 *Lumen Gentium*, no. 36.
23 John Courtney Murray, S.J., "Declaration On Religious Freedom: Its Deeper Significance," *America*, April 23, 1966, p. 593.

their own stability, truth, goodness, proper laws, and order. . . . But if the expression, the independence of temporal affairs, is taken to mean that created things do not depend on God, and that man can use them without any reference to their Creator anyone who acknowledges God will see how false such a meaning is. For without the Creator the creatures would disappear. For their part, however, all believers of whatever religion have always heard His revealing voice in the discourse of preachers. But when God is forgotten, the creature itself grows unintelligible.[24]

We have already quoted from the same document of Vatican II the further assertion of this independence of Church and state and the need for a cooperation which is wholesome and mutual in the service of man.[25] The same document continues:

Holding faithfully to the Gospel and exercising her mission in the world, the Church consolidates peace among men, to God's glory. For it is her task to uncover, cherish, and ennoble all that is true, good and beautiful in the human community.[26]

However the great "new start" offered to the discussion of Church and state by Vatican II is found in its *Declaration on Religious Freedom*. Rather than considering the age-old principle that "error has no rights," the Council develops its discussion along the lines of the "inviolable rights of the human person and of the constitutional order of society."[27] The substance of the *Declaration on Religious Freedom* is stated succinctly by the Council as follows:

The Synod further declares that the right to religious freedom has its foundation in the very dignity of the human person, as this dignity is known through the revealed Word of God and by reason itself. This right of the human person to religious freedom is to be recognized in the constitutional law whereby society is governed. Thus it is to become a civil right. It is in accordance with their dignity and persons — that is, beings endowed with reason and free will and therefore privileged to bear personal responsibility — that all men should be at once impelled by nature and also bound by a moral obligation to seek the truth, especially religious truth. They are also bound to adhere to the truth, once it is known and to order their whole lives in accord with the demands of truth.[28]

In his annotation of the document, Father Murray states:

The doctrinal substance of the Declaration . . . defines what religious freedom is and affirms its status as a human — and therefore civil — right. A right is a moral claim made on others that they either give me something or do something for me or refrain from doing something. Two questions always arise. First, what is the moral claim I make on others, or in

---

[24] *The Church in the Modern World*, no. 36.
[25] *Ibid.*, no. 76.
[26] *Ibid.*
[27] *Declaration on Religious Freedom*, no. 1.
[28] *Ibid.*, no. 2.

other words, what is the object or content of my right? Second, on what grounds do I make this moral claim, or in other words, what is the foundation of my right?

The Declaration first defines religious freedom in terms of its object or content. The moral claim that every man makes on others — on individuals, groups, political or social powers — is that they refrain from bringing coercion to bear on him in all matters religious. This claim is twofold. First, no man is to be forced to act in a manner contrary to his personal beliefs; second, no man is to be forcibly restrained from acting in accordance with his beliefs. The affirmation of this latter immunity is the new thing, which is in harmony with the older affirmation of the former immunity.

It is to be noted that the word "conscience," found in the Latin text, is used in its generic sense, sanctioned by usage, of "beliefs," "convictions," "persuasions." Hence the unbeliever or atheist makes with equal right this claim to immunity from coercion in religious matters. It is further to be noted that, in assigning a negative content to the right to religious freedom (that is, in making it formally a "freedom from" and not a "freedom for"), the Declaration is in harmony with the sense of the First Amendment to the American Constitution. In guaranteeing the free exercise of religion, the First Amendment guarantees to the American citizen immunity from all coercion in matters religious. Neither the Declaration nor the American Constitution affirms that a man has a right to believe what is false or to do what is wrong. This would be moral nonsense. Neither error nor evil can be the object of a right, but only what is true and good. It is, however, true and good that a man should enjoy freedom from coercion in matters religious.

This brings up the second question, concerning the *foundation* of the right. The reason why every man may claim immunity from coercion in matters religious is precisely his inalienable dignity as a human person. Surely, in matters religious, if anywhere, the free human person is required and entitled to act on his own judgment and to assume personal responsibility for his action or omission. A man's religious decisions, or his decision against religion, are inescapably his own. No one else can make them for him, or compel him to make this decision or that, or restrain him from putting his decision into practice, privately or publicly, alone or in company with others. In all these cases, the dignity of man would be diminished because of the denial to him of that inalienable responsibility for his own decisions and actions which is the essential counterpart of his freedom.[29]

From such an orientation, namely that of human dignity and the resultant personal rights of man, the Vatican Council, in this document, enters into many of the areas of attrition between Church and state, involving what we have called mixed matters. The important thing to note is that many of the claims made by expositors of Catholic doctrine on Church and state, that the state owes support to the Church precisely

---

[29] *The Documents of Vatican II*, ed. by Walter M. Abbott (New York: America Press, 1966), footnote 5, pp. 678–679.

because the Church is true and has prior claims, are denied in this document. While there is a request that the state support religion in general, it denies the vocation of the state to assess supernatural claims, and consequently rests its case with the simple demand to be free. We summarize the teachings of this document, in the areas of disputed matters, as follows:

1) *The obligation of the state to favor the practice of religion:*

The religious acts whereby men, in private and in public and out of a sense of personal conviction, direct their lives to God transcend by their very nature the order of terrestrial and temporal affairs. Government, therefore, ought indeed to take account of the religious life of the people and show its favor, since the function of government is to make provision for the common welfare. However, it would clearly transgress the limits set to its power were it to presume to direct or inhibit acts that are religious.[30]

2) *The rights of the Catholic Church in comparison with other religious sects:*

The freedom or immunity from coercion in matters religious which is the endowment of persons as individuals is also to be recognized as their right when they act in community. Religious bodies are a requirement of the social nature of both man and of religion itself.[31]

The freedoms listed here are those which the Catholic Church claims for herself. The Declaration likewise claims them for all Churches and Religious Communities. Lest there be misunderstanding, however, it is necessary to recall here the distinction between the content or object of the right and its foundation. The content or object always remain freedom from coercion in what concerns religious belief, worship, practice or observance, and public testimony. Hence the content of the right is the same for both the Catholic Church and for other religious bodies. In this sense, the Church claims nothing for herself which she does not also claim for them. The matter is different, however, with regard to the foundation of the right. The Catholic Church claims freedom from coercive interference in her ministry and life on the grounds of the divine mandate laid upon her by Christ Himself. It is Catholic faith that no other church or community may claim to possess this mandate in all its fullness. In this sense the freedom of the Church is unique, proper to herself alone, by reason of its foundation. In the case of other Religious Communities, the foundation of the right is the dignity of the human person, which requires that men be kept free from coercion, when they act in community, gathered into Churches, as well as when they act alone.[32]

3) *Religious education in schools:*

---

[30] *Declaration on Religious Freedom*, no. 3.
[31] *Ibid.*, no. 4.
[32] *Documents of Vatican II*, annotation of Father Murray, p. 682.

Since the family is a society in its own original right, it has the right freely to live its own domestic religious life under the guidance of parents. Parents, moreover, have the right to determine, in accordance with their own religious beliefs, the kind of religious education that their children are to receive. Government, in consequence, must acknowledge the right of parents to make a genuinely free choice of schools and of other means of education. . . . Besides, the rights of parents are violated if their children are forced to attend lessons or instructions which are not in agreement with their religious beliefs. The same is true if a single system of education, from which all religious formation is excluded, is imposed upon all.[33]

4) *Suppression of other religions in areas where one religion predominates:*

If, in view of peculiar circumstances, obtaining among certain peoples, special legal recognition is given in the constitutional order of society to one religious body, it is at the same time imperative that the right of all citizens and religious bodies to religious freedom should be recognized and made effective in practice.[34]

This paragraph is carefully phrased. The Council did not wish to condemn the institution of "establishment," the notion of a "religion of the State." A respectable opinion maintains that the institution is compatible with full religious freedom. On the other hand, the Council did not wish to canonize the institution. A respectable opinion holds that establishment is always a threat to religious freedom. Furthermore, the Council wished to insinuate that establishment, at least from the Catholic point of view, is a matter of historical circumstance, not of theological doctrine. For all these reasons, the text deals with the issue in conditional terms.[35]

5) *The duty of the state to protect against abuses perpetrated in the name of religion:*

Furthermore, society has the right to defend itself against possible abuses committed on pretext of freedom of religion. It is the special duty of government to provide this protection. However, government is not to act in arbitrary fashion or in an unfair spirit of partisanship. Its action is to be controlled by juridical norms which are in conformity with the objective moral order. . . . For the rest, the usages of society are to be the usages of freedom in their full range. These require that the freedom of man be respected as far as possible, and curtailed only when and insofar as necessary.[36]

6) *The norms of "common welfare" or "public order" and freedom as a purpose of human society:*

These norms rise out of the need for effective safeguard of the rights of all citizens and for peaceful settlement of conflicts of rights. They flow from

---

[33] *Declaration on Religious Freedom*, no. 5.
[34] *Ibid.*, no. 6.
[35] *The Documents of Vatican II*, annotation of Father Murray, p. 685.
[36] *Declaration on Religious Freedom*, no. 7.

the need for an adequate care of genuine public peace, which comes about when men live together in good order and true justice. They come, finally, out of the need for a proper guardianship of public morality. These matters constitute the basic component of the common welfare: they are what is meant by public order.[37]

Secular experts may well consider this to be the most significant sentence in the Declaration. It is a statement of the basic principle of the "free society." The principle has important origins in the medieval tradition of kingship, law, and jurisprudence. But its statement by the Church has an accent of blessed newness — the newness of a renewal of the tradition. The renewal, already hesitantly begun by Pius XII, was strongly furthered by John XXIII. Catholic thought had consistently held that society is to be based upon truth (the truth of the human person) directed toward justice and animated by charity. In "Pacem in Terris," John XXIII added the missing fourth term, freedom. Freedom is an end or purpose of society, which looks to the liberation of the human person. Freedom is the political method par excellence, whereby the other goals of society are reached. Freedom, finally, is the prevailing social usage, which sets the style of society. This progress in doctrine is sanctioned and made secure by "Dignitatis Humanae Personae."[38]

7) The acknowledgment of the state and its powers or rights:

He [Christ] acknowledged the power of government and its rights, when He commanded the tribute to be given to Caesar. But he gave clear warning that the higher rights of God are to be kept inviolate: "Render, therefore, to Caesar the things that are Caesar's, and to God the things that are God's" (Mt 22:21).[39]

8) The right of civil disobedience when state legislation opposes the recognized will of God:

At the same time, however, they (the Apostles) did not hesitate to speak out against governing powers which set themselves in opposition to the holy will of God: "We must obey God rather than men" (Acts 5:29). This is the way along which countless martyrs and other believers have walked through all ages and over all the earth.[40]

9) The right of the Church to a condition of legal privilege in society:

. . . The Church should enjoy that full measure of freedom from which her care for the salvation of men requires. . . . This freedom . . . is so much the property of the Church that to act against it is to act against the will of God. The freedom of the Church is the fundamental principle in what concerns the relations between the Church and the government and the whole civil order.[41]

---

[37] Ibid.
[38] Documents of Vatican II, annotation of Father Murray, p. 687.
[39] Declaration on Religious Freedom, no. 11. Cf. section 3 of this chapter.
[40] Ibid. Cf. also Acts 4, 19–20.
[41] Ibid., no. 13.

This statement, together with the declaration of religious freedom as a human right and the annunciation of the principle of a free society, must rank as one of the central doctrinal utterances of the Declaration. Its importance is emphasized by the fact that Paul VI quoted it in his address on December 9 to political rulers: "And what is it that this Church asks of you, after nearly two thousand years of all sorts of vicissitudes in her relations with you, the powers of earth? What does the Church ask of you today? In one of the major texts of the Council she has told you: she asks of you *nothing but freedom* — the freedom to believe and to preach her faith, the freedom to love God and to serve Him, the freedom to live and to bring to men her message of life." This doctrine is traditional; it is also new. Implicit in it is the renunciation by the Church of a condition of legal privilege in society. The Church does not make, as a matter of right or of divine law, the claim that she should be established as the "religion of the State." Her claim is freedom, nothing more.[42]

10) *The relation of religious freedom in civil society and the Christian freedom which obtains inside the Church:*

In the formation of their consciences, the Christian faithful ought carefully to attend to the sacred and certain doctrine of the Church. The Church is, by the will of Christ, the teacher of truth. It is her duty to give utterance to, and authoritatively to teach, that Truth which is Christ Himself, and also to declare and confirm by her authority those principles of the moral order which have their origin in human nature itself.[43]

The Council directs a word of pastoral exhortation to the Christian faithful. They are urged, in particular, to form their consciences under the guidance of the authority of the Church. It might be noted here that the Council intended to make a clear distinction between religious freedom as a principle in the civil order and the Christian freedom which obtains even inside the Church. These two freedoms are distinct in kind; and it would be perilous to confuse them. Nowhere does the Declaration touch the issue of freedom within the Church. Undoubtedly, however, it will be a stimulus for the articulation of a full theology of Christian freedom in its relation to the doctrinal and disciplinary authority of the Church.[44]

7. Conclusion

The Second Vatican Council has obviously presented us with a great step forward in clarifying the basic notions of the Church-state discussion. The teachings of the Council are to be applauded as a welcome up-dating. Christians are asked "to appreciate their special and personal vocation in the political community."[45] The Christian's apostolate to the state in

---

[42] Documents of Vatican II, annotation of Father Murray, p. 693.
[43] Declaration on Religious Freedom, no. 14.
[44] Documents of Vatican II, annotation of Father Murray, p. 693.
[45] The Church in the Modern World, no. 75.

which he lives is a continuation or extension of his fundamental vocation to "seek the kingdom of God by engaging in temporal affairs and by ordering them according to the plan of God."[46] Bishops, too, are also reminded of their responsibility to cooperate with civil authority.[47] The shepherds of Christ's flock must help provide all men with material as well as spiritual nourishment if they are to fulfill their mandate from Christ.

However, even though it is clear that Church and state must work toward a mutual collaboration in the building of a better world in order to attain the fulfillment of the kingdom of God, there are many serious difficulties in implementing the long-awaited principles afforded by the Second Vatican Council. To be a citizen of two worlds and to reconcile this dual citizenry in practice will call for a great number of difficult prudential judgments. The Church must patiently seek a delicate balance, refraining from "injecting herself into the government of the earthly city,"[48] while at the same time "in discharging their apostolic office, which concerns the salvation of souls, bishops of themselves enjoy full and perfect freedom and independence from any civil authority."[49] The Church must serve human society as a conscience, but it would be contrary to its own acknowledgment of human rights to impose its conscience by force on others.

Vatican II has set the stage for a profound dialogue between Church and state, between the sacred and the profane, between the Christian and the world. Now the dialogue must be begun in earnest. Herein lies the great work of implementation to be performed by the theologians and the Christians of the present and of the future.

> The Church cannot, by shutting itself up and remaining passive within its own sanctuaries, desert its divinely providential mission to form the complete man; for it is by that means that the Church collaborates continually in the construction of a solid foundation for human society. This mission is essential to the Church. . . . The harmonious development of all human inclinations and energies, the construction of the most durable basis for good human relations. . . . Through them [the faithful] *the Church is the very soul of human society.*[50]

---

[46] *Constitution on the Church*, no. 31.
[47] *Decree on the Bishops' Pastoral Office*, no. 19.
[48] *Decree on the Missionary Activity of the Church*, no. 12.
[49] *Decree on the Bishops' Pastoral Office*, no. 19.
[50] Pope Pius XII, *Address to the newly-created Cardinals*, February 20, 1946.

CHAPTER TWELVE

The Christian's Vocation to Holiness

Therefore, in the Church, everyone whether belonging to the hierarchy, or being cared for by it, is called to holiness, according to the saying of the Apostle Paul: "For this is the will of God, your sanctification" (1 Th 4:3; Eph 1:4).

— Vatican II, *Lumen Gentium*, No. 39

1. *The Biblical Concept of Holiness*

The Lord said to Moses: "Say to all the congregation of the people of Israel; you shall be holy, for I the Lord, your God, am holy" (Lev 19:2).

In the Old Testament, the sacred writers often used the term "holy" in the absolute sense exclusively of God's uncreated and completely unique majesty. His holiness is presented as something unreachable and inaccessible; it is totally above everything that is created.[1] God calls himself holy because his very essence or name is holy.[2] Before God no man can

---

[1] Cf. 1 Sam 6:20; Ex 15:11; 1 Sam 2:2.
[2] E.g. Ps 99:3, 5, 9; Lev 11:44; 19:2; 20:26; etc.

dare call himself holy.[3] Basically, the *constitutive* holiness of God is a concept of separateness from whatever is profane. The prophets strongly stress the *moral* aspect of God's holiness, although this idea is older than the prophets. God's moral holiness reveals itself as the opposite of human sinfulness. Isaiah sees God's holiness both in the *absolute* sense and also as a *moral* quality in contrast to his own sinfulness.[4] For the prophets in general, God is the absolutely stainless one, and this characteristic stands out all the more as men sin the more against this divine holiness.[5]

In the usage of these Old Testament writers, the holiness of God is both the reason and the norm for all human holiness. God demands holiness in men because he is a jealous God.[6] However, especially in Isaiah this jealousy and strict justice of God, the Holy One of Israel, gives place to redemptive mercy and to a love which forgives sins and which relents.[7] Consequently, in order to mediate this redemptive mercy and love, Yahweh demands of Israel that it be "a kingdom of priests, a holy nation" (Ex 19:4). The people of Israel are called to be holy because they are closely bound to God by the covenant. Israel must be "a holy people," because God has chosen it to be "a people peculiarly his own" (Lev 20:26; Dt 7:6; 26:19 etc.). Furthermore, the holiness of this people presupposes individual holiness, as is evident from the fact that the more pious are called "holy" by reason of the sanctity of their personal lives.[8]

The moral holiness of this people, which means its withdrawal from the contagion of sin, is safeguarded by *cultic* or *ritual* holiness, which is the holiness of the people expressing their complete orientation toward God in worship. Consequently, all of the worshiping people of Israel, but most especially the priests, were obliged to keep themselves free from all sin and uncleanness precisely because of God's holiness.[9] This cultic holiness also embraces a certain *material* and *exterior* holiness which is symbolic of the interior holiness of God's people.

In the New Testament the exclusively material factors of Old Testament holiness disappear. The holiness of the city Jerusalem, of Sion, the Meeting Tent and its court, the Holy of Holies, etc. gives way to a new emphasis which places all its stress on personal and moral holiness, even though material factors and objects still play a role, as in the sacraments. God's holiness is seldom referred to in the New Testament. More often,

---

[3] Job 4:17; 15:14; 25:4 ff.
[4] Is 6:3–7.
[5] Am 2:7; Dt 32:4.
[6] Jos 24:19.
[7] Is 41:14; 43:3, 14; 47:4; cf. also Hos 11:9.
[8] Cf. Ps 16:3; 34:10.
[9] Lev 11:44–45; 18:21; 20:3, 7; 22:32.

but still not frequently, reference is made to Christ's holiness as the basis and model of human holiness.[10] Christ is holy because he is the Son of God[11] and possesses the fullness of the Holy Spirit.[12] Christ is himself made holy by the Father,[13] and therefore his whole life is completely free from even the slightest moral fault.[14] The early Christians were so convinced of this that they referred to Christ as "God's holy servant" (Acts 4:27) and as the holy and innocent high priest of our salvation.[15] This, too, was the testimony which Jesus gave of himself: "Can one of you convict me of sin?" (Jn 8:46.)

> I shall not talk with you any longer, because the prince of this world is on his way. He has no power over me, but the world must be brought to know that I love the Father and that I am doing exactly what the Father told me (Jn 14:30-31).

The term "holy" is used most frequently of the Spirit of God in the New Testament, because this Spirit has the special function of sanctifying or making Christians holy, as he had already made Jesus holy.[16] This Holy Spirit is the unique possession of the Christian community[17] in whom he effects the work of sanctification.[18]

> Out of his infinite glory, may he give you the power through his Spirit for your hidden self to grow strong, so that Christ may live in your hearts through faith, and then, planted in love and built on love, you with all the saints have the strength to grasp the breadth and the length, the height and the depth; until, knowing the love of Christ, which is beyond all knowledge, you are filled with the utter fullness of God (Eph 3:16-19).

It is this same Spirit who not only effects the sanctification of the faithful but also maintains the community in the purity of the revealed doctrine which they believe. He is the "Advocate, the Holy Spirit, whom the Father will send in my name, to teach you everything and remind you of all I have said to you" (Jn 14:26).

Just as in the Old Testament the people of Israel was a "chosen people" of Yahweh, so in the New Testament there is the "chosen people" united to God in Christ, which is obliged and called to be holy.

> But you are a chosen race, a royal priesthood, a consecrated nation, a people set apart to sing the praises of God who called you out of the dark-

---

[10] Cf. 1 Pet 3:15; 1 Jn 2:20.
[11] Cf. Lk 1:35.
[12] Cf. Mk 1:24; Lk 4:34.
[13] Cf. Jn 10:36.
[14] Cf. 1 Pet 2:22; 3:18; 1 Jn 3:5.
[15] Cf. Heb 7:26.
[16] Cf. Lk 1:35; Mt 3:11.
[17] Cf. Acts 2:4; 4:31.
[18] Cf. Rom 15:16; 2 Th 2:13.

ness into his wonderful light. Once you were not a people at all and now you are the People of God; once you were outside the mercy and now you have been given mercy (1 Pet 2:9–10).

This new People of God, called to holiness in Christ, is one without national limitations, and the basis of their holiness is no longer the old covenant, but union with Christ[19] by means of which union the "new People of God" are sanctified in the Holy Spirit.

> I, Paul, . . . send greetings to the Church of God in Corinth, to the holy people of Jesus Christ, who are called to take their place among all the saints everywhere who pray to our Lord Jesus Christ . . . (1 Cor 1:1–2).

The new community, embracing both Jews and Gentiles, is by reason of its vocation to holiness, called simply by Paul "the holy ones" and "the saints" (Rom 1:7; 15:25; 1 Cor 1:2). This new People of God is to be withdrawn from the world of sin, darkness, and Satan[20] so that, chosen and beloved by God, the members of Christ are positively called to charity[21] and to the inheritance of God.[22]

The individual is received into this community of Christ and his personal sanctification takes place through the forgiveness of his sins[23] and his reconciliation with God[24] by means of faith[25] and baptism.[26] In the New Testament holiness is a spiritual and moral character much more than in the Old Testament, and the emphasis falls upon personal purity. From the Sermon on the Mount to the Pastoral Epistles a "pure heart" is demanded as the hallmark of the Christian.[27]

2. The Holiness of Christ and the Christian

> Husbands should love their wives just as Christ loved the Church and sacrificed himself for her to make her holy. He made her clean by washing her in water with the form of words, so that when he took her to himself she would be glorious, with no speck or wrinkle or anything like that but holy and faultless (Eph 5:25–27).

We have already seen that, when God uttered his Word into this world, that Word formed a new creation, gathered earthly man to itself to

---

[19] Rom 15:7–12.
[20] Cf. Acts 26:18; Col 1:12–13.
[21] Cf. Col 3:12 ff.
[22] Cf. Eph 1:18; 2 Th 2:13–14.
[23] Cf. 1 Cor 6:11.
[24] Cf. Rom 5:9–10.
[25] Cf. Acts 26:18; Jude 3; 2 Th 2:13.
[26] Cf. Eph 5:26.
[27] Cf. Mt 5:8; 1 Tim 1:5; 2 Tim 2:22.

become one with him. It was in Christ, the Word of God, that the transcendant and totally unique separateness of God's holiness and the infinitely removed creatureliness of man were finally and totally bridged by a union of complete mutual self-giving love. This is the essence of Christ's mediatorial role. Because he was God, his own humanity was filled with substantial holiness; and because he was a man, he was able to communicate this holiness to men. Because he lived in space and time, somehow he also sanctified space and time; because he ate food and walked upon the earth, in a sense food became holy and the whole earth was sanctified. Because he entered history, he made human history the history of salvation and sanctification. This is what the author of Hebrews meant when he wrote:

> At various times in the past and in various ways, God spoke to our ancestors through the prophets; but in our own time, the final epoch of man, he has spoken to us through his Son, the Son that he has appointed to inherit everything and through whom he made everything there is. He is the radiant light of God's glory and the perfect copy of his nature, sustaining the universe by his powerful command; and now that he has destroyed the defilement of sin, he has gone to take his place in heaven at the right hand of divine majesty (Heb 1:1–3).

We have also seen that Christ comes as king, priest, and prophet. He becomes our one mediator and the channel through whom God's life and holiness comes to man. From his fullness all must receive. It is in his own blood that a new and final call to man is made in the covenant of his own blood. It is the call to the fulfillment of the new creation, the new People of God. By incorporating his total membership into himself the holiness of Christ becomes the holiness of his whole Church.

The water used in baptism, by which we are incorporated into Christ, symbolizes not only the spiritual cleansing that takes place when one receives that sacrament; but it is also the symbol of growth. Water is necessary for every living being, plant, animal and man, if it is to grow. Consequently, water is an apt symbol also for the new supernatural life of God which is given by participation to the Christian through his incorporation into Christ. The soul, before baptism, is a spiritual desert, dry, sterile, lifeless, producing only dead works. "Amen, amen, I say to you, unless a man be born again of water and the Holy Spirit, he cannot enter the kingdom of God" (Jn 3:5). The dust from which every man is made, in the moment of baptism, is endowed with the animation of God's own life. The water and the words are the instruments used in this remarkable moment, but, as we have seen in our chapter on the liturgy, it is Christ who is acting, communicating the fullness of his own life to the Christian. He welcomes the new Christian into his kingdom. At this moment, the baptized is brought into the People of God, brought into a new and eternal covenant with God. Christ breathes a new life into the nostrils of the living chaos that is unredeemed man. The new Christian is a new being, a new creation, because of this merciful intervention of Christ, to whom the newly baptized man is now grafted. His whole being is transformed; the impress of Christ is upon him forever. All things now belong to him because he belongs to Christ and Christ belongs to his Father.[28] Now, he lives no longer himself, but Christ lives in him.[29]

By a man's very entrance into the kingdom of God, the People of God, and the Body of Christ, through the rite of initiation which is baptism, his personal sanctification is in one sense already achieved; his sins are forgiven and he is reconciled with God. At the same time baptism represents his vocation; with baptism he enters upon his life work; his sanctification and purification. Paul makes this quite clear, echoing the emphasis of Christ's Sermon on the Mount.[30] The Christian accepts with his membership in Christ the vocation to contribute to the health and growth of Christ's Body. By the commission of his Lord and Head, he is to bear fruit:

> I am the vine, you are the branches. Whoever remains in me, with me in him, bears fruit in plenty; for cut off from me you can do nothing. Anyone who does not remain in me is like a branch that has been thrown away — he withers; . . . It is to the glory of my Father that you should bear much fruit, and then you will be my disciples (Jn 15:5–8).

Whatever is said about Christian holiness, it is basically a growth in assimilation to God, who is love. God, we have seen, personifies the state of holiness by his very nature, and man participates in his holiness by sharing God's nature, and more specifically he grows in this participation and likeness by moral purity. Obviously, both this assimilation to God and man's growth in purity of heart is expressed most perfectly when his life is dominated by the God who is love[31] and by love for this God. It is true that charity alone does not constitute Christian perfection, but where there exists the habit of charity, there also coexists the other virtues and infused gifts by which man grows in his likeness to God. This explains the contention of St. Thomas that, more than faith or hope, charity attains God as he is in himself. Charity effects a closer union, so that the one loved is present in some way in the lover and the lover is drawn by his affection to union with the one loved, each

---

28 Cf. 1 Cor 3:23.
29 Cf. Gal 2:20.
30 Cf. 2 Cor 7:1; 1 Cor 7:34; 1 Tim 1:5; 2 Tim 5:8.
31 Cf. 1 Jn 4:16.

abiding in the other. The Christian vocation to holiness as a participation in the holiness of God and realizing its perfection most clearly in the virtue of charity, is neatly summarized by St. John in his First Epistle:

2:28 And now my dear children, abide in him. . . . Since you know that He is holy, you are also well aware that everyone who lives a holy life is a child of God.

3:2 We know that when he appears, we shall be like him, because we shall see him just as he is. Everyone who cherishes this hope in God strives to be holy, just as he is holy. . . . No one who abides in him sins; no one who sins has either appreciated or understood him.

He who lives a holy life is holy, just as God is holy. He who commits sin springs from the devil, because the devil has been sinning from the beginning. The Son of God made his appearance for the purpose of destroying sin, the work of the devil. No one who is a child of God sins, because the life-germ implanted by God abides in him, and so, he cannot sin [maliciously and habitually]. He is a child of God. Here is the sign which reveals who are God's children and who are the devil's: Whoever fails to live a good life is no child of God; neither is he who fails to love his brother.

3:14 We know that we have passed from death [of sin] to life [of grace in and through Christ] because we love our brothers. He who does not love abides in death. [He does not share the life of God, or participate in the holiness of God.]

3:16 Jesus taught us the meaning and manner of love [We know what love is from the fact that Jesus laid down his life for us in redeeming us]. We, too, ought to lay down our lives for our brothers.

3:24 He who keeps his commandments abides in God and God in him. It is the Spirit abiding in us who gives us the assurance that God abides in us.

4:4 You, little children, are born of God. . . . We are born of God.

4:7 Beloved, let us love one another, because love takes its origin in God, and everyone that loves is a child of God and knows God. He who has no love does not know God, because God is love. And God's love was made manifest among us by the fact that God sent his only-begotten Son into the world that we might have life [a participation in God's own life of love through Christ] through him. . . . Beloved, if God so loved us, we in turn ought to love one another.

4:12 No one has ever seen God, yet if we love one another, God abides in us and our love for Him reaches perfection. . . . God is love, and he who abides in love abides in God and God in him.

4:17 This love has become perfect through our cooperation . . . because, we in this world are likened to Christ [in heaven]. . . We exercise mutual love, because He loved us first. If anyone says: "I love God," yet hates his brother, he is a liar. Why? Because he who does not love his brother whom he sees, cannot love God whom he does not see. Besides, we have received this commandment from God: He who loves God must love his brother also.

5:6	He [Jesus] it is who came to make us victors by purifying and re-deeming us, and by the effusion of the Spirit. He made victory possible for us not merely by the water of baptism, but both by the water and by his own blood.

5:20	In fact, we are incorporated into this true one, God's Son, Jesus Christ. He is the true God and eternal life.

Consequently, the holiness to which every Christian is called, and which is already achieved essentially in the assimilation to God that is effected by baptism, is subject to growth. The growth of this assimilation or likeness to God is gained through personal, conscious, and free union with God, characterized by a love for and the doing of God's will, made known through Christ. It is this adherence to God's will that pervades the whole existence of the Christian who is united to God; and the greatest of all the commandments of this will is that love which unites as its object both God and neighbor. In the First Epistle of St. John, which we have quoted in part, the two themes are interwoven into one fabric: love of God — love of our fellowmen. They are such a unity that one cannot be had without the other. It is this love which augments our essential or constitutive holiness. It is this love which has a dynamism all its own. It is to be a continuous process of growth, intimately linked with human personality, its transformation, and divinization.

Of this love Christ is not only the channel of the graces which make this possible for us, but he offers in his own life a portrayal of a human nature completely united to God. It is from the fullness of God's life that was in Christ that we receive our life in and through Christ, which affords us our supernatural intimacy with God; it is the unfathomable riches of God given to us through Christ.[32] It is the meaning of Christ's own words: "I am come that they may have life, and have it abundantly" (Jn 10:10).

We might say that this fact of our Christian existence staggers the imagination, except for the fact that it does not represent so much a challenge to the imagination as to faith. When the Gentile Christians in Asia Minor were being persecuted, and were lapsing into pagan customs, St. Peter wrote to them from Rome:

Therefore, fervently and unaffectedly love one another from the bottom of your hearts. Because you have been born anew, not from a perishable, but

---

[32] Cf. Eph 3:8.

from an imperishable life-germ, through the living and eternal Word of God. In contrast, all things are like a plant, and their glory is like the bloom of a plant. The plant [eventually] withers and its bloom droops [and dies] but the Lord's word endures forever (1 Pet 1:22–25).

This new life, sacred and supernatural, which circulates in the Christian is a life that he must develop, defend, and nourish with the means given by Christ through the Church. Peter exhorts the persecuted neophytes in the same letter:

As obedient children do not conform yourselves to the evil desires which ruled you when you were in ignorance. On the contrary, after the model of the Holy One who called you, become yourselves holy in your entire conduct. So it is written, "You shall be holy, because I am holy" (1 Pet 1:14–16).

Peter tells these people that they are "a chosen race, a royal priesthood, a holy nation, a people that is God's possession" (1 Pet 2:9). God's predilection and choice has made them "living stones [of] a spiritual edifice, so as to be a holy priesthood to offer up spiritual sacrifices which will be acceptable to God through Jesus Christ" (1 Pet 1:5; 2 Tim 15:8). This participation in God's holiness, however, is offered not to individuals as such but rather is meant to create and form a People of God, because the life that animates this People and binds them together is not a common blood line, but the life of grace and holiness in the human soul of Christ, from whose fullness all the members of this People receive a share.

You are an edifice built on the foundation of the apostles and prophets with Christ Jesus himself as the chief cornerstone. In him the whole structure is being closely fitted together by the Spirit to become God's temple consecrated in the Lord. In him [Christ] you, too, are being fitted by the Spirit into the edifice to become God's dwelling place (Eph 2:20–22).

This is the Church that is the household of God, the assembly of those redeemed by Christ, filled with life by the Holy Spirit, who sanctifies, inspires, and guides. In this house men offer God homage and adoration; and each soul is itself a "holy temple of God," sanctified by the very presence of God. This divine presence within the Christian consecrates him as sacred, far more sacred than the most magnificent church, altar, or chalice. The Christian is set aside for God's use; not only set aside but divinized by sharing in God's life and God's holiness. His very soul has received the internal anointing of the Holy Spirit, who penetrates all his human faculties and consecrates them to the divine service, elevates them with new powers, and adapts them to the loving presence of God who abides in the Christian.

3. The Dynamics of Holiness

Personality is, in a psychological usage of that word, the expression of the person. When God creates a human being, this human being is endowed with remarkable natural endowments, which strive for self-expression. It is possible that all of the endowments could remain sterile, and unproductive if he does not use them. We call this use the dynamics of human personality and this self-expression the exercise of personality. So it is with the Church, that is the priestly community and People of God, so heavily endowed by God with supernatural powers. The *Constitution on the Church* of Vatican II, in speaking of this People of God, describes the dynamics of this corporate personality:

> Christ the Lord, High Priest taken from among men (Heb 5:1–5), made the new People "a kingdom of priests to God the Father" (Apoc 1:6; 5:9–10). The baptized, by regeneration and the anointing of the Holy Spirit, are consecrated as a spiritual house and a holy priesthood, in order that through all those works which are those of the Christian man they offer spiritual sacrifices and proclaim the power of Him who has called them out of darkness into His marvelous light (1 Pet 2:4–10). Therefore, disciples of Christ . . . should present themselves as a living sacrifice [gift] holy and pleasing to God (cf. Rom 12:1). Everywhere on earth they must bear witness to Christ and give an answer to those who seek an account of that hope of eternal life which is in them (cf. 1 Pet 3:15).
>
> . . . But the faithful, in virtue of their royal priesthood, join in the offering of the Eucharist. They likewise exercise their priesthood in receiving the sacraments, in prayer and thanksgiving, in the witness of a holy life and by self-denial and active charity.
>
> It is through the sacraments and the exercise of the virtues that the sacred nature and the organic structure of the priestly community is brought into operation. Incorporated in the Church through Baptism, the faithful are consecrated by the baptismal character to the worship of the Christian religion. Reborn as Sons of God they must confess before men the faith which they have received from God through the Church. More perfectly bound to the Church by the sacrament of Confirmation, they are endowed by the Holy Spirit with special strength so that they are more strictly obliged to spread and defend the faith, both by word and by deed, as true witnesses of Christ.
>
> Taking part in the Eucharistic Sacrifice, which is the font and apex of the whole Christian life, they offer the divine victim to God, and offer themselves along with it. . . . Strengthened at the holy table by the Body of Christ they then manifest in a concrete way that unity of the People of God which is suitably signified and wondrously brought about by this most holy sacrament.
>
> . . . . Fortified by so many and such powerful means (the Mass and Sacraments) of salvation, *all the faithful*, whatever their condition or state, are

called by the Lord, each in his own way, to that perfect holiness whereby the Father Himself is perfect.[33]

4. Epilogue on the Layman

In the following chapter of this text we will deal with the specific vocations within the Christian vocation, namely that of layman, religious and priest. However, in connection with the subject matter of this chapter, it is perhaps necessary to add this epilogue. Very sadly, the term *layman*, when spoken, has too often been charged with the inflection "only a layman," as though he were a second class citizen in the People of God. Too often, also, the distinction has been made between the *active* (the hierarchy) and *passive* (laity) Church. By way of further distortion of the truth the term "vocation" has been used in such a way that might conclude that only religious and priests have vocations. Hopefully, the Church is now outgrowing these badges of ignorance, which tend to be divisive within the People of God and the Body of Christ. Every member of this People and Body shares a common nobility, and is committed to the same common mission and fulfillment. All are sanctified by the same grace, and all are called to the same holiness. Christian perfection is the same for all: pope, bishops, priests, religious, and laity. All are consecrated by the same baptism and destined for the same salvation. There was no sound of qualification in the voice of Christ when he enjoined: "Be perfect as your heavenly Father is perfect" (Mt 5:48).

The *Constitution on the Church* tells us what we know, that in the Church everyone does not proceed via the same path, ". . . nevertheless all are called to high holiness and have received an equal privilege of faith through the justice of God, and if by the will of Christ some are made teachers, pastors, and dispensers of mysteries on behalf of others, yet all share the same true quality of dignity and vocation to build up the Body of Christ."[34] The same Constitution also tells us that "the laity are gathered together in the People of God and make up the Body of Christ under one Head. Whoever they are, they are called upon, as living members, to expend all their energy for the growth of the Church and its continuous sanctification since this very energy is a gift of the Creator and the blessing of the Redeemer."[35] However, because the vocation of the layman within the People of God and the Body of Christ is specified

---

[33] *Lumen Gentium*, no. 10–11.
[34] *Ibid.*, no. 32.
[35] *Ibid.*, no. 33.

by a unique function, what we might call "lay spirituality" can be distinguished from the spirituality of the priest or religious. We shall take this up at length in the following chapter.

The hundredfold promised by Christ to those who would leave all things for love of him is the inheritance of all Christians who are inwardly detached from the things of this world. We have wrongly misconstrued this promise to be the hope chest of those who pronounce the vows of priest or religious. The surrender that Christ asks, to be rewarded with a hundredfold, is the surrender of self, in love. This is truly the surrender of love, which asks nothing for itself, but seeks only to give, to contribute to the destiny and fulfillment of the People of God. The opposite of this love is self-seeking, a blinding sort of affliction that has eyes only for gain and acquisition, and that calculates only: "what's in it for me?" The self-centered person is one who walks along through life looking only at his own feet. The world about him is hostile, threatening, unyielding, and it is his opponent in a sad little game of chess. The man who loves does not clutch his possessions to his heart, because he seeks to share them; he is not anxious for his own glory, security, and his own great name. The hundredfold comes to those who die with Christ, who submit to the death which he himself commanded: the dying to self and selfish interests.

> I tell you the plain truth: Unless the grain of wheat falls into the earth and dies, it remains just one grain; but once it has died, it bears abundant fruit. He who holds his life dear destroys it; he who sets no store by his life in this world will preserve it for eternal life. Whoever would be in My personal service must follow me [he says this as he approaches his own passion and death]; and then, wherever I am, there too, my servant will be (Jn 12:24–26).

This is the torch the layman must carry into the darkened parts of our world, which he alone can enter; he is commissioned to do this by his baptism, strengthened to do it in his confirmation. He must make God present in his lonely environs; he must shape the world into a Christian world, dominated by love. In his family-life he is a co-creator with God, a co-teacher, and a co-ruler. And in all his life, he is a co-redeemer with Christ, filling up with himself the things that are wanting to the passion of Christ; he is forever shaping the world he lives in, redeeming it with Christ. His is a life of love and service; and wherever love and service come alive in this world, the redemption becomes active in that part of the world. And this is the point of unity in all Christian striving for holiness; all Christians, each according to his state and opportunities are men and women of love, redeeming and sanctifying the world with Christ. This is the universal vocation, in which the layman participates so vitally, to diffuse the life and powers of God which are his holiness. This is the prophetic holiness he displays in his witness to Christ within the secular city. This is his particular and absolutely essential way of actualizing the People of God and the Body of Christ, by wrestling with this world, mastering it, loving it, laying down his life for it, and laying it at the feet of Christ. He uses it, but as its Lord would use it; he gives his mind to it, but his thoughts are shaped by God's thoughts; but above all, he loves it, just as God loved it when he sent his only-begotten Son into the world to redeem it.[36] Within himself he shares God's own life and outside of himself he diffuses this life with his holiness to the world.

> They [the laity] are in their own way made sharers in the priestly, prophetical and kingly functions of Christ, and they carry out for their own part the mission of the whole Christian people in the Church and in the world.[37]

---

[36] Cf. Jn 3:16.
[37] Lumen Gentium, no. 31.

CHAPTER THIRTEEN

Laity and Religious in the Life of the Church

For just as in one body we have many members, yet all the members have not the same function, so we, the many are one body in Christ, and as part of the body we belong to one another (Rom 12:4–5).

Yet a man must so respond to God's call that, without consulting flesh and blood (Cf. Gal 1:16), he can devote himself wholly to the work of the Gospel. This response, however, can be made only when the Holy Spirit gives his inspiration and strength. . . . Therefore, the Christian must be ready to stand by his vocation for a lifetime, and to renounce himself and all those whom he thus far considered as his own, and instead to become "all things to all men" (1 Cor 9:22).

— Vatican II, Decree on the Missionary Activity of the Church, no. 44

Although we intend to differentiate the lay vocation from that of the religious in this chapter, following the example of Vatican II, actually the distinction, as the Council makes clear, is not canonical.

From the point of view of the divine and hierarchical structure of the Church, the religious state of life is not an intermediate state between the clerical and the lay states. Rather, the faithful of Christ are called by God from both these states of life so that they might enjoy this particular gift in the life of the Church, and thus each in his own way be of some service to the salvific mission of the Church.[1]

Clerics are those, according to Canon Law, who are ordained to the major holy orders. A religious is one who by vow embraces the life of the commandments and the counsels and thereby renders a special and specified witness to the Lord. Consequently, it is clear that members of religious orders, who are ordained to major holy orders, are both clerics and religious. Yet there are other religious, such as lay brothers and religious sisters, who are not ordained to these major orders, and thus canonically would be classified as lay people. Still, there is a basis for distinguishing between the states of the layman and the religious, according to the means of perfection used and the witness rendered in each of these states. Acknowledging such a distinction the Fathers of Vatican II addressed themselves in separate chapters, in the *Constitution on the Church*, to the laity in the Fourth Chapter and to religious in the Sixth Chapter.

1. Old Prejudices and New Lights Concerning the Laity

The word *laity* is derived from the Greek word *laos*, which in Sacred Scripture is used frequently to designate the *People of God*. However, in the more technical language of the Church, almost from the beginning, it was used to describe a state of life which had to be somehow classified in order to be differentiated from the state of the clergy and monks. The truth is that this lay state describes Christians who sanctify themselves in the midst of the world, by using the things of this world rather than withdrawing from them. However, as Canon Law gradually took form in the Church, the layman was unfortunately defined negatively by his not being a cleric.

Very often theological error has its own favorite quotations from the Scriptures. And in the undeserved insult to the lay-state that has been a part of our Christian heritage, the attempt to submerge the laity sought justification in the words of Paul to the Corinthians: "I would have you free from concern. He who is unmarried is concerned about the interests of the Lord, how he may please the Lord. But he who is married is concerned about worldly interests, how he may please his wife. Thus

---

[1] *Lumen Gentium*, no. 43.

his interests are divided" (1 Cor 7:32-34). Obviously, Paul did not mean that this "division" is necessarily a bad thing, but simply a different means of sanctification. At least this must be the interpretation as the Church now reads her Sacred Scriptures. But over the course of the centuries, by the overtones at least of Catholic ascetical literature, the lay state came to be considered a concession to the frailty of human nature. Pope Urban II (1088-1099), in an official document, wrote: "From the Church's beginnings, two ways of life have been opened to the faithful: one, to sustain the frailty of the weak (the lay state), the other to perfect the happy life of the strong . . . (clerical or religious state)."

The attitude of Pope Urban unfortunately was not an isolated or unique ignorance, but sadly represented the consensus thinking of a clerically dominated Church. It tended to deprive the layman of an *active* role in the affairs of the Church. It relegated the layman to the category of the carnal, weak, and worldly, and tended to distort the whole theology of the People of God. Such an attitude also has other distorted theological ramifications. It tends to define Christian life in terms of the renunciation of a supposedly evil world. It is blind to the natural values of the temporal order, and it is totally removed from the concept of the Body of Christ which is the Church.

As such a vision and posture tended to dominate ecclesiastical thinking, the function and nature of the Church fell into obscurity among Christians, and the lamentable heresy of personal isolation for sanctity became more and more the approved version of true holiness. The layman not only lost his status, but his sense of significance and the vision of his very important role in the People of God.

As a result, the definitive theology of the layman is not only looking for an author, but until very recently the theology of the layman was looking for contributors. Pope Paul VI once remarked to the International Congress of the Lay Apostolate that this new appreciation of the role of the layman and the recognition of his status is *the charism* of the modern Church. However, very often newly-found appreciation and recognition stumble for words, and the first search of those who have tried to articulate this new appreciation and recognition of the lay state was for a definition of this state and a description of the function of the layman within the Church. We have already alluded to the fact that, up to now, the layman has been defined by his not being a cleric. Some redress of this imbalance is afforded in the *Constitution on the Church* of Vatican II in its chapter "On The Laity." There has also been a wealth of recent literature attempting a theology of the layman.

One author, who acknowledges that his thought is based on that of

Karl Rahner, has described the layman as a Catholic whose state is characterized by marriage, ownership, and self-determination.[2] Another eminent author bases his description on the fact that the Greek word *laos* means "the people," and in Scripture is used in reference to the People of God. Consequently, the lay person is a member of the People of God assembled in the Church but set apart from the hierarchy — a separation, he says, which implies a reference to the profane or secular.[3] Still another author sees two aspects of the Church: one, the communal aspect, the collectivity of the assembled faithful who have an active function in achieving the work of God and in doing the work of the world, and second, the institutional or hierarchical aspect, the aggregate of the means of sanctification. The first aspect sees the Church as a community, working together for a common destiny to be achieved in this world; the second sees the Church as an institution, with hierarchical and prophetic offices, a kind of blueprint of the Church drawn up by Christ, and legitimately implemented by the successors of the apostles. The author feels that the second aspect has been so overstressed that we have lost our vision of the Church as a community, working together to redeem the world; consequently, we have subjected the layman to centuries of undeserved obscurity and inferiority. He feels that we must now develop the communal aspect and learn to see the layman, consequently, as the man for whom, in the work confided to him by God, the reality of things in themselves becomes the area of his redemptive apostolate. This reality of things in themselves and their natural values are not swallowed up and destroyed simply because they must be related to a higher, supernatural principle and order.[4]

In his own work,[5] Father Rahner investigates the positive and the negative aspects of the layman's identity. He denies the historical overtones that *layman* suggests the profane, the ignorant, the non-ecclesiastical, the indifferent. The layman is not the passive object of the hierarchical powers in the Church. More positively, the layman's role in the Church does not determine his role in the world but vice versa. The specific responsibility of the layman in the world specifies his responsibility in the Church. The layman has a specific place in the Church; he is a member of the Church and he exercises his function wherever the

---

[2] John D. Gerken, *Toward a Theology of the Layman* (New York: Herder and Herder, 1963), p. 10.

[3] Edward Schillebeeckx, *The Layman in the Church* (Staten Island: Alba House, 1963), p. 35.

[4] Yves Congar, *Lay People in the Church* (Westminster, Md.: Newman, 1957), p. 22 ff.

[5] Karl Rahner, *Theological Investigations* (Baltimore: Helicon, 1963), Vol. II, pp. 318–330.

Church confronts and contacts the world and the temporal order. The layman, as no one else in the Church can do, must render the grace which God invests in him historically tangible. This is the charism or grace which characterizes the function of the layman within the Church. As a member of the Body of Christ, he is without question charged with a serious responsibility to assist the Church in her mission. His service of the Church is the Church's mission. However, the dedication of the layman to this responsibility and mission must complete, not destroy, his nature as a layman.

The *Constitution on the Church* does not succeed totally in refining a positive and dynamic definition of the layman or his function within the Church. In fact, it even slips into the old regret of defining by opposition, saying that the laity is meant to include "all the faithful except those in holy orders and those in the state of Religious Life especially approved by the Church."[6] In a more effective part of the same paragraph, the *Constitution* says:

> What specifically characterizes the laity is their secular nature. . . . By their very vocation, they seek the kingdom of God by engaging in temporal affairs and by ordering them according to the plan of God. They live in the world, that is in each and all of the secular professions and occupations. They live in the ordinary circumstances of family and social life, from which the very web of their existence is woven. They are called there by God that, by exercising their proper function and led by the Spirit of the Gospel, they may work for the sanctification of the world from within as a leaven.[7]

Perhaps all these definitions and descriptions converge into a reasonably clear portrait, although theological thinking will have to eliminate many areas of shadow. This much at least is clear: every state of life within the Church is a role of specific service, which is indispensable to the mission of the whole People of God and Body of Christ, which is the Church. Consequently, it is dissatisfying to characterize the layman by opposing him to the cleric or religious, by saying what he is not. Somehow the layman must seek the self-identity and arrive at some kind of a self-image in terms of his service to the world and therefore to the Church.

2. The Layman and the World

The world is not evil or sinful in itself. What God created he saw as very good. It is only because of man's sinful use of the good things which

---

[6] *Lumen Gentium*, no. 31.
[7] *Ibid.*

God has made that this world stands in need of redemption, and this redemption can be achieved only by men who think rightly about the things of this world, knowing that they are good, and using them accordingly. This redemption can be achieved only by the layman, for through him alone can the Church seriously affect the temporal order.

All creation awaits with eager longing the manifestations of the sons of God. For creation was made subject to vanity not by its own choice but by the will of man who made it subject [to vanity], yet with the hope that creation itself would be delivered from its slavery to corruption, to enjoy the freedom that comes with the glory of the children of God. For we know that all creation groans and travails in pain until now (Rom 8:19–22).

The "creation" to which Paul refers is that which is to be gathered under one Head, Christ.[8] It embraces the "all things" that belong to the Christian, who belongs to Christ, who in turn belongs to God.[9] It is the world in which men save or lose their souls: the world of newspapers, television, movies, industry, factories, schools, and families. Only by the influence of Christians who know that these things are good and who use them accordingly, can this world of creation come to enjoy the freedom from vanity for which it groans. Obviously, this is the enormously important work of Christians who are willing to stay in the world, to wrestle with it, and in the sense indicated to redeem it. This is the vocation of the layman.

We have already alluded to Paul's concept of the Church as the "Body of Christ," and to his insistence on the community of the members of this Body, the common life and destiny as well as the diversity of parts and functions of these members.

God has put the members, every last one of them in the body as he wished so that the eye cannot say to the hand "I have no need of you," nor the head to the feet, "I have no need of you." On the contrary, much rather are those members of the body necessary, which seem the weakest (1 Cor 12:4–31; cf. Rom 12:4–6).

Obviously the layman is that hand of the Church which holds the values of the temporal, secular order: and, if the Church is destined to Christianize this world, to gather it under one Head, Christ, then this hand holds the destiny and mission of the Church in a very vital way within its grasp.

The vocation of the layman certainly implies an active role in the mission of the Church. Rahner sees the layman giving that specific witness to Christ which testifies that the Church and its program of life can and do exist harmoniously among men. The committed layman is a living

---

8 Cf. Eph 1:10.
9 Cf. 1 Cor 3:23.

illustration of the fact that the Christian vocation does not do violence to the nature of man or deny the natural values of creation but rather embellishes man as a human being and safeguards the values of creation. In the layman alone, according to Rahner, there can be the perfect illustration of this fact. Rahner believes that such a perfect illustration is impossible in the lives of religious, who are defined in their state of life by vows and community life.

The life of the vows testifies to a spirit of belief that the center of human existence in the Mystical Body is found outside the natural; the religious reminds the world that true and full perfection lies outside the realm of nature in the supernatural bounty of God, and that the highest aspirations of man lie beyond and above the highest goods of nature. The witness of religious life reminds men that we have not here a lasting city, but are destined for a life in which there is no giving or taking in marriage, no mine and thine of individual possession, and no conflict of wills. In his vows of chastity, poverty and obedience, the religious, in a sense, lives this life of the hereafter in the here and now.

However, if the Mystical Body is designed for such an eschatological state and finality, it is nevertheless in actual existence in the world of nature also. If the religious witness is to that which is above the goods of this world and beyond the here and now, the layman's witness is to the harmony of grace and nature in this world, through which man passes on his way to his eternal destiny. Father Gerken puts it this way:

> The life of the Church exists on the existential plane as well as on the sacramental. That life, because it exists in visible creatures, must manifest itself. There are two essential characteristics of that life: first it is cosmic or worldly, that is, it can and must express this life; second, it is eschatological and transcendental, that is, it looks to its full perfection in the supernatural life of Jesus Christ who is to come at the end of time and give to the Church the fullness of this life. Consequently, these characteristics must manifest themselves in the daily (existential) life of the Church. Only a permanent surrender of the highest goods of man can manifest in the daily life of the Church this transcendental-eschatological characteristic. Only an embracing of the lay life can manifest the cosmic or worldly characteristic of the Church's life. These manifestations can be true manifestations of the Church's life only if each group admits that the other's way of life is a true expression of the Christian life. This admission, this living in the unity of love of the Church, is the full sign of the Church's interior life.[10]

In other words, the Church must witness externally her inner reality or interior life, and this life has firm roots both in this world and in the world to come. Both must be manifest in the witness of the corporate Church, and witnessing to the inner life of the Church in the here and

---

[10] Gerken, op. cit., p. 70.

now is the work of laymen. The classic rejection of religion on the grounds that it is concerned only with a world to come, while the poor starve and die, must be rebutted by the testimony and witness of the life of the Church in this world, and the concern of the Church for the values which we call "natural." This is what is meant by the *consecration of the world,* of which Pope Pius XII spoke, the "new order" which he envisioned.

It would be a mistake to separate the witness of the layman and that of the religious so completely that one could conclude that all cosmic witness is the responsibility of the layman and all eschatological and transcendental witness is the duty of the religious who forfeit the goods of this world by vow. Rahner explicitly disclaims this error. It is rather a question of a purpose or a role which specifies a state, and which provides a basis for a theoretical and theological distinction between the lay and religious vocations. Obviously, religious will to some limited extent deal with the things of this world, and the laity will to some extent surrender them when called upon to do so by a higher purpose. *The Constitution on the Church* tells us:

> The Holy Spirit "allotting His gifts to everyone according as He wills" (2 Cor 8:11) distributes special graces among the faithful of every rank. By these gifts He makes them the fit and ready instruments to undertake the various tasks and offices which contribute towards the renewal and building up of the Church. . . . Each individual part contributes through its own special gifts to the good of other parts and of the whole Church.[11]

When the Word of God was made flesh, God made his most incredible entrance into human history, clearly revealing that he would make human history the history of salvation and redemption. Still the graciousness of God does not coerce men but rather tries to win them back by love. In a sense, the sins of men are all a form of idolatry, the worship of false gods which promise so much more than the God who first gave man his life. In a sense now the world of man that God wishes to redeem had taken itself for its own destiny in a monstrous idolatry; and the civilization of man has been buried in earthliness. In man's rebellious departure from God, he has not only lost God but has distorted the true meaning of the world that meets his senses and asks him questions. The world can have meaning and be truly understood only in the light of its origins. To know what a thing is you must know where it came from.

In asserting his own liberty and independence of God, man has lost his true liberty as a child of God; he has fallen into the enslavement of the creatures to which he turned and to which he offered the incense of his adoration. Yet deep within the heart of man lie two restless spirit-

---

[11] *Lumen Gentium,* no. 18.

ual aspirations: the quest for God and the quest for civilization. These two aspirations really form a unity in man, for man instinctively seeks unity between the natural and the supernatural aspects of God's work; he instinctively seeks to put each in the service of helping to understand the other. He cannot live comfortably with the torture of double vision; he cannot departmentalize his life and mind. Such disunity would be disquieting to man, for harmony is the law of God within him.

So man constructs civilizations and cultures, even without knowing it, so that he might respond more fully to the supernatural summons of his God to enter a life of divine unity and love. Only a truly religious orientation can give meaning to the temporal aspects of man's life; and conversely, only a true temporal orientation can open man's vision to the invitations of God to life in all its fullness, in the human condition.

Yet there is an autonomy in each of these dimensions of human life and activity, the natural and the supernatural, and man must respect this metaphysical separation. But such autonomy is not one that precludes unity and mutual influence. Unless faith serves to unify civilization, as Christopher Dawson has maintained, civilization will collapse and degenerate into complete secularism. The lord of creation, who is man, will be mastered by his subject; he will gouge and claw to possess what he can, and will violate the rights of others, and scorch the earth with his hot desires. And this way can lie only the deepest human agony.

It is the urgent and imperative task of the Catholic layman to supply from the abundance of the faith that fills him a correct orientation of the temporal aspects of human life. He is consecrated by his role in the Body of Christ, to civilization and to temporal goals, as a part of God's work. By contrast, the function of the religious and priest would seem to be to safeguard, primarily at least, the supernatural goals and realities of life. To do this, the priest and religious must be in close touch with the progress and pitfalls of civilization. But it is the Catholic layman who must assume the responsibility to promote civilization itself, and to direct it to those natural ends which are truly human. In doing this, he will dispose man for God's grace, and render the world ready to reply to the love of God who is love.

3. The Messianic Offices of Christ in the Church

Father Yves Congar distinguishes, as we have seen, between the communal and the institutional or hierarchical aspects of the Church. Under the first aspect, the communal, the Church is seen as a collectivity and a community; under the second, the Church is viewed rather according to its structure, which is hierarchical. Father Congar laments that the second aspect has been overstressed and the first seriously neglected. Both are, of course, true aspects of the Church. Christ did structure his Church to be hierarchical, built on the foundation of the apostles and their successors, who have historically delegated a part of their own powers to the priesthood. The bishops of the Church, as the successors of the apostles, are the recipients not only of the offices to rule, to teach, and to sanctify the Church, but are given the charismatic graces needed in the discharge of these responsibilities. These offices, because they are originally those of Christ the Messiah, are called the messianic offices. We usually distinguish the messianic role of Christ by the titles of priest (the office of sanctifying), prophet (the office of teaching), and king, (the office of ruling). While it is true that the hierarchy (the bishops together with the Roman Pontiff) possesses the supreme power of these offices, if we consider the Church as an institution, it is nevertheless true that the whole Church participates in these messianic energies of Christ because Christ continues to live in his entire Body and redeem the world through all its members. According to Father Congar's distinction, if we consider the Church under its institutional aspect, it is the hierarchy that possesses the messianic offices; however if we consider the same Church under its communal or community aspect, it is the whole Church that exercises these redemptive functions of Christ. Father Congar writes:

> The Church is hierarchically royal, sacerdotal, and prophetical in order that she may transmit the life that is in Christ to men; (all) the faithful incorporated into Him live spiritually by a life that is kingly, priestly and prophetical.[12]

Jesus Christ is, of course, the one Lord and High Priest of his Church, and he was ordained such by his Father.[13] However, the priestly powers that are his he has delegated to others, in varying degrees. Historically, the notion of *priesthood* is related to the offering of *sacrifices*. In general, those religious sects which offer a sacrifice have a priesthood; those which do not refer to their clergy as "ministers" rather than as priests. The priesthood, which involves the power of holy orders, is called the hierarchical priesthood; the universal priesthood, shared by all the faithful as a participation in the priesthood of Christ the one Lord, and the one High Priest of all, is commonly called "the priesthood of the faithful."[14] Congar gives the following succinct formulation of the levels of Christian priesthood:

---

[12] Congar, *op. cit.*, p. 108.
[13] Cf. Heb 5.
[14] Cf. Bishop Emile-Joseph de Smedt, *The Priesthood of the Faithful* (New York: Deus Books [Paulist Press], 1962).

One alone is Priest, Christ, who is Alpha, Omega and the Way. Between alpha and omega his priesthood is shared in sacramentally, with a view to the sacramental celebration of the sacrifice: (a) by all at Baptism (and Confirmation), in order to join in that celebration; (b) by some, hierarchically, at Ordination, in order to carry out that celebration. All are priests through their spiritual life in Christ, which is the priesthood of the last and final reality.[15]

The Constitution on the Church declares that Christ bestows upon the laity

. . . they share in His priestly function of offering spiritual worship for the salvation of men. . . . For all their works, prayers and apostolic endeavors, their ordinary married and family life, their daily occupations, their physical and mental relaxation if carried out in the spirit, and even the hardships of life if patiently borne — all these become "spiritual sacrifices acceptable to God through Jesus Christ" (1 Pet 2:5).[16]

The laity are an integral and essential part of the priestly People of God, and they discharge a priestly function in their participation in the liturgy and by their own private acts of love and sacrifice. In the liturgical sacrifice the layman is not a passive spectator. In fact, it is the whole Mystical Body that offers the whole Christ in the Mass. It remains true, of course, that the hierarchical priest alone has the powers of consecration, which is the essential moment of offering, but it is really Christ, the one High Priest of all, who consecrates through his ordained priest.

St. Peter refers to the Christian community as "a holy priesthood, to offer spiritual sacrifices acceptable to God through Jesus Christ" (1 Pet 2:5). He also insists that all Christians together are now "a chosen race, a royal priesthood, a holy nation, a purchased people" (1 Pet 2:9). John, in the book of revelation (Apocalypse), writes: (You) have made them for our God a kingdom and priests, and they shall reign over the earth" (Apoc 15:10). Later he writes ". . . They will be priests of God and Christ, and will reign with him a thousand years" (Apoc 20:6).

It is interesting to note that a great preponderance of theological writing by the Fathers, theologians, and the Magisterium of the Church,[17] refers these texts to the priesthood of the faithful and not to that of the clergy. The classic interpretation of the Fathers is that every Christian shares in the priesthood of Christ because he is a member of Christ; from the moment he puts on Christ, he is made a sharer in his priestly worship of the Father. The pre-Reformation tradition always contrasted the priesthood of the faithful, not to the priesthood of holy orders, but to the non-

---

[15] Congar, op. cit., p. 164.
[16] Lumen Gentium, no. 33.
[17] Cf. P. Dabin, Le sacerdoce des fidèles dans les livres saints (Paris, Bloud and Gay, 1941); le sacerdoce royal des fidèles dans la tradition ancienne et moderne (Paris, Desclée de Brouwer, 1950).

priesthood of the non-baptized. Baptism was rightly regarded as a form of consecration to the service and worship of God, and the *laity*, in its original connotation, meant a consecrated People. Only gradually did it come to be used to denote those who are not members of the clergy.

The priesthood of the faithful is a reality, not a mere metaphor; it involves a status and the vocation to perfection, and to divine worship; and it is conferred by the sacraments of initiation. As indicated, it is not only their participation in the offering of the Mass, but the living out of that offering. Since they are inseparably joined to Christ as members to Head, the offering of the Mass not only includes the life and death of Christ, but the life and the dying of every Christian.

In his encyclical, *Mediator Dei*, Pope Pius XII fully endorses the teaching of St. Thomas Aquinas that the Christian is deputed, in virtue of his sacramental character and consecration, to offer the Mass with the ordained priest and to participate in other official Christian acts of worship. The People of God is indeed a priestly people, and this priesthood includes all Christ's members. Christ also has entrusted his *kingly* office to the whole Church. It is evident that if the will of God alone rules the Church and the function of the kingly office of Christ now is to mediate that will of God, then all participate in this messianic function. The royal power of Christ is pre-eminently a power of service, the service of the Mystical Body. No legislator would act wisely who did not consult the needs and suggestions of those he governs. The hierarchy needs a continual feedback of ideas and representations from the entire Church to assist its own graces and wisdom; and the laity has a clear obligation to support this need.

The layman further participates in the royal power of Christ in his *active acceptance* of the government of the hierarchy, which has the ultimate power of discretion in the pursuit of the will of God. Only through this acceptance, and a corporate sensitivity to the will of God as forwarded to us through the hierarchy, can this royal power attain its full effect. The whole royal People of God is called upon to accept this will by the very active process of making that will its own and translating it into action. In both its exercise of free speech and in its obedience, the laity erects lines of communication and dialogue between head and members, and charges the whole Church with the living presence of Christ the King and the full influence of His royal power.

Finally, the *Constitution on the Church* makes specific reference to the *prophetic* office of the laity. It is perhaps one of the most dynamic challenges that stands before the layman.[18] The layman is called to make

---

[18] Cf. our chapter on "Free Speech and Public Opinion in the Church."

a productive and original contribution to the effective fulfillment of this messianic office of Christ performed by the Church. It is an area of almost unlimited possibility. Essentially, the *prophet* is the mouthpiece or spokesman of God, for through him God speaks to his People. To prophesy, in the last analysis, means to *teach*, and that which the prophet of Christ must teach is Christ himself. Again, in this office as in the other two messianic offices, the hierarchy holds the ultimate power of discrimination and discernment of spirit in the conservation and explanation of God's revelation to man.[19] However, this revelation must be kept relevant for each and every generation; it must be learned in living a way of life, for Christian revelation is not a body of speculative knowledge as much as a program of life. Consequently, God's revelation to man must be re-thought and re-worded by and for each changing generation. In the discharge of this responsibility, the whole Christian community and People of God must accept its own very important role. The Holy Spirit who works in and vivifies the whole community will express himself through the guidance he gives to the whole Body of Christ. This is the *sensus fidelium* (the sense or instinct of the faithful) to which *The Constitution* alludes, and which has always been regarded in the Church as normative in the effort of the Church to understand God's revelation.

Of course, the layman must be a prophet to his world of secular concern. His voice of prophecy must arise and surmount the sounds of conflict that distract the inhabitants of our modern world. Whether he be a factory worker, a scientist, a politician or a farmer, he is primarily identified as a member of the Body of Christ and to his world and to those whose lives cross his he must be a mystical reincarnation of Christ. "I live now, no longer I, but Christ lives in me" (Gal 2:20). If a Christian is deeply imbued with the conviction that the things of this world are from God and consequently good, and that man, as the lord of creation, must think of them rightly and use them accordingly, he will prophesy from his factory, construction job, laboratory, learned journal, from city hall, business office, or within his own household. The redemption of the world is at work wherever there is such a Christian. The bedrock truth is put clearly in *The Constitution on the Church:*

> Christ the Great Prophet, Who proclaimed the kingdom of His Father both by the testimony of His Life and the power of His words continually fulfills his prophetic office until the complete manifestation of glory. He does this not only through the hierarchy who teach in His name and with His authority, but also through the laity whom He has made His witnesses and to whom He has given an understanding of the faith (*sensu fidei*) and

---

[19] Cf. our chapter on "Authority in the Church," esp. to the section on the magisterial prerogatives and office.

an attractiveness in speech (cf. Acts 2:17–18; Apoc 10) so that the power of the gospel might shine forth in their daily social and family life.

. . . so, too, the laity go forth as powerful proclaimers of a faith in things to be hoped for (cf. Heb 11, 1) when they courageously join to their profession of faith a life springing from faith. This evangelization, that is, this announcing of Christ by a living testimony as well as by the spoken word, takes on a specific quality and a special force in that it is carried out in the ordinary surroundings of the world.

In connection with the prophetic function, that state of life which is sanctified by a special sacrament, is obviously of great importance, namely, married and family life. For where Christianity pervades the entire mode of family life, and gradually transforms it, one will find there both the practice and an excellent school of the lay apostolate. . . . The Christian family loudly proclaims both the present virtues of the kingdom of God and the hope of a blessed life to come.[20]

In these times of *aggiornamento* the Church is redressing the imbalances of the past, is apologizing to the newly "emerging layman,"[21] and attempting to restore him to his proper and very important status in the Church. The future role of the layman within the Church and in confrontation with the world is filled with mystery and challenge, but, in a sense, he is the master of his own fate and future. Rebellious attitudes are silly and immature, not to mention that they are un-Christian. Still the layman must, in all charity and with due respect for the divinely appointed offices of authority in the Church, assert himself with firmness and determination. Christ redeemed the world as priest, king, and prophet; and the *entire* Church, which is his Body, must continue to redeem the world in the exercise of these messianic offices. In each of them, both in their hierarchical and communal aspects, the laity has a vital role. In a very true sense, the future of the Church is in lay hands, as is the consecration of the world which they are called to redeem, not to forsake.

The basic demand of Christ in the Christian is *holiness*. The holiness and perfection of the layman will be achieved in the world, by using the things of this world, or it will not be achieved at all. The layman must "grace" the world, communicate the fruits of Christ's redemption to the world out of the abundance of his own grace-filled soul. His "spirituality" or avenue of perfection will involve him deeply in the good world that God has created and which man has at times abused. The Christian layman's attitudes toward love, sex, money, other men, and religion must resound with the spirit of Christ. He will offer the whole Christ, Head

---

[20] *Lumen Gentium*, no. 35.

[21] Cf. Donald Thorman, *The Emerging Layman* (Garden City, New York: Doubleday, 1962).

and members, to the Father in the sacrifice of the Mass, but his own life will be on the paten of offering because he is a member of Christ. There are no facile solutions to the problems he will face in the world, but he alone is competent to work toward these solutions, since it is his unique vocation to redeem the world by being in it. He alone can effectively put these solutions into practice.

The term laity is here understood to mean all the faithful except those in Holy Orders and those in a religious state sanctioned by the Church. These faithful are by Baptism made one body with Christ and are established among the People of God. They are in their own way made sharers in the priestly, prophetic, and kingly functions of Christ. They carry out their own part in the mission of the whole Christian people with respect to the Church and the world.[22]

A secular quality is proper and special to laymen[23] . . . by their very vocation, they seek the kingdom of God by engaging in temporal affairs and by ordering them according to the plan of God. They live in the world, that is, in each and in all of the secular professions and occupations. They live in the ordinary circumstances of family and social life, from which the very web of their existence is woven.

They are called there by God so that by exercising their proper function and being led by the spirit of the gospel they work for the sanctification of the world from within, in the manner of leaven. . . . The layman is closely involved in temporal affairs of every sort. It is therefore his special task to illumine and organize these affairs in such a way that they may always start out, develop, and persist according to Christ's mind, to the praise of the Creator and the Redeemer.[24]

Therefore, by their competence in secular fields and by their personal activity, elevated from within by the grace of Christ, let them labor vigorously so that by human labor, technical skill, and civic culture created good may be perfected for the benefit of every last man, according to the design of the Creator and the light of His Word.

Moreover, let the laity also by their combined efforts remedy any institutions and conditions of the world which are customarily an inducement to sin, so that all such things may be conformed to the norms of justice and may favor the practice of virtue rather than hinder it. By so doing, laymen will imbue culture and human activity with moral values. They will better prepare the field of the world for the seed of the Word of God. At this time they will open wider the Church's doors, through which the message of peace can enter the world.[25]

Each individual layman must stand before the world as a witness to the resurrection and life of the Lord Jesus and as a sign that God lives. As a

---

[22] Note that the Council attempts a positive definition of the layman in terms of his baptism and active role within the People of God.

[23] Cf. the whole of the Decree on the Church in the Modern World.

[24] The first three paragraphs here are from Lumen Gentium, no. 31.

[25] Ibid., no. 36.

body and individually the laity must do their part to nourish the world with spiritual fruits (Cf. Gal 5:22), and to spread abroad in it that spirit by which are animated those poor, meek, and peacemaking men whom the Lord in the gospel calls blessed (Cf. Mt 5:3–9). In a word, "what the soul is to the body, let Christians be to the world."[26]

4. Religious Life in the Life of the Church

Presently someone approached him and said: "Rabbi, is there something good that I can do so as to win eternal life?" He said to him: "Why do you consult me about something good you could do? There is One who is absolutely good! If you want to enter eternal life, keep the commandments." "Which commandments?" the young man asked. And Jesus said: "These: 'Do not murder; do not commit adultery; do not steal; do not bear false witness; honor father and mother; and love your neighbor as yourself.'" "I have observed all these things," the young man replied, "what am I still lacking?"

"If you want to be perfect," Jesus said to him, "go and sell all your possessions and give the proceeds to the poor — for which you will have an investment in heaven; then come back and be my follower" (Mt 19:16–21).

When we consider the religious state, it must be, as with the lay state, in the context of the life of and service to the Church. It is precisely this perspective that *The Constitution on the Church* reflects in its chapters on these two states of life.[27]

From the point of view of the divine and hierarchical structure of the Church, the religious state of life is not an intermediate one between the clerical and lay states. Rather, the faithful of Christ are called by God from both these latter states of life so that they may enjoy this particular gift in the life of the Church and thus each in his own way can forward the saving mission of the Church.[28]

As a special manner or way of life by which one responds to the universal call to holiness, religious life is defined by the Council[29] in terms of the evangelical counsels of chastity, poverty, and obedience. The religious, whether living as a solitary or in a religious community, embraces by vows the life of the commandments and the counsels in his state of life and witness to Christ. As a state of life, the religious state is not an in-between state, distinct from the clerical[30] and the lay state, but represents rather an added commitment of members of both these states to

---

[26] *Ibid.*, no. 38.

[27] Cf. Chap. 4 on The Laity, and Chap. 6 on Religious.

[28] *Lumen Gentium*, no. 43.

[29] *Ibid.*

[30] Cf. *Code of Canon Law*, Canon 108, No. 1: ". . . those marked for the divine ministry at least through first tonsure."

Christian perfection, and one which embraces the life of the counsels. *The Constitution on the Church* portrays this state of life in terms of an added commitment of religious to Christian perfection which constitutes a fuller imitation of Christ and a special sign to the world of the continued saving presence of Christ in his Church and in the world.[31]

If, however, the religious state represents an added commitment and a more intense dedication and assimilation to Christ, it cannot be judged as though it were a question of addition and subtraction. The religious commits himself to the commandments and the counsels; therefore, his is the better way. Such logic is open to grave delusion. The commandments are the heart of the Christian life and of Christian perfection, especially the commandment of love. Our dedication and assimilation to Christ is achieved mainly in our imitation of the love of Christ and fidelity to the commandments. The counsels and religious vows are not added commandments or even added heights of perfection; they are rather special means to insure the attainment of Christian perfection which is epitomized in perfect love. All Christians are called to the same heights of perfection. Some are called by God to achieve this perfection in and through the means of secular involvement; others are called to achieve this perfection in and through the means of the evangelical counsels. God calls some to achieve this perfection in the lay state and others he invites to achieve this perfection in the religious state, ". . . thus organizing the saints for the work of the ministry, which consists in building up the Body of Christ, until we all attain the perfect unity in faith and a deep knowledge of the Son of God" (Eph 4:13).

5. Religious Vows and Christian Perfection

The Code of Canon Law defines religious life as "a stable and communal way of life in which the faithful, besides the precepts common to all, propose to observe as well the evangelical counsels of Christ through the vows of obedience, chastity, and poverty."[32] In this definition the "precepts common to all" describe the essence of Christian perfection, as we have remarked, and all Christians by virtue of their incorporation into the Body of Christ, through baptism, are to strive for the perfection outlined in the general command or precept of Christ: "Be perfect, then, as your heavenly Father is perfect" (Mt 5:48). In the encounter between Christ and the rich young man, related above, Jesus delineates the lines of demarcation between the commandments and the counsels. He tells the

---

[31] *Lumen Gentium*, no. 44.
[32] *Code of Canon Law*, Canon 487.

young man to keep the commandments if he would enter eternal life. He also indicates as a means or guarantee of this observance of the commandments a life that embraces the counsels as well as the commandments. If one reads on in the text cited, he hears Jesus describing the attachment to richness as an obstacle to entrance into the kingdom of heaven: "I tell you frankly: a rich man will find it difficult to enter the kingdom of heaven. I repeat: it is easier for a camel to pass through the eye of a needle than for a rich man to enter the kingdom of God" (Mt 19:23–24). And he subsequently praises the single eye that is willing to renounce for the kingdom of God: "And everyone who has left houses, brothers, sisters, father, mother, children or land for the sake of my name will be repaid a hundred times over, and also inherit eternal life" (Mt 19:29).

Everyone who is baptized is consecrated by that baptism and is marked with an indelible character. This character not only marks the person as a member of Christ's Body and the People of God, but marks him with a participation in the death and resurrection of Christ. Christ entered into his glory by his submission to suffering, through his passion and death, thereby determining our itinerary of salvation. Somehow the Christian must go with Christ, participate in his passion and death and thus enter into his resurrection. This is precisely the significance and the accomplishment of baptism. In baptism we die with Christ and we rise with Christ.[33]

Religious vows are not a second baptism, though many theologians have compared the effects of baptism to the effects of these vows. There can be no such thing as a second baptism but only renewals of the consecration effected in baptism. In these renewals the Christian chooses Christ all over again, and reconsecrates himself to Christ's redemptive work.

Religious profession of vows is not strictly a renewal of baptism, although it clearly embraces renewal. It is rather a serious and generous decision to live out the consecration of baptism, the confirmation and assimilation to Christ and dedication to his work, by the very decisive act to forego everything which could be an obstacle to this new divine life acquired in the regeneration of baptism. This is the *positive* aspect of religious profession: its choice to live a life of assimilation and dedication to Christ. The *negative* aspects are the separation, the renunciation, and the self-denial implied and accepted in these vows. Somehow these are the eye-catching aspects of religious profession, but they have no meaning or value unless one sees them as a means to identification with Christ. The renunciation of religious profession is the fullness, in a sense, of the radical renouncement which baptism implies.

---

[33] Cf. Rom 6:1–11.

Do you not know that all of us who have been baptized into union with Christ Jesus have been baptized into union with his death? Yes, we were buried in death with him by means of baptism, in order that, just as Christ was raised from the dead by the glorious power of the Father, so we also may conduct ourselves by a new principle of life. Now since we have grown to be one with Him through a death like his, we shall also be one with him by a resurrection like his. We know that our old self has been crucified with him, in order that the body enslaved to sin may be reduced to impotence, and we may no longer be slaves to sin; for he who is dead is once and for all through with sin. But if we have died with Christ, we believe that we shall also live with him, since we know that Christ, having risen from the dead, will die no more. . . . The death that he died was a death to sin once and for all, but the life that he lives is a life for God. Thus you too must consider yourselves dead to sin, but alive to God in Christ Jesus (Rom 6:1–11).

The baptized Christian, therefore, is dead to sin (the negative aspect or renunciation), but alive to God in Christ Jesus (the positive aspect or assimilation to Christ). It is this death and this life that is realized with a total fullness in the religious profession of the vows. It not only implies a separation from sin but from everything that could be an occasion of separating one from Christ, and attaching a man to any other master other than Christ. When we speak of religious as being separated from the world by their vows, this is not to say that religious should be tucked away safely in a sequestered ivory tower. They, like all Christians, are meant to be a leaven in the mass, the salt of the earth, a light to and within the world. The world from which religious separate themselves in religious profession of vows is the world of carnal desires and man's own will,[34] the world that does not acknowledge Christ,[35] the world for which Christ refused to pray.[36]

Paul generally equates sin with lust,[37] and to renounce sin means to refuse to submit to all earthly lust. These lusts are scripturally represented by earthly possessions, bodily pleasures, and self-will. Of course, there is a regulated and Christian use of earthly possessions, bodily pleasures, and one's own will. But these things so easily tyrannize a man, and accordingly, the religious renounces at a high cost all possibility of such tyranny by his vows of poverty, chastity, and obedience. This renunciation, however, is a good for the Christian and religious only in the context of liberation. The detachment implied in the vows has value only in the light of the attachment and conformation to Christ which it serves to

---

[34] Cf. Jn 1:13.
[35] Cf. Jn 1:10.
[36] Cf. Jn 17:9.
[37] Cf. Rom 1:26–27; 5:12–19; 7:24–25; 11:17–22; 1 Cor 4:4; 5:9–10; 6:9–10; 10:1–13; Eph 5:5.

guarantee. Human nature abhors a vacuum, and the vows of religious life are not meant to make this of any human being.

The important thing is not to define the religious state in terms of its negative characteristics; such a definition would make religious life seem a stifling, prohibitive, and isolating program of human disintegration. Rather, religious life must be defined in terms of assimilation to Christ who himself chose this way of life. It must be defined in terms of the love of Christ, and there is no more eloquent expression of love than imitation and sharing the life of the beloved.[38]

The Church has newly awakened to the reality that its Lord is a living and triumphant Lord; the radiant Christ of Easter. There is a general emphasis today in the Church on the importance of the resurrection. The Lord of the Church is triumphant, and baptism, while it represents a dying with Christ to sin, also represents a rising with Christ. The Christian, emerging from the waters of baptism, is risen and victorious with Christ.[39]

The vows of a religious are meant to express the attitude of a resurrected person. They are the expression not only of death to sin but of complete belonging to God in Christ. Chastity, which is the basic vow in that it represents the fundamental choice of a religious, must leave the heart free to be possessed by God, for this vow makes Christ the sole spouse of the heart; it presumes a complete sense of belonging and expresses a total consecration. It is the most perfect expression of the new, divinized, risen-with-Christ life which is given in baptism. It is a life of the farthest extremity from the death of sin and the lusts of the flesh. It is the perfect expression of a new man, risen with Christ, for whom nothing of the old, of the partial, or of this world can for itself make sense or have value.

The liberation of the vow of poverty is a liberation from all selfish grasping, an emancipation from the riches that tend to possess their possessor, a liberation to a life of love. It is, at the same time, a gesture of confidence by a man or woman who is above the goods of this world and who is not anxious about them; it is a refusal to be subject to the things of this earth. The religious emancipates himself by this vow from the competition of men who seek to possess the earth and are forever anxious about losing their possessions. Poverty is the attitude of a man who has found a greater treasure, far more valuble than the petty treasures of this world; the love of Christ. The religious, in his posture of poverty, has no time or enthusiasm for the acquisition of riches, for play-

[38] Cf. Henri Holstein, "The Mystery of Religious Life," Review for Religious 20 (1961), pp. 312–329.

[39] Cf. Francis F. Durrwell, The Resurrection (New York: Sheed and Ward, 1962).

ing the stock markets of this world, and fretting about the preservation of his capital. He frees himself by his vow for an undivided self-donation, not so much for the peace that will come to him in being free from the monopolizing desires of possessions, but that he might give himself totally to his Lord, and, in him, to all men. The desire to be poor in order that one might be unencumbered and free from worry would be selfish, not Christian. Religious poverty can have meaning only when it is a liberation to live a life of love and dedication to the interests of the Lord. If chastity is the basic vow, because it chooses the Lord alone, poverty refuses to allow any self-interest to detract from this choice.

It is only from the choices of chastity and poverty that *obedience* can assume its value and meaning. Defined in terms of its negative characteristics, religious obedience could seem like infantile submission, a recession from and abdication of intelligence and free choice. The dynamism of the vow of obedience is the dynamism of love: to seek the good pleasure of the beloved.[40] If obedience involves the submission of self and the emptying of self, its positive thrust must always be the good pleasure of God. What a person called to the married state does in his choice of a partner in marriage, the religious does in his vow of chastity. And just as the choice of marriage precludes and prohibits competition for one's heart, so the vow of poverty is a voluntary forfeiture of those things which can preoccupy the human mind and heart. Finally just as the married person seeks the good pleasure of his spouse, so does the religious in his profession of obedience dedicate himself to the pursuit of the good pleasure, will, and love of Christ. There is an inner consistency in these vows. It has been said that religious poverty and obedience are meaningless unless they are chaste, and at the same time chastity and poverty are caricatured by the absence of obedience. It would be as though a man chose a woman in marriage, and moved into the same house with her, but did nothing to please her thereafter. Chastity and poverty without this desire to please God in obedience would be meaningless.

The three vows together represent the total and complete commitment to Christ. This is why there must be a question of *vows*; complete commitment is not a generous impulse made in a moment of fervor. Complete commitment is a definitive thing which engages the whole person for his whole life and embraces his whole future. We have insisted that religious consecration does not ambition a perfection higher than the perfection to which all Christians are called; but rather seeks this perfection through the *means* of religious consecration. The vows of the

---

[40] Cf. Jn 4:34; Mk 3:35.

religious are the means of his consecration and commitment and the guarantee of his fidelity in them. Commitment is not an abstraction, a thing of incense and flowers; it is a way of life. A man or woman, consecrated by religious vows, does not really choose poverty, chastity, and obedience so much at the altar of his vows as in his day-after-day being poor, chaste, and obedient, in imitation of his Lord. The religious, by his profession, walks the undemanded mile, the surrender of lawful pleasures and possessions that might have been his in order to imitate Christ more fully and love more perfectly.

Of this consecration, *The Constitution on the Church* says:

> By such a bond a person is totally dedicated to God, Who is loved beyond all things. In this way, that person is ordained to the honor and service of God under a new and special title. Indeed, through Baptism a person dies to sin and is consecrated to God. However, in order that he may be capable of deriving more abundant fruit from this baptismal grace, he intends, by the profession of the evangelical counsels in the Church, to free himself from those obstacles, which might draw him away from the fervor of charity and the perfection of divine worship. By this profession of the evangelical counsels, then, he is more intimately consecrated to divine service.[41]

6. The Religious as a Witness to Christ

The Greek word for witness, *mártus*, is used thirty-five times in the New Testament. In the Synoptic Gospels and in the Pauline Epistles, and sometimes in Acts, it is used to designate someone who gives testimony to a fact because of what he has seen or heard.[42] However, a specific Christian connotation is attached to the word by Luke and Peter.[43] It is used of the apostles as eyewitnesses and earwitnesses of what they had seen and heard and can verify by their testimony. However the object of this testimony is something special; at first it was particularly concerned with the resurrection of Christ,[44] without which all Christian preaching about Christ would be in vain.[45] But eventually the object of this testimony broadened and eventually came to designate rather specifically the apostles themselves. However, in the beginnings of the post-biblical usage of the word, *mártus* came to designate a martyr, that is, one who is a witness of Christ even unto death.[46] It was in this latter sense that the

---

[41] *Lumen Gentium*, no. 44.
[42] Cf. Mt 18:16; Mk 14:63; Acts 6:13; 1 Th 2:10; 1 Tim 6:12, etc.
[43] Cf. Lk 24:48; Acts 1:8; 1 Pet 5:1.
[44] Acts 1:21; 4:33.
[45] 1 Cor 15:14–17.
[46] Cf. Acts 22:20; Apoc 1:5; 3:14, in which Jesus himself is called "the faithful witness," or martyr, who gives his life.

early Church spoke of those who consecrated themselves to Christ by the renunciation of the vows as martyrs. The title was thought fitting because such a person truly gave his life for Christ as a sign to the world of Christ's presence.

In the order of sign and symbol, the religious is a martyr for Christ. He is a reminder to the world that man is not made for this world and he clearly manifests the kingdom of God that is to come.[47] We have spoken of the witness of the religious to Christ as transcendental and eschatological, meaning that he is a living reminder to man that, good as this world is, it can never satisfy the heart of man (transcendental); and that man has not here on this good earth a lasting city (eschatological). Many theologians, notably Karl Rahner, have speculated that such witness can be effectively rendered only if some in the Church voluntarily sacrifice some of the highest human goods.

The religious also manifests the heavenly kingdom, for in heaven there is no mine or thine, no giving or taking in marriage, no opposition of wills; every heart in the New Jerusalem belongs to God in undivided love. The religious manifests the heavenly kingdom in a way that is especially visible: under the sign of sacrifice, the sign of the cross. He professes, by his very way of life and his vows, to strive for that freedom from attachments to possessions, to people, to himself, which is the necessary emptying for the fulfillment of love. He becomes the chalice emptied and in readiness for the possession of God.

> One day when great crowds were journeying along with him, he turned around and said to them: "If anyone comes to follow me and does not hate his father and mother, his wife and children, his brothers and sisters, and even his own life, he cannot be my disciple. He who comes to follow Me but will not shoulder his cross, cannot be my disciple" (Lk 14:25–27).

> With Christ I am nailed to the cross. And I live, now not I, but Christ lives in me. And the physical life that I now live, I live by faith in the Son of God, who loved me and sacrificed himself for me (Gal 2:20).

Of course, the religious embodies for the whole People of God the life of the counsels, and reminds them of their life in Christ and of the life to come. However, it would be unjust not to add that the religious must look to the other members of God's People who are a complementary sign and symbol to him. There is the danger that religious, being removed from the world in one sense, may also be isolated from it. Living apart in communities of their own there can perhaps be a tendency to limited vision. The religious must look to the laity, not succumbing to the world, but wrestling with it and trying to redeem it. In one sense,

---

[47] *Lumen Gentium*, no. 44.

the vows and community life are an emancipation from struggles in which the laity must be engaged; and the religious can very often find in their example a new sense of dedication, a new meaning of detachment, and a new dimension of true holiness.

Of the witness rendered to the universal Church by religious, *The Constitution on the Church* says:

> The profession of the evangelical counsels, then, appear as a sign which can and ought to attract all the members of the Church to an effective and prompt fulfillment of the duties of their Christian vocation. The People of God has no lasting city here below, but looks forward to one which is to come. This being so, the religious state by giving its members greater freedom from earthly cares more adequately manifests to all believers the presence of heavenly goods already possessed here below.
>
> Furthermore, it not only witnesses to the fact of a new and eternal life acquired by the redemption of Christ. It foretells the resurrected state and the glory of the heavenly kingdom. . . . The religious state reveals in a unique way that the kingdom of God and its overmastering necessities are superior to all earthly considerations. Finally, to all men it shows wonderfully at work in the Church the surpassing greatness of the force of Christ the King and the boundless power of the Holy Spirit.[48]
>
> Religious should carefully keep before their minds the fact that the Church presents Christ to believers and non-believers alike in a striking manner and daily through them. Through them the Church portrays Christ in contemplation on the mountain, in His proclamation of the kingdom of God to the multitudes, in His healing of the sick and the maimed, in His work of converting sinners to a better life, in His solicitude for youth and His goodness to all men, always obedient to the will of the Father Who sent him.[49]

We have said that religious life can be understood only in the context of the life of the Church, and have insisted that withdrawal from the world in the case of religious does not mean isolation from the world, and certainly it is important to realize that the witness of religious must not be misconstrued as an evasion of the great commandment in which all Christian perfection resides: love of one's neighbor.[50] We have seen that theologians of "encounter" insist that man must encounter God in bodily fashion. God must somehow be rendered sensibly perceptible to man. The religious, by reason both of the self-despoliation of his state and his active concern for the needs of his neighbor, must be a special place of encounter with Christ for man. By reason of his religious com-

---

[48] *Lumen Gentium*, no. 44.
[49] *Ibid.*, no. 46.
[50] Mt 22:37–40; Gal 5:14.

mitment, he is personally trying to live the life that Christ led and to experience personally what Christ experienced.[51]

In his Constitution on Religious Life, Pope Pius XII states very clearly that religious life is essentially a life of charity, a life of love which embraces both God and neighbor:

> Since the perfection of Christian life consists especially in charity, and since it is really one and the same charity with which we must love God alone above all and all men in Him, Holy Mother Church demands of all nuns who canonically profess a life of contemplation, together with a perfect love of God, also a perfect love of the neighbor; and for the sake of this charity and their state of life, religious men and women must devote themselves wholly to the needs of the Church and of all those who are in want.[52]

Finally, religious witness may be said to be a representation of the mystery of the Church. Paul portrays the Church as the Bride of Christ.[53] The whole Church is the Bride of Christ and reflects total submission to him.[54] Religious witness reflects and manifests this spirit of loving submission to Christ in a striking manner.[55] Pope Pius XII called religious ". . . the children of the Church's predilection . . . [because they have] given their whole lives to Christ in order to follow Him freely on the arduous path of the evangelical counsels. . . ."[56] The religious has been called "an intense Christian," in that he has renewed his baptismal dedication in the dedication of his vows and consequently bears witness to the deepest reality of the Church's inner life: its union with Christ as Spouse. And the particular eloquence of his witness is the joy with which he makes this loving submission.

> The joy of religious life is perhaps the most constant and the most efficacious trait of its witness. This is so precisely because it manifests itself spontaneously without being conscious of itself and without imposing itself upon those it meets. . . . the joy of their Lord which they know well that no one can take from them.[57]

---

[51] Cf. Edward Farrell, The Theology of Religious Vocations (St. Louis: Herder, 1951).
[52] Pope Pius XII, Sponsa Christi.
[53] Eph 1:4; 5:22–32; 2 Cor 11:2–5.
[54] Eph 5:24.
[55] Cf. Lumen Gentium, no. 46.
[56] AAS 39 (1947), p. 114.
[57] Henri Holstein, "The Mystery of Religious Life," Review for Religious, 20 (1961), p. 329.

Bibliography

CHAPTER ONE: THE CHANGING CONCEPT OF THE CHURCH

Congar, Yves, M.-J., Tradition and Traditions (New York: Macmillan, 1967).
Dodd, C. H., The Apostolic Preaching and Its Developments (New York: Harper, 1954).
Dulles, Avery, Dimensions of the Church (Glen Rock, N. J.: Newman-Paulist, 1967), Woodstock Papers.
Hales, E. E. Y., Pope John and His Revolution (New York: Doubleday, 1964).
Häring, Bernard, The Johannine Council (New York: Herder & Herder, 1964).
Küng, Hans, The Council, Reform and Reunion (New York: Sheed & Ward, Inc., 1960; Doubleday Image, 1964).
———— The Council in Action (New York: Sheed & Ward, 1964).
———— Structures of the Church (New York: Nelson, 1964).
Latourelle, René, Theology of Revelation (New York: Alba House, 1966).
Mackey, James R., A Modern Theology of Tradition (New York: Herder & Herder, 1963).
Moran, Gabriel, Catechesis of Revelation (New York: Herder & Herder, 1965).
———— Theology of Revelation (New York: Herder & Herder, 1966).
Newman, John Henry, An Essay on the Development of Christian Doctrine (New York: Longmans, Green, 1949).
———— On Consulting the Faithful (New York: Sheed & Ward, 1962).
Novak, Michael, The Open Church (New York: Macmillan, 1964).
Scott, William, "The Phenomenon of Change in the Church," in The Role of Theology in the University (Milwaukee: The Bruce Publishing Company, 1967).
Tavard, George, The Church Tomorrow (New York: Holt, Rinehart, and Winston, 1965; Doubleday Image, 1966).

CHAPTER TWO: THE MYSTERY OF THE CHURCH

Butler, Basil, The Church and Infallibility (New York: Sheed & Ward, 1964).
Cerfaux, Lucien, The Church in the Theology of St. Paul (New York: Herder & Herder, 1959).
Congar, Yves, M.-J., The Mystery of the Church (Baltimore: Helicon, 1960).
———— The Mystery of the Temple (Westminster, Md.: The Newman Press, 1962).

217

De Lubac, Henri, *The Splendour of the Church* (New York: Sheed & Ward, 1965; paperback reprint Paulist Deus Books).

Lefebvre, George, *The Mystery of God's Love* (New York: Sheed & Ward, 1961).

Rahner, Karl, *The Christian Commitment* (New York: Sheed & Ward, 1964).

Schnackenburg, Rudolf, *God's Rule and Kingdom* (New York: Herder & Herder & Herder, 1966).

Stanley, David, *The Apostolic Church in the New Testament* (Westminster, Md.: The Newman Press, 1966).

CHAPTER THREE: A BIBLICAL IMAGE OF THE CHURCH: THE BODY OF CHRIST

In addition to the works of Cerfaux, Schnackenburg, and Stanley mentioned in the bibliography for Chapter Two the following are most pertinent here:

Grossouw, William, *In Christ: A Sketch of the Theology of St. Paul* (Westminster, Md.: The Newman Press, 1952).

Guerry, Emile, *In the Whole Christ* (New York: Alba House, 1960).

Masure, Eugene, *The Sacrifice of the Mystical Body* (Chicago: Regnery, 1957).

Mersch, Emile, *The Theology of the Mystical Body* (St. Louis: B. Herder, 1951).

Mura, Ernest, *The Nature of the Mystical Body* (St. Louis: B. Herder, 1963).

Wickenhauser, Alfred, *Pauline Mysticism: Christ in the Mystical Teaching of St. Paul* (New York: Herder & Herder, 1960).

CHAPTER FOUR: A SECOND BIBLICAL IMAGE OF THE CHURCH: THE PEOPLE OF GOD

Here again the works of such biblical scholars as Cerfaux, Schnackenburg, and others to whom we have referred are pertinent. In addition the following works ought to be consulted:

Hanssler, Bernard, *The Church and God's People* (Baltimore: Helicon, 1963).

McCabe, Herbert, *The People of God* (New York: Sheed & Ward, 1964).

Minear, Paul S., *Images of the Church in the New Testament* (Philadelphia: Westminster, 1960).

Norris, Frank B., *God's Own People* (Baltimore: Helicon, 1962).

CHAPTER FIVE: THE CHURCH AS THE PRIMORDIAL SACRAMENT

Cooke, Bernard, *Christian Sacraments and Christian Personality* (New York: Holt, Rinehart, and Winston, 1965).

Rahner, Karl, *The Church and the Sacraments* (New York: Herder & Herder, 1963).

Schanz, John, *The Sacraments of Life and Worship* (Milwaukee: The Bruce Publishing Company, 1966).

Schillebeeckx, E., *Christ the Sacrament of the Encounter With God* (New York: Sheed & Ward, 1963; paperback edition, Sheed & Ward, 1966).

Semmelroth, Otto, *Church and Sacrament* (Notre Dame, Ind.: Fides, 1965).

CHAPTER SIX: ENCOUNTER WITH CHRIST IN THE
CHURCH AND IN THE WORLD

Bekker, Wilhelm, *God's People on the March* (New York: Holt, Rinehart, and Winston, 1965).

Burns, Patrick (ed.), *Mission and Witness* (Westminster, Md.: The Newman Press, 1964).

Cox, Harvey, *The Secular City* (New York: Macmillan, 1965).

Guardini, Romano, "The Church, Encounter with Christ," in *The Church: Readings in Theology* (New York: Kenedy, 1963).

McKenzie, John L., *The Power and the Wisdom* (Milwaukee: The Bruce Publishing Company, 1965; paperback, 1967).

Rahner, Karl, *The Dynamic Element in the Church* (New York: Herder & Herder, 1964).

Schnackenburg, Rudolf, *The Church in the New Testament* (New York: Herder, 1963).

CHAPTER SEVEN: THE HISTORICAL FOUNDATION
OF THE CHURCH

Here too the works of Cerfaux, Stanley, Schnackenburg, and others to whom we have referred previously, are of utmost value. Likewise valuable are the books by Hanssler, McCabe, and Norris listed under Chapter Four. In addition, the following should be consulted:

Heaney, John J. (ed.), *Faith, Reason and the Gospels* (Westminster, Md.: The Newman Press, 1961).

Jones, Alexander, *God's Living Word* (New York: Sheed & Ward, 1961).

LeRoux, Jean-Marie, *The New People of God* (Notre Dame, Ind.: Fides, 1963).

Quesnell, Quentin, *This Good News: An Introduction to the Catholic Theology of the New Testament* (Milwaukee: The Bruce Publishing Company, 1965; paperback edition, 1967).

CHAPTER EIGHT: AUTHORITY IN THE CHURCH

Butler, Basil C., *The Idea of the Church* (Baltimore: Helicon, 1962).

Callahan, Daniel, *Honesty in the Church* (New York: Scribners, 1965).

Clarke, W. Norris, *Authority and Private Judgment* (Glen Rock, N. J.: The Paulist Press, 1962).
Dubay, William, *The Human Church* (New York: Doubleday, 1966).
McKenzie, John L., *Authority in the Church* (New York: Sheed & Ward, 1966).
Todd, John M. (ed.), *Problems of Authority* (Baltimore: Helicon, 1962).

CHAPTER NINE: FREE SPEECH AND PUBLIC OPINION IN THE CHURCH

In addition to the books of Callahan and Dubay listed in the bibliography of the previous chapter, the following are important:

Küng, Hans, *Freedom Today* (New York: Sheed & Ward, 1966).
McGoey, John, *The Uncertain Sound* (Milwaukee: The Bruce Publishing Company, 1967).
Rahner, Karl, *Free Speech in the Church* (New York: Sheed & Ward, 1960).
Thorman, Donald J., *The Christian Vision* (New York: Doubleday, 1967).

CHAPTER TEN: THE LITURGY AND THE CHURCH

Bouyer, Louis, *Liturgical Piety* (Notre Dame, Ind.: The University of Notre Dame Press, 1964).
Casel, Dom Odo, *The Mystery of the Christian Religion and Other Writings*, edited by Burkhard Neunheuser (Westminster, Md.: The Newman Press, 1962).
Crichton, John, *The Church's Worship* (New York: Sheed & Ward, 1964).
——— *Changes in the Liturgy* (New York: Alba House, 1965).
Davis, Charles, *Liturgy and Doctrine* (New York: Sheed & Ward, 1961).
Diekmann, Godfrey, *Come, Let Us Worship* (Baltimore: Helicon, 1961; Doubleday Image edition, 1966).
Hovda, Robert (ed.), *Sunday Morning Crisis* (Baltimore: Helicon, 1963).
King, James, *The Liturgy and the Laity* (Westminster, Md.: The Newman Press, 1963).
Leonard, William (ed.), *Liturgy for the People* (Milwaukee: The Bruce Publishing Company, 1963).
Martimort, Aimé, *The Liturgy and the Word of God* (Collegeville, Minn.: The Liturgical Press, 1959).
McManus, Frederick, *Sacramental Liturgy* (New York: Herder & Herder, 1967).
McNaspy, C. J., *Our Changing Liturgy* (New York: Hawthorn, 1966).
Powers, Joseph, *Eucharistic Theology* (New York: Herder & Herder, 1967).
Roguet, Aimon, *Christ Acts Through the Sacraments* (Collegeville, Minn.: The Liturgical Press, 1966).
Vagaggini, Cyprian, *Theological Dimensions of the Liturgy* (Collegeville, Minn.: The Liturgical Press, 1960).

CHAPTER ELEVEN: CHURCH AND STATE

Bennett, John C., *Christians and the State* (New York: Scribners, 1958).
Bonhoeffer, Dietrich, *Ethics* (New York: Macmillan, 1955).
Cullmann, Oscar, *State in the New Testament* (New York: Scribners, 1956).
Littell, Franklin H., *From State Church to Religious Pluralism* (New York: Doubleday Anchor, 1962).
Love, Thomas T., *John Courtney Murray: Contemporary Church-State Theory* (New York: Doubleday, 1965).
Maritain, Jacques, *Man and the State* (Chicago: University of Chicago Press, 1951).
Murray, John Courtney, *We Hold These Truths* (New York: Sheed & Ward, 1961; Doubleday Image edition, 1964).
—— (ed.), *Freedom and Man* (New York: Kenedy, 1965).
—— (ed.), *Problems of Religious Freedom* (Westminster, Md.: The Newman Press, 1965).
Niebuhr, Reinhold, *Man's Nature and His Communities* (New York: Scribners, 1965).
—— *Reinhold Niebuhr on Politics*, edited by Harry R. Davis and Robert C. Good (New York: Scribners, n.d.).
Niebuhr, Reinhold and Heimert, Allan, *Nation So Conceived* (New York: Scribners, 1963).
Zahn, Gordon C., *German Catholics and Hitler's Wars* (New York: Sheed & Ward, 1962).

CHAPTER TWELVE: THE CHRISTIAN'S VOCATION TO HOLINESS

Adam, Karl, *The Spirit of Catholicism* (New York: Doubleday, 1955; Doubleday Image edition, 1959).
Berrigan, Daniel, *They Call Us Dead Men* (New York: Macmillan, 1965).
Bouyer, Louis, *Christian Initiation* (New York: Macmillan, 1960).
Evely, Louis, *That Man Is You* (Westminster, Md.: The Newman Press, 1964).
—— *We Dare to Say Our Father* (New York: Herder & Herder, 1965).
Hastings, Cecily, *The Point of Catholicism* (New York: Sheed & Ward, 1958).
Huyghe, Gerard, *Growth in the Holy Spirit* (Westminster, Md.: The Newman Press, 1965).
Lavelle, Louis, *The Meaning of Holiness* (New York: Pantheon, 1954).
Merton, Thomas, *Life and Holiness* (New York: Herder & Herder, 1963; Doubleday Image edition, 1965).
Montague, George, *Maturing in Christ* (Milwaukee: The Bruce Publishing Company, 1965; paperback edition, 1967).
O'Neill, Joseph E., *The Encounter With God* (New York: Macmillan, 1962).
Pelikan, Jaroslav, *Fools for Christ* (Philadelphia: Fortress, 1955).

Rahner, Karl, *Christian in the Marketplace* (New York: Sheed & Ward, 1965).

Wroblewski, Sergius, *Christian Perfection for the Layman* (Chicago: Franciscan Herald Press, 1963).

CHAPTER THIRTEEN: LAITY AND RELIGIOUS IN THE LIFE OF THE CHURCH

Beha, Sister Helen Marie, *Living Community* (Milwaukee: The Bruce Publishing Company, 1967).

Bertrams, Wilhelm, *The Celibacy of the Priest* (Westminster, Md.: The Newman Press, 1963).

Callahan, Daniel, *The Mind of the Catholic Layman* (New York: Scribners, 1963; paperback edition, 1965).

Congar, Yves, *Lay People in the Church* (Westminster, Md.: The Newman Press, 1957; revised edition, 1965).

———— *Laity, Church, and World* (London: Birchall and Sons, 1960).

Evoy, John, and Christoph, Joseph van, *Personality Development in the Religious Life* (New York: Sheed & Ward, 1962).

Geaney, Dennis, *You Shall Be Witnesses* (Notre Dame, Ind.: Fides, 1963).

Gerken, John D., *Toward a Theology of the Layman* (New York: Herder & Herder, 1963).

Legrand, Lucien, *The Biblical Doctrine of Virginity* (New York: Sheed & Ward, 1963).

McGoey, John, *Sins of the Just* (Milwaukee: The Bruce Publishing Company, 1965).

Muckinhern, Sister Charles Borromeo, *The Implications of Renewal* (Notre Dame, Ind.: Fides, 1967).

O'Gara, James (ed.), *The Layman in the Church* (New York: Herder & Herder, 1962).

Riga, Peter, *Catholic Thought in Crisis* (Milwaukee: The Bruce Publishing Company, 1964).

Schillebeeckx, Edward, *The Layman in the Church* (New York: Alba House, 1963).

Suenens, Leon, *The Nun in the World* (Westminster, Md.: The Newman Press, 1963).

Tavard, George, *The Church, the Layman and the Modern World* (New York: Macmillan, 1959).

Thorman, Donald, *The Emerging Layman* (New York: Doubleday, 1962; Doubleday Image edition, 1964).

Index

44809